CAMBRIDGE LIBRARY COLLECTION

Books of enduring scholarly value

Medieval History

This series includes pioneering editions of medieval historical accounts by eye-witnesses and contemporaries, collections of source materials such as charters and letters, and works that applied new historiographical methods to the interpretation of the European middle ages. The nineteenth century saw an upsurge of interest in medieval manuscripts, texts and artefacts, and the enthusiastic efforts of scholars and antiquaries made a large body of material available in print for the first time. Although many of the analyses have been superseded, they provide fascinating evidence of the academic practices of their time, while a considerable number of texts have still not been re-edited and are still widely consulted.

Yorkshire Deeds

Published between 1909 and 1955, this ten-volume collection contains deeds relating to all of Yorkshire, from the twelfth to the seventeenth century. The deeds are of local historical interest, and provide topographical, philological and genealogical information, as well as insights into daily life. The majority of the records here are presented as abstracts, while documents in the vernacular that are of greater interest or importance are printed in full. Where possible, the documents are dated. Thorough background information and discussion of the deeds is included, as are notable physical descriptions, in particular of the seals. Each volume concludes with an index of people and places. Published in 1948, Volume 9 was edited by M.J. Hebditch (later M.J. Stanley Price), the librarian of the Yorkshire Archaeological Society. This is the first volume in the series to focus on the East Riding, and contains documents largely from the Yorkshire Archaeological Society and Archer-Houblon collections.

T0371308

Cambridge University Press has long been a pioneer in the reissuing of out-of-print titles from its own backlist, producing digital reprints of books that are still sought after by scholars and students but could not be reprinted economically using traditional technology. The Cambridge Library Collection extends this activity to a wider range of books which are still of importance to researchers and professionals, either for the source material they contain, or as landmarks in the history of their academic discipline.

Drawing from the world-renowned collections in the Cambridge University Library and other partner libraries, and guided by the advice of experts in each subject area, Cambridge University Press is using state-of-the-art scanning machines in its own Printing House to capture the content of each book selected for inclusion. The files are processed to give a consistently clear, crisp image, and the books finished to the high quality standard for which the Press is recognised around the world. The latest print-on-demand technology ensures that the books will remain available indefinitely, and that orders for single or multiple copies can quickly be supplied.

The Cambridge Library Collection brings back to life books of enduring scholarly value (including out-of-copyright works originally issued by other publishers) across a wide range of disciplines in the humanities and social sciences and in science and technology.

Yorkshire Deeds

VOLUME 9

EDITED BY M.J. HEBDITCH

CAMBRIDGE
UNIVERSITY PRESS

CAMBRIDGE UNIVERSITY PRESS

Cambridge, New York, Melbourne, Madrid, Cape Town,
Singapore, São Paolo, Delhi, Mexico City

Published in the United States of America by Cambridge University Press, New York

www.cambridge.org
Information on this title: www.cambridge.org/9781108058483

© in this compilation Cambridge University Press 2013

This edition first published 1948
This digitally printed version 2013

ISBN 978-1-108-05848-3 Paperback

YORKSHIRE DEEDS

Vol. IX

Ebor̄aceñ archiep̄o toti̇g̱ cl̄o Dn̄o Ꝑt̄ ⁊ Om̄ib; s̄c̄e ecc̄l̄ie fil̄s. Gillebt̄ d̄l
meinil de Turkilleb; s̄ct̄. Sciaꞇ me Assensu ⁊ concessione Steph̄i p̄mogen-
iꞇu ⁊ hedis mei ⁊ Joh̄eñ sponse mee dedisse ⁊ hac p̄sent̄ c̄art̄a mea con-
fi̇rmasse deo ⁊ s̄ce marie Bellelande ⁊ monachis ibidem deo serui̇entib;
ꞇocā illā cult̄ur̄ t̄r̄e mee ꝗm p̄dict̄i monachi saꞇauerunt in t̄r̄ra
de turkilleb; ūsuꝶ Angorelñ p̄ eisdem metas ⁊ diuisas qu̇as Walꞇ⸗ d̄l ꞁe
inl̄ pat̄ meus p̄ambulauiꞇ. Concesse ⁊ eis ⁊ ofirmau̇i saꞇare ad latit-
d̄ine p̄dicte cultur̄e ūsuꝶ oꞃiente̅ in longum quantu̅cu̅ꝗ; hedes mei
uꞇ Ego ip̄e uꞇ hoꞃes de turkilleb; t̄r̄am ꞃsdam iuxta p̄dictā cult̄
ꞃam ūsuꝶ oꞃiente saꞇaꞇdo p̄longauerim. hanc a̅u̅ donctione feci
deo ⁊ p̄dict̄is monachis ꞁ p̄̄s ⁊ p̄petua̅ elemosina ꝗsdam liba̅.
soluta̅ ⁊ quieta̅ ab om̄i t̄reno ꞁeruicio ⁊ exactione sec̄l̄ari ꞁ p̄petu-
um p̄ salute a̅īe mee ⁊ Sꞯoꞃꞟ mee ⁊ p̄t̄rꞯ ꞁ matꞯꞯ mee ⁊ om̄niu̅
Anꞇecessoꞃ ⁊ hedu̅ meoꞃ; s̄z Ego ⁊ hedes mei ha̅c donctionem
manutenebim̄ ⁊ warantizabim̄ p̄dict̄is monach̄ coꞇꞇ om̄s hoꞃes
⁊ p̄petuu̅. hiꞟ t̄estib;. Witt̄o dauel. Philippo f̄r̄e sꞯoꞃꞟ mee Steph̄o
filio meo. Petꞯo f̄r̄e meo. Gualt̄io canonico cell̄io de Roueb; Oliuo
filio Guncertiꞟ de Trese. Symone dispensaꞇoꞃe meo. Rob̄ꞇo dic̄o filio Ro-
ꞇa de Buskt.

THE YORKSHIRE
ARCHÆOLOGICAL SOCIETY

FOUNDED 1863   INCORPORATED 1893

RECORD SERIES

VOL. CXI

FOR THE YEAR 1946

YORKSHIRE DEEDS

VOL. IX

EDITED BY

M. J. HEBDITCH, M.A.

PRINTED FOR THE SOCIETY

1948

MADE AND PRINTED IN GREAT BRITAIN
BY JOHN WHITEHEAD AND SON LTD., BOAR LANE, LEEDS

CONTENTS

ILLUSTRATION

INTRODUCTION

The ownership of the documents printed in this volume is as follows:

Archer-Houblon MSS. (in the custody of Y.A.S.), Nos. 1–25, 30–54, 73–99, 214–215, 252, 257, 282–285, 297–299, 302–311, 320–322, 326–327, 334–337, 347–365, 429–434, 441, 449, 461.

The Vicar and Churchwardens of Bramley, Nos. 55–69, 186–189, 242, 243, 367, 459.

The Duke of Devonshire (Bolton Abbey Muniments), Nos. 26–28, 101, 102, 108–109, 295.

The Dorman Museum, Middlesbrough, No. 234.

Major le G. G. W. Horton-Fawkes (Farnley Hall Muniments, in the custody of the Y.A.S.), Nos. 29, 105–107, 138–139, 190–213, 216–219, 259, 262–264, 279, 290, 293, 313–315, 318–319, 325, 330–333, 338–342, 366, 383, 435–440, 446, 450–454, 458, 460, 487.

The Duke of Leeds (Hornby Castle Muniments, in the custody of the Y.A.S.), Nos. 312, 369–381.

Miss A. Norfar, 34, London Street, Edinburgh, No. 328.

Major T. W. Slingsby, Romanby Park, Northallerton (in the custody of the Y.A.S.), Nos. 236–241, 287.

The Yorkshire Archæological Society, Nos. 70–72, 100, 103–104, 110–137, 140–185, 220–233, 235, 244–251, 253–256, 258, 260–261, 265–278, 280–281, 286, 288–289, 291–292, 294, 296, 300–301, 316–317, 323–324, 329, 343–346, 368, 382, 384–428, 442–445, 447–448, 455–457, 462–486, 488–506.

The documents printed in this volume range from the twelfth to the sixteenth century, and although all parts of the county are represented, the majority of those printed here relate to the East Riding. The greatest number of these deeds of the eastern part of the county are taken from the large Archer-Houblon collection. They include many deeds concerning Beverley, some of which are of greater interest than the usual stereotyped grants of property.

The West Riding is represented by the first instalment of the Farnley Hall Muniments, and by part of a large series relating to Snaith and district, which have been presented to the Society by Dr. E. G. Millar. The Bramley deeds were lent for transcription through the kindness of Mr. A. Dobson, and supplement those printed by the Thoresby Society in their volume of *Calverley Charters*. The Slingsby documents are the remainder of a collection printed in earlier volumes of this series. It will be noticed that there are many single documents relating to individual places throughout the county. These are, for the most part, transcripts of deeds in the Society's possession and the result of a policy which aims at printing eventually all the medieval deeds in the keeping of the Society.

Mr. C. T. Clay has drawn my attention to two points of interest. In no. 101, Thomas de Multon issues a charter with reference to services due to the manor of Skipton, when he should obtain it. The first chapter of Mr. Clay's recent volume of Early Yorkshire Charters for Skipton supplies the reason for Thomas's expectations. His hopes, which did not, in fact, materialise, dated back to various claims made when the manor passed into the king's hand after the death of Aveline de Forz in 1274.

The mention of Lord de Brewse as holding land in Weaverthorpe, no. 455, elucidates the puzzle presented in the *Complete Peerage*, New ed., wherein Thomas de Brewse is described as holding, *inter alia*, the manor of Werthorpe, an imaginary place, apparently confused with Weaverthorpe.

The volume provides material which adds to the manorial history of the county, notably in the deeds relating to Easthorpe, Escrick, Londesborough, Sessay and Harswell. The first Harswell deed is more than usually explicit for its date of 1288.

The organisation of medieval life is exemplified in a number of documents, particularly the Inspeximus of Marmaduke Darelle (no. 384). The complexities of working the open field system with its scattered strips is well demonstrated in nos. 256, 262; while among the many field names which occur, those such as Trysterlandes, Stonelandes, Sowrelandes and Stonirode imply further difficulties met with in tilling the soil.

A number of uncommon words may be found, such as *wodwosh*, *rona*, and *frunte*. The latter, with *steuenyour* and *perrettes*, has not been fully explained. There is mention of one unusual saint's day, that of St. Hilarion the monk, which is used for the dating of a Gowdall deed.

The few fifteenth-century deeds in English have been printed as they stand, and show well the use of the vernacular at the time (nos. 287, 374).

In connection with the seals, attention is again drawn to the importance in the authenticity of a document of the actual seal. Nos. 33 and 430, for the further strengthening of the deeds, bear seals which were considered to be easily recognisable and well known, in addition to the seals of the authors of the deeds. No. 430 establishes the existence of a seal of the deanery of Dikering and shows a portion of what was doubtless a fine piece of work.

The most interesting seal described here is that appended to no. 330. No perfect example of the abbey seal of Byland seems to be known.[1] This example shows clearly the letters ERIVM in the second half of the legend, and presumably represents [MONAST]ERIVM; but that this word is not in the genitive case is curious. It suggests, however, that the Byland legend must have differed from that on the Cistercian abbey seals of Rievaulx and Jervaulx of similar design, where the words S' ABBATIS ET CONVENTVS are not free from doubt.

In the printing of the deeds, the practice of the preceding volume has been followed, with the addition of the words 'Warranty' and 'Sealing clause' where those clauses occur in the original.

The thanks of the Society are due to the owners of documents who have kindly permitted transcripts to be made and printed. In this connection I must add that the first transcripts of the Archer-Houblon deeds—many of them lengthy and in poor repair—were made by my late husband, William Hebditch, who had hoped to edit this volume.

My thanks are due to Prof. C. E. Whiting for his help on several points, and in particular to Mr. Clay, who has patiently corrected mistakes, read the proof sheets, and helped and advised at every turn.

M. J. HEBDITCH.

<hr/>

[1] See the frontispiece to Vol. V of this series of *Yorks. Deeds*, and the examples given in *Archæologia*, lxxviii, 13.

YORKSHIRE DEEDS

Acaster Malbis.

1. Wednesday before St. Lawrence, 15 Edward III [Jan. 31, 1340–1]. Indenture[1] witnessing that an agreement has been reached between Sir William Malbys of the one part and Sir Roger Bygot of the other part, touching the covenants to be made between them; namely, that the said Sir William shall enfeoff one or two discreet men in whom he trusts in the manors of Acaster Malbys and Coupmanthorp in fee simple, and they shall re-enfeoff Sir William in the said manors for the term of his life, with remainder to William Malbys, his son and the heirs male of his body. And if William, the son, should bring an action of waste (*port seon breue de wast*) against Sir William, the latter shall come into court by his attorney and acknowledge that he has no right in the said manors except for the term of his life. And in respect of the annuity granted by Sir William to William, his son, and Isabel, his wife, in Fyueleye,[2] if the said William and Isabel should bring an action for the annuity against Sir William, then he shall come into court by his attorney and acknowledge his obligation. Also in respect of the annuity of 10*li.* per annum which Sir William granted to Thomas and John, his sons, in Southotrington, Sir William shall give surety to Sir Roger Bygot that William, the son, and Isabel will be discharged of the said annuity until they take possession of the said manor of Southotrington; further, if the acquittance by Thomas and John is not sufficient in law for William and Isabel until Thomas and John come of age, then Sir William shall make surety for Thomas and John to acquit William and Isabel from the said annuity of 10*li.* until the full age of Thomas and John. The said Sir Roger and John de Bukton shall make a bond of 40 marks payable to Sir William at Martinmas next, and they shall make a recognizance of 100 marks by Statute Merchant, payable to Sir William at Whitsuntide and Martinmas, 40 marks at each term until the 100 marks are fully paid. These covenants are to be performed before Martinmas next. Alternate seals.[3] At Seteryngton. (*Archer-Houblon MSS.*, No. 1.)

[1] In French.

[2] Filey.

[3] Seal: red wax, broken; on a heater-shaped shield a chevron between three stags' heads erased.

Hdlingfleet.

2. Grant by Richard de Celar, son of the late Robert de Celar of Athelingflet, to John Gouk of Athelingflet and Alice, his wife, their heirs and assigns, of the moiety of a toft, formerly belonging to Robert Hunekok of Athelingflet, which lies in length on the north side of the house of the late Robert and stretches to the end of his garden (*ad buttam gardini quondam predicti Roberti*), together with a chamber built upon it, and 2 roods of moor pertaining to the said moiety, and all other appurtenances; to hold with free ingress and egress, paying yearly to the grantor and his heirs a pair of white gloves at Christmas for all service, suit of court, homages, reliefs, exactions and demands. Warranty. Sealing clause.[1] Witnesses: John de Hustuayt, Adam de Celar, John de Slengisby, Stephen de Egmanton, John Russel, Robert Cortwys, William Tebaud. (*Ibid.*, No. 3.)

3. Grant by Richard de Celar of Athelingflet to William Wlsi of Watreton and John Pitefut, their heirs and assigns, of a toft with appurtenances and easements, in the vill of Athelingflet, which lies 24 feet in width between the toft of John Gouk and the toft of Alice Lotercis, and in length from the king's highway of Athelingflet for 15 perches towards the south ditch behind the said toft; to hold freely, quietly, for ever, paying yearly to the grantor and his heirs a pair of white gloves at Christmas and to the chief lords of the fee 6*d.*, half at Palm Sunday and the other half at the Nativity of the B.V.M., for all services, exactions and demands. Warranty. Sealing clause.[2] Witnesses: John de Hustuayt, Adam de Celar, Robert Cortewys, John Gouk, John Russel, Stephen son of Robert, John de Slenggesby, Thomas de Egmanton. (*Ibid.*, No. 4.)

4. Grant by John son of Richard de Camera to Robert his son, and John his younger son (*Johanni filio meo juniori*), for their homage and service, of the whole of the croft which Sauari' formerly held, which lies between the land of the church of Adhelingflet and the lane (*lanam*) stretching from the vill of Useflet towards the moor, with its whole length and breadth and with all liberties and easements within the vill and without, pertaining to the said croft; to hold of the grantor, his heirs or assigns, to Robert and John, their heirs and assigns or to whomsoever they wish to give, sell, or assign the said croft, religious houses excepted, freely, quietly and fully, paying yearly a pound of pepper at the feast of St. Nicholas the Confessor [Dec. 6] for all secular service, suit of court and demand. Warranty. Sealing clause.[3] Witnesses:

[1] Seal: red wax, chipped, diam. ½ in.; two animals (perhaps a hare and a monkey) facing each other, in between them a chest [?].

[2] Seal: white wax, oval, 1¼ × 1 in.; a hawk [?] between two stars, facing sinister; ✠ SI.... DI DE CÉL[A]RIO.

[3] Seal: white wax, oval, large; chipped and blurred, ✠ ...[JOH]ANN[IS] DE ....

Sir John de Useflet, Walter his son, William son of Robert de Rednesse, Walter son of Geoffrey of the same, Robert the clerk of Haldanby, William his son, Robert de Celar, Robert Russel of Adhelingflet, Gervase the clerk. (*Ibid.*, No. 5.)

5. Grant by Robert de Dayuile to John son of Richard de Kamera and his heirs, for his homage and service, of a toft and a croft in the vill of Athelingflet, namely, that toft which Nicholas son of Roger formerly held of the grantor in the same vill, lying between the toft of Ranulf de Insula and the toft of Nicholas; and the toft is 2 perches in width, and the croft extends in length from the courtyard (*curia*) of the said Nicholas to the ditch of Fourestangeg and is 3 perches wide; to hold in fee and inheritance, freely, quietly and in peace, with all liberties and easements within the vill and without, paying yearly to the grantor and his heirs 4s. in equal portions at Whitsuntide and Martinmas for all services. Warranty. Sealing clause.[1] Witnesses: Sir Jocelin de Dayuile, Richard de Dayuile, Adam de Dayuile, Sir John de Useflet, Henry de Dayuile, Robert Ruff, Hugh Langle, Ranulf de Insula, Nicholas son of Roger the clerk. (*Ibid.*, No. 6.)

6. Quitclaim by Agnes daughter of Henry de le Celer of Athelingflet to John [Go]uk of Athelingflet·and Alice, his wife, his heirs and assigns, of all right and claim in a messuage with appurtenances in Athelingflet, which lies in length and breadth between the messuage of the said John on one side and a lane called Gof....e on the other, which messuage the said John and Alice hold by the gift and feoffment of John .... de Drax and Margery his wife, mother of the grantor's mother. Warranty. Sealing clause.[2] Witnesses: William de Hustwait, Stephen de Egmanton of Athelingflet, William de le Celer of the same, Stephen de le Celer of Athelingflet, John ....el. (*Ibid.*, No. 7.)

7. Grant by Ranulf de Adhelingflet, knt., to John de Thorintoft, his heirs and assigns, of a toft with appurtenances in Adhelingflet 24 feet wide and 15 perches long, from the king's highway in Adhelingflet towards the north, and on the east side of the grantor's toft; to hold to John, his heirs and assigns for their homage and service, freely and quietly, paying yearly 6d. of silver, 3d. at the Nativity of the B.V.M. [Sept. 8] and 3d. on Palm Sunday for all service except forinsec service. Warranty. Sealing clause. Witnesses: Sir John the chaplain, Robert de Celeir, Robert Russell, Robert the clerk, Thomas le Gant[?], Peter de Usfleit, Hugh de Langelay, William .... (*Ibid.*, No. 9.)

8. Grant by Robert the cook (*Cocus*), son of John de Thorneton, to Richard de Celer of Atlingflet, his heirs and assigns, of a toft with appurtenances in Atlingflet, 24 feet wide and 15

---

[1] Seal: green wax, broken; paw and leg of an animal.

[2] Seal: white wax, small, diam. ¾ in., chipped; clasped hands above two sprigs of foliage and a bird.

perches long, stretching from the king's highway in Atlingflet towards the north and between the houses of John Guk and Alice Lotric'; to hold freely, quietly and in peace, paying yearly to the chief lord of the fee 6 silver pennies, three at the feast of the Nativity of the B.V.M., and three on Palm Sunday, for all services and demands. Warranty. Sealing clause.[1] Witnesses: John de Hustewayt, Adam de Celer of Atlingflet, Thomas de Egmanton, John de Slingesby, Robert Cortewys. (*Ibid.*, No. 10.)

9. Friday before SS. Philip and James, the 16th year of our sovereign lord.[2] Bond[3] by William del Bour of Athelingflet to Alan du Celer of Athelingflet in the sum of 15s. to be paid to the said Alan or his attorney having these letters at Athelingflet at Michaelmas in the 16th year of our sovereign lord. For the performance of this he has bound himself and his heirs and executors and has pledged all right and claim which he has or may have in a messuage (*un mees*), a croft and a rood of land which William Gouk of Athelingflet holds of him on lease for a term of years. Alan to have power to enter the said tenements after the completion of William Gouk's tenancy and to hold them of the chief lords of the fee by the service and rent due and accustomed. Sealing clause.[4] Witnesses: William de Hustwate, Richard his brother, John de Useflet, Thomas Grant, Hugh de Burton. At Athelingflet. (*Ibid.*, No. 11.)

10. Morrow of Easter, 29 Edward I [April 3, 1301]. Bond by John de Dayuill and his heirs to John Gouk of Athelingflet or his attorney, in the sum of 13*li.* 8s. 9d. to be paid to the latter or his attorney at Athelingflet at Martinmas, 29 Edward I, without further delay or fraud. If John de Dayuill dies before payment his executors shall have no power to administer his goods until the said sum is paid. Sealing clause.[5] Witnesses: Adam de Celer, John Russell, Robert [C]ortewys. At Atlingflet. (*Ibid.*, No. 12.)

11. Monday the morrow of St. Luke the Evangelist [Oct. 19], 1310. Grant and confirmation by Alice, daughter of Ranulph Hycheuauler, to John Gouk and Alice his wife, their heirs or assigns, of a rood of land in the territory of Athlingflet, abutting in length on the land of the said John on the south and on the land formerly belonging to Jocelin Dayuile on the north, and lying in width between the land of William de Waterton on both

[1] Seal: white wax, round, badly damaged; a fleur-de-lis; ✠ SI ROB....

[2] The actual name of the king is not mentioned anywhere in the deed: the witnesses also appearing in Nos. 13 and 23 would suggest Ed. II.

[3] In French.

[4] Seal: red wax, diam. ½ in.; within a eusped circle a small bird, a stag and a third object undeciphered; ✠ RIV.SV.ROY.CO.V

[5] Seal: red wax, chipped, diam. 1 in.; within a circular band of scroll work, a shield of arms, on a fess between two fleurs-de-lis, a fleur-de-lis, impaling two bars differenced by a label. For a seal of John de Eyvill, lord of Egmanton, in 1321, and a note on the Deyville arms, see *Yorks. Deeds*, i, 213*n*.

sides; to hold of the chief lords of the fee by the due and accustomed services freely, quietly and in peace, paying to the grantor and her heirs 1*d.* at Christmas for all secular service and demand. Warranty. Sealing clause. Witnesses: William de Oustwayth, John de Slengesby, Stephen de Celar. At Athling[flet]. (*Ibid.*, No. 13.)

12. Friday after Whitsunday [May 31], 1314. Lease by Sir John de Eyuile to John Gouk of Adlingflet, Alice his wife, and William and Thomas, their sons, of a toft with a house built upon it in Adlingflet, which lies near the cemetery of the church of Adlingflet between the toft which John Godfray formerly held and the toft of the said John Gouk; to hold for the term of their lives or for the lifetime of the survivor, paying yearly 16*d.*, half at Martinmas and half at Whitsuntide, for all secular service and demand. Warranty. Reversion to the grantor and his heirs. Alternate seals. Witnesses: William de Hustwayt, Thomas de le Celer, Stephen de Egmuntun, William de le Celer, Stephen de le Celer. At Adlingflet. (*Ibid.*, No. 14.)

13. The Apostles Peter and Paul [June 29], 1314. Agreement[1] between William de le Bour of Athelingflet and John Gouk of Athelingflet and Alice, his wife. William grants to John and Alice all the lands and tenements with appurtenances which he has in the vill and territory of Athelingflet, also all annual rents and services which John Kob and Margery, his wife, Thomas de Slengesby and Alice, his wife, and Thomas de le Celar are bound to render to William for the dowers which they hold of the same in Athelingflet; to hold the said lands and tenements, rents and services from Michaelmas next for the 10 years following, performing for William and his heirs the due and accustomed service to the chief lords of the fee, except suit of court which William and his heirs shall do. Warranty. If John Gouk, Alice, his wife, their heirs and assigns hold the lands and tenements, rents and services beyond the said term they shall pay yearly to William or his heirs and assigns 60*s.* of silver, half at Martinmas and half at Whitsuntide. Further grants for himself and his heirs that if any dower from the aforesaid dowers reverts to him within the said term it shall remain to John and Alice and their heirs and assigns until the end of the said term, and they shall pay yearly to William and his heirs and assigns the value of the dower according to the estimation of lawful men, at Martinmas and Whitsuntide in equal portions. Alternate seals.[2] Witnesses: William de Hustwayt, Stephen de Egmanton, Stephen de le Celer, William de le Celer, William de Useflet. And John and Alice and their heirs and assigns shall maintain the thatch of William's house during the term in as good condition as when they received it. (*Ibid.*, No. 15.)

---

[1] Also a precisely similar agreement made a year later.

[2] Seal: white wax, diam. ¾ in.; a hawk preying on a smaller bird, both facing to sinister; legend blurred ....IS.

14. Thursday before St. Valentine, 9 Edward II [Feb. 12, 1315–6]. Indenture witnessing that John de Eyuill has received of John Gouk eight years rent, at 10s. 9d. per annum, for a tenement formerly belonging to William de la Chamber of Atthelingflet. Acquits John Gouk and his heirs. Alternate seals.[1] At Atthelingflet. (*Ibid.*, No. 17.)

15. Monday after the Annunciation of the B.V.M., 9 Edward II [March 29, 1316]. Release by John de Eyuill, lord of Athelingflet, to John Gouk of Athelingflet and Alice, his wife, of all the rent and service which they customarily pay for the lands and tenements which they hold of him, for the term of their lives or for the lifetime of the survivor, paying yearly to him or his heirs 2d., in equal portions at Whitsuntide and Martinmas, for all service, suit of court and demands. Warranty. After their deaths reversion to the grantor and his heirs. Alternate seals.[2] Witnesses: William de Ustewayt, Stephen de Egmanton, William de Celar, John Russell. At Adthelingflet. (*Ibid.*, No. 18.)

16. Tuesday after St. Ambrose the Bishop, 9 Edward II [April 6, 1316]. Grant and confirmation by William son of John de la Bour of Athelingflet to John Gouk of Athelingflet and Alice, his wife, and his heirs and assigns, of all the lands and tenements with appurtenances which the grantor has in two cultures in Athelingflet, of which one lies between the lane of Athelingflet on the north and the field of Fowquardby[3] on the south, and the other between the field which is called Castelandes on the east and the lane of Useflet on the west. Also in remainder the lands and tenements with appurtenances which Thomas de le Celer of Athelingflet holds for the term of the life of Ellen (*Elene*), who was the wife of John de Langelay, of the grantor's inheritance in the aforesaid culture near Fowquardby; also all the lands and tenements with appurtenances which John Cob and Margery his wife, and Thomas de Slengesby and Alice his wife hold as dower of the said Margery and Alice in the said two cultures, which after the death of the said Ellen, Margery and Alice should revert to the grantor; to hold the said cultures as well in demesne as in reversion, of the chief lords of the fee by the due and accustomed services for ever. Warranty. Sealing clause.[4] Witnesses: William de Hustwayt of Athelingflet, Stephen de Egmanton of the same, William de le Celer of Athelingflet, Stephen de le Celer of the same, Robert Cortwys, Thomas de Slengesby, John Russel. At Athelingflet. (*Ibid.*, No. 19.)

17. Monday after the Apostles Peter and Paul [July 5], 1316. Lease by John de Eyuill of Athelingflet to John Gouk of Athe-

---

[1] Tongue, but seal missing.
[2] Seal: white wax, diam. 1 in. Same as to No. 10.
[3] Fockerby.
[4] Tongue and seal both missing.

lingflet and Alice, his wife, of all his land in the field of Atheling-flet which lies in length from le Radecance to the field which is called le Intakes, and in width between the land of the abbot of Selby on the west and the lane of Athelingflet on the east; also a culture of land in the same vill called Aldbrek which extends in length from le Radecance to the field called Morediklandes, and in width between the land of the said abbot of Selby on the west and the field called Biornhilles on the east; to hold from Michael-mas, 1316, for 6 years free of all services. Warranty. Alternate seals. Witnesses: Stephen de Egmanton, William de Hustwait, William de le Celer, Stephen de le Celer, William de Useflet. At Athelingflet. (*Ibid.*, No. 20.)

18. Monday, St. Valentine, 10 Edward II [Feb. 14, 1316–7]. Appointment by William de la Mar of Usflet of Walter Tebaud of Haldanby as his attorney to deliver seisin to John Gouk of Athelingflet of a croft with a building on it, situate in Atheling-flet, and of 4 selions of land, as appear in the charter of feoffment. In witness whereof he has caused these letters to be made patent.[1] (*Ibid.*, No. 21.)

19. Thursday after St. Gregory the Pope, 10 Edward II [March 17, 1316–7]. Lease by John de Eyuill, lord of Atelingflet, to Emma Augryme and Richard her son, of a messuage with a croft and half a bovate of land with appurtenances in the vill and territory of Atellingflet, which Thomas Augryme formerly held of John; to hold for the term of their lives freely and quietly, paying 11s. of silver in equal portions at Whitsuntide and Martin-mas for all secular services, exactions and demands, except suit of court at Atellingflet. Warranty. Reversion to John and his heirs after their deaths. Sealing clause.[2] Witnesses: William de Hustwayt, Thomas de Slengsby, Stephen de Celar, Thomas de Celar, John Gouk. At Thorneton super Swale. (*Ibid.*, No. 22.)

20. Sunday before the Ascension [May 28], 1318. Grant by John Gouk of Athelingflet to Thomas his son and the heirs of his body, of a toft with a croft and the houses built on the said croft in Athelingflet, near a lane called Gousfelan on the east, which the grantor had of the gift of William de la Mar; to hold with all commodities, liberties and easements, of the chief lord of the fee by the due and accustomed services. Warranty. Sealing clause.[3] Witnesses: William de Hustewayt, Thomas de Celar, Thomas de Slengkesby, Stephen de Celar, Robert Huttyng, William de Celar. (*Ibid.*, No. 23.)

21. Saturday after St. Valentine, 13 Edward II [Feb. 16, 1319–20]. Appointment by William de la Bour of Adlyngflet of

---

[1] Seal : fragment of red wax.

[2] Seal: as to No. 10.

[3] Seal: white wax, small, oval; a device of leaves arranged similar to a fleur-de-lis.

Robert du Celer or John son of Robert de Haldenby as his attorney to deliver seisin to William Gouk and Joan, his wife, of the whole of his moor in the moors of Adlyngflet, according to the form of his charter made to the said William and Joan. Sealing clause. At Adlyngflet. (*Ibid.*, No. 24.)

22. Sunday after St. Valentine, 13 Edward II [Feb. 17, 1319–20]. Grant and confirmation by William de la Boure of Adlyngflet to William Gouk of Adlyngflet and Joan his wife, his heirs and assigns, of all the moor which he has in the moors of Adlyngflet, with a piece of ground (*cum fundo*) 2 perches wide lying between the moor of William du Celer and the moor formerly belonging to Adam du Celer, and extending in length from the croft of William de Hustwait, which is called Morecroft, towards the vill of Thorn as far as the moor of Adlyngflet stretches. Also in remainder all the moor with a piece of ground which Thomas de Slengesby and Alice his wife hold as dower of Alice of the grantor's inheritance; also all the moor with a piece of ground which John Cob and Margery his wife hold as dower of Margery of the grantor's inheritance in Adlyngflet; to hold all the said moors and grounds as well in reversions as in demesnes of the chief lords of the fee by the due and accustomed services. Warranty, Sealing clause.[1] Witnesses: Thomas de Egmanton, William de Hustwait, John de Usflet, Stephen du Celer, Robert du Celer, Robert de Haldanby. At Adlyngflet. (*Ibid.*, No. 25.)

23. Sunday before the Annunciation of the B.V.M., 14 Edward II [March 22, 1320–1]. Quitclaim by William de Camera of Athelyngflet to William Gouk and his heirs, of all right and claim which he has in two selions of arable land; and in two parts of half an acre of meadow, with appurtenances, in Athelyngflet, of which selions, one called Foulsikeland lies in the east field between the land of Thomas du Celer and Robert Utting, and the other in the field called le Croftes between the land which is called Nicholas Croft and the land which John Cob and Margery his wife hold as her dower; and the meadow lies between the meadow of the said William Gouk and the meadow which Thomas de Slengesby and Alice his wife hold as dower. Also in remainder the whole of the land which Thomas de Slengesby and Alice his wife hold as dower of Alice in Foulsikeland and the land which John Cob and Margery his wife hold as dower in the same selion called Foulsikeland, and the whole of the meadow which Thomas de Slengesby and Alice his wife hold as dower; to hold of the chief lord of the fee by the due and accustomed services. Warranty. Sealing clause.[2] Witnesses: Thomas de Egmanton, John de Usflet, Thomas de Slengesby, Stephen du Celer, Robert Uttyng, Richard Rewe. At Adelyngflet. (*Ibid.*, No. 26.)

[1] Tag, but seal missing.

[2] Seal: white wax, small, oval, badly chipped; a hawk [?] preying on another bird, both facing to sinister.

24. Thursday after St. Michael [Oct. 1], 1321. Grant by Robert de Celar of Adhelingflet to William Wlsi of Waterton, living in Adhelingflet, his heirs and assigns, of 4 selions of arable land and one rood, with appurtenances, in the territory of Adhelingflet, of which 2 selions lie in the south field in length and width between the land of Thomas de Slengesby on the north and the land of Peter Brekesikel on the south, and 2 selions and a rood lie in the same field in length and width between the land of Thomas de Slengesby on the south and the land of Peter Brekesikel on the north; to hold freely, quietly and in peace, of the chief lords of the fee by the due and accustomed services for ever. Warranty. Sealing clause.[1] Witnesses: Thomas de Egmanton, William de Hustwayt of Adhelingflet, Stephen de Celar of the same, Alan de Waterton, Robert Uttyng of Adhelingflet, William son of Ingram de Waterton, Richard Gonall of Burton. At Adhelingflet. (*Ibid.*, No. 27.)

25. Friday after St. Martin the Bishop, 15 Edward II [Nov. 13, 1321]. Lease[2] by Richard Augrim of Adlingflet to Thomas de Egmanton of Folquardby and his heirs, of 6 acres of land with appurtenances in the fields of Adlingflet for 10 years; to hold freely, quietly and in peace, paying yearly to Robert de Eyuill and his heirs 5s. 6d. at Whitsuntide and Martinmas in equal portions for all services. Warranty. Sealing clause. Witnesses: William de Hustwayt, John de Ousflet, Thomas de Slengesby, Stephen de Celar, John Russell. At Adlingflet. (*Ibid.*, No. 28.)

Appletreewick.

26. Grant by William de Deserto, with the assent of Emma his wife, to Marton priory in pure and perpetual alms, of 3 roods of land in the territory of Apeltrewic, lying between the path from Kale and the stream of Dib[3] near the culture of the canons of Marton called Simund Riding towards the east; to hold of the grantor and his heirs free from all service, custom and secular exaction. Warranty against all men. Witnesses, William de Hertlingt[un], Alexander de Rauthecliue, Thomas de Apeltrewic, Andrew de Apeltrewic, Alan de Dractun, Roger de Wdehuses.[4] (*Duke of Devonshire, Bolton Abbey Estate MSS.*)

27. Grant and quitclaim by William son of Edward to Marton priory of a bovate of land with appurtenances in Apeltrewic which he had held of the priory. Warranty. Witnesses:

[1] Seal: brown wax, small, oval, $1\frac{1}{8} \times \frac{1}{2}$ in.; a garb [?]; ✠ CREDE [M]ICHI.

[2] Also quitclaim of the same to the same dated March 14, 1321-2. Same witnesses.

[3] Kail hill above Woodhouse to NW. of Appletreewick, and the river Dibb which flows to the Wharfe near Woodhouse.

[4] Seal missing. Medieval endorsement: Willelmus de Deserto de iij rodis terre in Apiltreuuic; and the number ix.

Hugh de Kaltun, William de Martun, John de Haltun, William de Hertlingtun, Thomas de Apeltrewic.[1] (*Ibid.*)

28. Grant by Andrew the clerk of Appeltrewik to Marton priory in free, pure and perpetual alms of all his land in Wdehuses from the site of his house (*mansionis*) as far as the bridge of Hertlingtun', saving to him the entirety of his croft and of the site of his barn, namely 3 roods of land; and if more than that then the residue; to hold of the grantor and his heirs. Warranty against all men. Witnesses, Eustace de Rilliston', William de Hertlingtun', William the forester, Henry de Eluetheham, Thomas de Appeltrewik, Thomas de Crakahou, Ralph the clerk.[2] (*Ibid.*)

Batley.

29. March 10, 26 Henry VI [1448]. Indenture by which Thomas Sayuell, knt., William Mirefeld and Robert Neuyll, esqs., with the assent of Mary, widow of Thomas Eland, esq., also of Robert, son and heir of Thomas, grant to George Popelay, junior, and his heirs, a yearly rent of 6s. 8d. for the term of 21 years next following, to be received at Whitsuntide and Martinmas in equal portions from all the lands and tenements with appurtenances called Brokerodes in the territory of Batelay which the grantors recently had of the gift and feoffment of Thomas Eland; the first payment to be made at Whitsuntide 1449. Power to grantee to enter and distrain if the rent is in arrears in part or wholly, until satisfaction is obtained. Sealing clause.[3] At Batelay. (*Farnley Hall MSS.*, No. 51.)

Beverley.

30. Gerard son of Stephen de Cottyngham swears on the tomb of St. John of Beverley that he will pay or cause to be paid in perpetuity a yearly rent of 2s. from his shop (*selda*) in the meat market in Beverley which he has sold to Thomas de Grimeston, in equal portions at Whitsuntide and Martinmas; if he, his heirs or assigns shall fail to pay this rent, Thomas or any of his assigns may enter the said shop and hold it as a feoffment without contradiction by Gerard or his heirs. He swears that he and his heirs will observe this promise made before these worthy (*fidedignis*) witnesses: William de Tuluse, bailiff of the lord archbishop, Andrew Matfray, Dennis de Balne, Adam Cachelune, Alexander de Scaureburg. Sealing clause. (*Archer-Houblon MSS.*, No. 68.)

31. Grant by John son and heir of Robert the apothecary (*apotecharii*), burgess of Beverley, to Master Thomas de Grimeston,

---

[1] Seal missing. Medieval endorsement: Willelmus filius Erwardi de una bouata terre in Apeltrewyck; and the number iij.

[2] Seal: red wax, round, diam. 1¼ in.; a fleur-de-lis; ✠ SIGILL': ANDREE: D: WD'. Medieval endorsement: Andreas de Appeltrevyk de tota terra quam habuit in Wodhuse; and the number xiij.

[3] Three seals: of red wax; (1) diam. ⅝ in., an owl to dexter; (2) small gem, undeciphered; (3) undeciphered.

clerk, his heirs or anyone to whom he may wish to give it, of all right and claim which he has or may have by any right, circumstance or escheat in all lands, rents, houses and tenements whatsoever in the vill of Beverley, which belonged to Robert, his father, and which may belong to him and his heirs after the death of Isabel, his mother or Matilda, Isabel or Collet, his sisters; to hold to Thomas and his heirs in peace and without impediment. In proof that this grant is without craft or guile he has offered a bodily oath (*corporale prestiti iuramentum*) over the tomb of the Blessed John of Beverley. Sealing clause. Witnesses: Master Robert de Lesset,[1] Thomas de Huton, Robert Inghelbert, Bartholomew Tyrel, Robert de Randes, John Minghot. (*Ibid.*, No. 70.)

32. Quitclaim by Peter de Faucumbargia, son of Walter, to God and the altar of the Blessed John of Beverley and the canons there serving God, in pure and free alms, of Odo de Rise, son of Roger, with all his sequel and chattels. Sealing clause. Witnesses: William, Robert, John, Ingram (*Hingelram*), Thomas, Adam, chaplains of the church of Beverley, William, then steward (*senescaldo*) of Sir Peter de Faucumbargia, Peter his brother, rector of Rise, Robert Vauasur, Stephen, son of Alexander, Ingram, clerk of Beverley, Walter, clerk of the church of Holy Trinity, Beverley. (*Ibid.*, No. 69.)

33. John le Gras,[2] canon of the Church of Beverley, moved by divine charity and for the safety of his soul, grants to God and the Virgin Mary and all saints, for a chaplain to celebrate divine service in perpetuity in the chapel of the Blessed James on the bridge of Hull (*ad pontem de Hull*) which belongs to the grantor's prebend of the church of Beverley, for his soul, the souls of his parents and benefactors, and of those who help in the maintenance of the bridge of Hull and in repair of the causeway on either side of the bridge, a yearly rent of 20s. in Beverley, to be received each year of the grantor and his heirs, namely: from a messuage in which William Gerard lives 5s.; from Gregory of London from the house of Reginald Barber 2s.; from two shops (*seldis*) in the fish market of Beverley which Richard the goldsmith and William the parchment-maker hold of the grantor, 5s.; and from two stone houses in Keldegate lying between the land of William Paulyn and Ivo de Benechle 8s.; which same chaplain is to be appointed by the canon of that canonry to which that chapel is attached, and he is to be perpetually resident there, and to celebrate divine service in the same chapel for the dead, daily, except on Friday on which he shall celebrate the feast of the Holy Cross, and on Saturday on which he shall celebrate the feast of the Glorious Virgin, and on Sunday on which he shall celebrate

---

[1] Robert de Lesset was a witness to a grant dated 1273 (*Beverley Chapter Act Book*, ii, 294).

[2] Before 1279 when Walter of Gloucester was collated to the prebend made vacant by the death of John le Gras (*Beverley Chapter Act Book*, ii, 137).

the feast of the Holy Trinity; and let him say each . . . . mass, the special prayers for the grantor's soul, for the souls of his parents and benefactors, and of those by whose rents the chantry is to be supported, and of those by whose offerings (*suffragiis*) the bridge and causeway are repaired [*the document is here damaged*: *the following words and portions of words can be deciphered—" Et* . . . . *per me* . . . . *res meos pro canonica et notoria causa* . . . . *t* . . . . *depositus Ego* . . . .*ores mei alium ydoneum preficiemus capellanum infra tres menses. Et* . . . . *t per capitulum Beuer'* . . . . *os tres menses ibidem preficiat'.*"]

And if within this time the Chapter has not appointed a chaplain, the grantor appoints in his place and in place of his successors, the more discreet (*saniorem*) part of the commonalty (*communitatis*) of Beverley to present to the said Chapter an honest and suitable chaplain to carry out the office. And if the Chapter will not admit him he puts in his place and in place of his heirs, the said commonalty of Beverley to collect the rent, which is to be reserved until a chaplain is installed, so that neither the grantor and his successors nor the Chapter can interfere with the taking of these rents. The chaplain to have the same power of distraining for the rents as the grantor has.

For the further strengthening of this grant he has caused the seal[1] of the Chapter of Beverley and the seal of the commonalty of Beverley to be affixed along with his own; part of the deed to remain with the Chapter, part with the commonalty of Beverley and part with the grantor and his heirs. Witnesses: Master . . . . of St. Leonard, Master Robert de Schardburg, Master Robert de Fangfosse, Master Adam de Northfolc, Master John de Pening-st . . . ., Dom.[?] William de Calverle, then canons of the Chapter of Beverley, Richard de Burton, William de Swyna, Peter de Wylgby, Peter Pollard, Robert de Lautorp, then vicars choral of Beverley, Richard le Carect', Gilbert de Snayth, Christopher de Barton, Christopher Tunde, Alexander de Bilton, John Fr[au]nceys, Roger Ousyns, Robert de W[inter]ingham, Richard de Brimston, Andrew de Neubald, burgesses of Beverley.

Dorso: It is to be noted that all chaplains of the prebends of St. John of Beverley celebrating within the vill or without, as the chaplain of *Hule bredge* and other chaplains, shall owe obedience to the Chapter and shall be corrected by the Chapter, so that all so celebrating, within the vill or without, as is aforesaid, shall have from the canons bread and wine and candles from the Sacristan. [*This in a different and probably later hand.*]   (*Ibid.*, No. 135.)

34. 12 Kal. July [June 20], 1299. Writ of William de Lincoln, canon and brother (*concanonicus et confrater*) to the Chapter of Beverley: he presents William Nithegal of Lincoln, priest, to a vicarage pertaining to his prebend in the church of Beverley; he

---

[1] Seals and tags missing.

requests the Chapter to admit his presentee. At Beverley.[1] (*Ibid.*, No. 137.)

35. May 26, 1315. William de Melton, canon of Beverley, to the Chapter of the same, explaining that the affairs of the king to which he must attend, prevent him from being present in the Chapter of Beverley on the Thursday next after the Nativity of St. John the Baptist [June 26] to treat of the urgent affairs of the church of Beverley as specified in the citation. He therefore appoints Master John de Nassington and Dom. William de Sothill as his proxies. Sealed[2] with the seal he uses as Provost of Beverley (*sigillum meum quo utor in prepositura mea Beuerl' presentibus est appensum*). In London. (*Ibid.*, No. 139.)

36. Monday before the Purification of the B.V.M., namely, 4 Kalends February [Jan. 29], 1329[-30]. Will of Alan de Humbelton,[3] vicar of the church of the blessed John of Beverley. *Inprimis*, he leaves his soul to Jesus Christ, Blessed Mary and the whole court of heaven, and his body to be buried within the church of the blessed John, or without according to the disposition of his executors. Item: in wax about his body two and a half stone (*duas petras et dimidiam*). Item: in all other funeral expenses 60s. Item: to the fabric of the said church 100s. Item: to the choir of the same, a psalter. Item: a chalice and two pieces of serge (*duo sergia*) one of blue and one of red for the high altar of the same church. Item: to the eight vicars of the same church 40s., to each vicar 5s. Item: to each chaplain present at his exequies 6d. Item: to each clerk being a stall holder (*clerico stallario*) 3d. and to each wearing the monastic garb (*portanti habitum*) 2d. and to each of the eight choir boys 2d. Item: to Dom. John de Risindon[4] one pyx of crystal with his best altar cloth and towel. Item: to Dom. William Bynd', chaplain, for celebrating divine service for two years, 3 selions of land which he [Alan] bought of William Gudmode lying near Westwode and the land which he bought of Henry Cinctfowle near Chapellan, and if the said William is unwilling to celebrate for the testator's soul during the said time, he leaves the said selions to Dom. John Bynder his nephew if he wishes to undertake the duty. Item: he leaves to Alan his boy (*garconi meo*) his house and the land which he bought of Henry Cinctfowell and the land which he bought of Margaret Ben, and the chest standing in the vicars' chamber with a copper pot, two gallon vessels with a broken posnet and a broken ewer. Item: to Beatrice, daughter of John Spicer, a house and garden

---

[1] Seal: whitish wax, oval, badly chipped; device not deciphered; legend LINC COLNIA CL....

[2] Seal: small fragments of red seal showing part of figure under crocketed canopy. Attached by a tongue of parchment cut from bottom of document.

[3] The Senior of the vicars choral.

[4] Assessor of the Chapter of St. John of Beverley (*Beverley Chapter Act Book*, i, 60).

which he bought of Benedict de Wadesworth. Item: for the augmentation of his obit and that of his father 2s. to the vicars of the said church from the houses and lands which he bought of Richard de Welwikthorp in Northwod, and 2s. for a light on the beam before the altar of St. John from the same tenement. Item: the house and lands in Flymyngate which he bought of the executors of Alice, wife of Walter de Beswyk, and a house and garden in Keldgate which he bought of Richard Roce and the house in which Rouland lives to be sold and the money given to the priests, widows and orphans of Beverley for the grantor's soul. Item: he leaves to Cecily his sister a robe of blue cloth with a tabard and half a mark. Item: to Mariot his sister a robe of russet and half a mark. Item: to Margaret, wife of John le Spicer, a red robe with two hoods and a chest which stands in his house. Item: to the three boys of Beatrice formerly wife of Alan de Boynton 6s. Item: to the boys of John Spicer 8s. Item: to William, son of Mariot his sister, a tapestry (*unam tapetam*), two linen sheets, a mattress and half a mark. Item: to Simon de Langetoft 6s. 8d. Item: to William, son of Thomas his brother, a copper pot, two gallon pots with the whole of what he owes him, that he shall do the like for the grantor's soul (*ita quod faciat pro anima mea*). Item: to his brother John *unum kundill'* [candelabrum] with 6d. rent from the house of William Raudman. He wishes his breviary (*portiforium*) to be fixed on a certain column[1] in the church just as the *Speculum Misteriale* is fixed. Item: to Sir John de Hornse a chest standing in his chamber and half a mark. Item: to John Spicer a chest standing near his bed and half a mark. Item: to Juliana, wife of William Tannatone, a red furred bodice. Item: to Thomas formerly his cook 3s. Item: to John Knyght two linen sheets and 2s. Item: to Hugh Barker two copes, a better and a worse, with a better surplice and a book which begins *cum exodo . . . genesi*, with a book of the Gospels. Item: 100s. to be distributed to the poor on the day of his burial. Item: to Alan, his boy, a spoon (*patellam*) and a cloth of little value. Item: to Agnes, his washerwoman (*lotera*) 3s. Item: to Dom. Nicholas de Hugat, provost[2] of the said church, a drinking horn and a gilt cup and to Alice the provost's sister another gilt cup. Item: three silver cups are to be sold and the money given to the poor of Beverley. Item: to Alan de Fitelyng, his nephew, 100s. on condition that he makes a pilgrimage for the testator to the Holy Land. Item: he leaves to Alan, his boy, all his teazles (*cardones*) and bales of canvas and linen (*et walos canabum et linum*). Item: to Nigel and Alan, servants in the dormitory, half a mark. Item: to Robert de Mollescroft 12d. Item: to Richard, page of the said Nigel (*Ricardo pagio dicti Nigelli*) 6d. Item: to

---

[1] See Wordsworth and Littlehales, *The Old Service Books of the English Church*, p. 281, for a description of such bookrests.

[2] See *Beverley Chapter Act Book*, ii, pp. lvi–lxii, for the life of this learned and active man.

Agnes Bullex, late wife of Adam Haunsayl, his mantle. Item: to Dom. William de Burton, chaplain, a red furred tabard. Item: to Dom. John de Risingdon a fur of mynever for a supertunic. Item: to Dom. John de Hornse a furred tabard with a furred hood *cendrini coloris*. Item: to Margaret, wife of John le Spicer, a fur of strandlyn [squirrel?]. Item: to Juliana, wife of William le Barker, a supertunic with hood with fur of *cendryn*. Item: to the Friars Preachers of Beverley half a mark. Item: to the Friars Minor of the same town half a mark. Item: to the brethren of the Brotherhood of St. Nicholas of Beverley half a mark. The house in which he lives, with the garden belonging to it and his grange outside the South Bar with the garden and rent belonging to the said grange, are to be sold and the proceeds distributed among his poor relations (*inter pauperes parentela mea*) as follows: to the boys of William *ad pontem* of Humbelton, to each of them half a mark, to Robert Pikard half a mark, to Alan his brother half a mark, to John de Humbelton their brother half a mark, to Robert, son of William the mason, half a mark and a cope, a surplice and two vestments (*rochets*). Item: all fruits standing on his land, as teazles, *perrettes* and madder, are to be sold and the proceeds, after his debts and final expenses have been paid, with the money from [the sale] of his house, garden and grange aforesaid, are to be distributed among the poor of Beverley according to the disposition of his executors, for the good of his soul. He appoints William his brother as his residuary legatee, and for the execution of his will he appoints John de Hornse, John le Spicer, and Alan, his boy. Sealed[1] with his seal and since his seal is unknown he has caused his will to be sealed with the seal of the assessor (*auditor*) of the Chapter of the church of St. John also.

Dorso: Proved before the assessor of the Chapter of St. John of Beverley and administration given to the executors named in the will. Sealed with the Chapter seal. In the Chapter at Beverley 7 Id. Feb. [Feb. 7], 1329[–30]. The proof approved by the Dean of Beverley 2 Id. Feb. [Feb. 12], 1329[–30]. (*Ibid.*, No. 140.)

37. April 6, 1352. William,[2] provost of the church of the Blessed John of Beverley, grants and gives licence under his letters patent, as far as lies within his power, for himself and his successors, to John de Wilton of Beverley to give a messuage with appurtenances in Beverley to the Chapter of the church of the Blessed John of Beverley, to provide a chapel in that church for the souls of the Lord Edward, late king of England and father of the present king, and of Dom. Nicholas de Hugate, late provost of the said church, and for the healthful state (*salubri statu*) of the same John and Alice his wife, while they are alive, and for their souls after

---

[1] Tags for six seals; fragment of brown wax on three of them.

[2] William de la Mar, provost of Beverley 1338–1360 (*Beverley Chapter Act Book*, ii, pp. lxii–lxvi).

death, and for the souls of the father and mother of the same John, and of Joan his late wife, and of all their benefactors and all the faithful departed; [the services] to be celebrated according to the ordinance of the same John. William similarly grants a separate licence to the Chapter to hold this messuage with appurtenances notwithstanding the Statute of Mortmain. William reserves for himself and his successors the services and customs due to him from this land if there were any, lest either John de Wilton and his heirs or the Chapter and their successors may be harmed by reason of the grant. Sealing clause.[1] At Northdalton. *Dorso*: *Licencia prepositi de tenemento ad manum mortuam tradito pro cantariam* [*sic*] *corporis Christi Johannis de Wilton*. (*Ibid.*, No. 141.)

38. May 26, 1353, and the first year of his second translation. John,[2] by divine permission Archbishop of York, Primate of England and Legate of the Apostolic See, to his beloved sons the archdeacon of the East Riding, his official, and the deans and all and singular the rectors, vicars, and parish priests of the said Archdeaconry to whom these present letters shall come, greeting and benediction. We have received the grave complaint of our beloved sons the provost and chapter of our Collegiate Church of the Blessed John of Beverley in our diocese, that whereas from ancient times there were due to the same church and the canons of the same, for their part support (*in partem sustentacionis*), portions of sheaves commonly called thraves payable yearly from certain fees and fields existing in the said Archdeaconry, by the devotion of the faithful and by adequate authority conferred and lawfully assigned; which said portions the lords, tenants or possessors of the fees, fields and tenements were accustomed to pay and fully deliver yearly to the said church and canons; and they, the canons, their servants and ministers in the name of the same, and of the aforesaid church, took the portions from the lords, tenants and possessors; and the present canons of the said church in their time (*pro eorum temporibus*) and their predecessors in their time were in possession of the right of taking and having all and singular the portions conferred and assigned as is aforesaid and throughout the time which the memory of man knoweth not to the contrary, peacefully and quietly; however certain degenerate and irreligious (*indevoti*) people, having no reverence for the glorious confessor and bishop St. John, have striven to withdraw certain portions of the said sheaves and for some time have withdrawn the same and unjustly retained them, thus basely depriving the canons and the church of St. John of their right, to the grave peril of their souls, the no small loss and annoyance of the said canons and church, and the scandal of many, and thus

[1] Tag and seal both missing.

[2] John Thoresby, translated from St. David's to Worcester in 1349, and from thence to York, 1352.

incurring the sentence of the greater excommunication. We therefore in the solicitude of our pastoral office, desiring to provide remedies against the said dangers, order you all and singular, in virtue of your obedience and under penalty of suspension from office should you be negligent or remiss in this matter, to denounce solemnly before clergy and people in every parish church under you on three Sundays or solemn occasions (*solempnes*), and on as many others as may seem necessary, that all who detain or withdraw the said thraves (*detentatores et subtrahentes*), and other such despoilers, as well as their aiders and abettors by deed or advice, have fallen under the sentence of the greater excommunication, likewise expressly forbidding anyone to presume to fall into such rashness in future, under pain of serious penalties to be inflicted by reason of our office, in addition to the canonical penalties aforesaid; you shall also enquire concerning the names of those who have so presumed and of their aiders and abettors; and those whom you shall find offenders (*reos*), you shall cite or cause the same to be cited to appear before us or our official in our church of York, on a law day assigned by you to the same, to show without delay if they know any reason why they ought not to be proclaimed as having fallen under the sentence of excommunication and further to be punished according to the quantity and nature of the business (*negocii*) as is laid down by the canons. You or one of you shall notify us concerning the day of the receipt of the presents, the names of the delinquents, the days of the warning and citation, the day assigned by you and whatever further you do in this matter. In our manor near Westminster.[1] (*Ibid.*, No. 142.)

39. Aug. 12, 1357. The Official of the court of York to the dean of Herthill and the vicars of the churches of Santon, Hesell, Watton, Hoton Crauncewyk, Kilnewyk and North Dalton, and all and singular parochial chaplains of the said churches and of others in the archdeaconry of the Estriding, greeting. Whereas our commissary general has given letters ordering you, the dean and vicars aforesaid to warn under pain of the greater excommunication all and singular parishioners cultivating lands within your or their parishes or in any of them, that they, the parishioners shall faithfully separate the whole tenth part (*integram decimam*), without any diminution or subtraction, of the fruits growing on their lands from the nine parts and shall place them in the fields where they grow in full and separately (*in campis ubi crescunt dimittant integraliter separaliter*), and that then they, or any others shall not lay hands on the said tithes nor move the same, nor bear them off or dispose of them in any wise without licence of the rector or vicar of the said churches or of their ministers [since they are] the possession of the canons and pre-

---

[1] There are indications that the document has either been sewn to another or some attachment has been made by threads. Evidence of more than one seal having been affixed to the dorse of the document; all have disappeared.

B

bendaries of the church of St. John of Beverley who have complained to us on this matter. Wherefore to you and each of you who shall receive this our present mandate, we order you to warn, under pain of the greater excommunication, all and singular your parishioners and others cultivating the land within your parishes and in any other parishes within the archdeaconry that concerning the thraves and tithes of all kinds due and pertaining to the church of Beverley and the canons and prebendaries of the same, they are to give such full satisfaction in the form and manner in which it has hitherto been customary to give satisfaction. At York. (*Ibid.*, No. 143.)

40. Oct. 1, 1362. Inspeximus by the dean of Beverley of the testament of Thomas de Burton son of William de Burton of Beverley, deceased, with proof of the same, the tenor of which is as follows: In the name of God, Amen. Sunday after St. Mary Magdalene [July 24], 1362. Thomas de Burton son of William de Burton of Beverley deceased made his testament in this wise. Inprimis, he left his soul to God and the B.V.M. and all saints, and his body to be buried . . . .[1] of the chapel of the B.V.M. in Beverley. Item: to Emma, his mother, a messuage with appurtenances in Beverley in Fischmarketgate lying between the land late belonging to Thomas de Ryse on the north and the land late of William de Carleolo, now in the hands of Richard de Holm', on the south for the whole length as is shown (*ad totam longitudinem sicut proportatur*); to hold to Emma his mother for the whole of her life with remainder to the testator's right heirs. Item: to Richard de Holm' another messuage with appurtenances in Beverley, adjacent to the said messuage, which formerly belonged to William de Carleolo and lies between the messuage he has left to his mother [on the north] and the land of the said Richard de Holm' on the south; to hold to Richard his heirs and assigns for ever of the chief lords of the fee by the services due and accustomed. Item: his horse to be sold to pay William Day of Wighton 15s. of silver for the money . . . . The residue of all his goods he left for the performance of his exequies; and he appointed Emma his mother executor of his testament.

Proved before the dean of Beverley Sept. 4, 1362. Sealed[2] with the seal of his office. At Beverley. (*Ibid.*, No. 144.)

41. Tuesday before the Nativity of St. John the Baptist [June 19], 1375, 49 Edward III. Grant by Richard de Rauenser, prebendary of the prebend of St. Martin[3] in the collegiate church of St. John of Beverley, to the canons and chapter of that church,

---

[1] Document torn and stained in places and writing difficult to decipher.

[2] Seal: fragment of small seal of green wax 1¼ in. long, pointed oval; bears a figure in a posture of devotion facing to sinister; legend broken away except for ACI.

[3] For the further possessions of this, the richest of the prebends, see *Beverley Chapter Act Book*, i, 215.

of a piece of land with appurtenances in Beverley 147 feet in length and 19 feet in width, which piece of land is part of the said prebend; to hold to the canons and chapter and their successors in perpetuity in exchange for a certain piece of land with appurtenances in the same vill 108 feet in length and 48 feet in width, near to the house of the said Richard; to hold of the chief lords of the fee by the due and accustomed services. Sealing clause. Witnesses: Adam Coppandale, John Tirwhyt, Thomas Geruays, William Frost, Thomas Jolyf, Geoffrey Howell. At Beverley. (*Ibid.*, No. 145.)

42. Aug. 5, 1391. Quitclaim by the chapter of the collegiate church of St. John of Beverley, with the consent of the provost of the same, to Doms. John de Normanby, John de Roston, and William de Nonyngton, chaplains, of all right and claim in a messuage with appurtenances in the vill of Beverley, situate opposite the chapel of Blessed Mary of Beverley between a lane called Viberlane on the north and Couperlane on the south, and the highway on the east and the tenement of Amand de Routhe on the west. Sealed[1] as well with the common seal of the chapter as with the seal of the provost of Beverley. At Beverley in the chapter house. (*Ibid.*, No. 147.)

43. June 28, 1400. To all the faithful in Christ, Robert de Louthorp, John Spretley, William Harpham, William Hoton, John Boynton, John Brydlyngton, Robert Green, Thomas Skyftlyng, and Robert Bryde, vicars choral of the church of the Blessed John of Beverley send greeting. Be it known that Master Simon de Euesham, late archdeacon of Richmond, granted to our predecessors, to us and our successors, vicars choral of Beverley, a yearly rent of 5s. from his tenement in Mynstermoregate in Beverley, which lay and lies between the land of Alice daughter of Matilda on one side, and the land late of Elias nephew of Angot; to be held in frankalmoin by us the said vicars choral and our successors in perpetuity; but in course of time the said yearly rent, by reason of the ruin and devastation of the tenement (*occasione ruine et vastacionis eiusdem tenementi*), remained and remains unpaid; we therefore the said vicars choral, by common consent, have assigned to Robert Manfeld, Roger Flex, and William Leke, clerks, their heirs and assigns, in perpetuity, 3s. per annum of this yearly rent of 5s. Warranty. For this release, Robert Manfeld, Roger Flex and William Leke covenant to pay to the vicars choral and their successors in perpetuity, for the said tenement, a yearly rent of 2s., payable in equal portions at Whitsuntide and Martinmas. If rent not paid within fifteen days of either of these two terms the vicars choral and their successors to have power to

---

[1] Seal: very dark brown wax, oval, *c.* 3 in. × 2 in., badly broken round edges; bears full length figure of ecclesiastic, vested, mitred and enthroned; legend, all chipped away except RLAC . . . . ES.; very fine impression. No indication that there has been another seal.

distrain on the tenement to the extent of the rent and arrears. Sealing clause.[1] Witnesses: John de Routh, clerk, Gerard Usflete, clerk, Nicholas Rys, John Kelk, William Rolleston, Richard Aglyon, John Holm. At Beverley. (*Ibid.*, No. 148.)

44. Aug. 25, 1402. Grant by the chapter of the collegiate church of Blessed John of Beverley to William Santon, chaplain of the chantry of St. Anne, founded in that church for the souls of Alexander Neuill, late Archbishop of York, and Robert Manfelde, provost of the church of Beverley, and of others, and his successors, chaplains of the same chantry, of a yearly pension of 11 silver marks, to be received yearly from the donors and their successors in the chapter house of the said church, by the hands of the custodians of the fabric, in four equal portions at Christmas, Easter, the Nativity of St. John the Baptist, and Michaelmas; to hold to William Santon and his successors in perpetuity. If part or whole of payment in arrears fifteen days after any of the set terms, power to distrain on all lands and tenements of the church within or without the Liberty of Beverley. Warranty. Alternate seals. Witnesses: Richard Chestirfield, president (*president'*), Master Adam Fenrothir, Robert Manfeld, provost, Roger Weston, canons, John Sprotley, John de Bridlyngton, John de Boynton, vicars. In the chapter house at Beverley. (*Ibid.*, No. 149.)

45. Feb. 7, 1416[-7]. Ordination in perpetuity of a chantry by the licence of Henry V, and of Henry, Archbishop of York, Primate of England and Legate of the Apostolic See.

Nicholas de Ryse of Beverley has given, granted and assigned to Dom. Robert Smyth, perpetual chaplain (*capellano perpetuo*), and his successors, for the celebration of divine service for the good estate (*pro bono statu*) of the said Nicholas and of Joan his wife, in the chapel of the Blessed Mary of Beverley at the altar of St. Nicholas in the same, 2 messuages, 10 acres of land and 3 acres of meadow, with appurtenances, in Beverley, lying as is more fully explained in the charters made to this end; to have and to hold to the same Dom. Robert Smyth, chaplain, and to each of his successors, of the then lord archbishop of York by the services due and by right accustomed, namely that the said Dom. Robert Smyth and each of his successors shall personally and continually reside in the chantry, notwithstanding any dispensation or excuse; and he and each of his successors shall daily celebrate mass, any canonical impediment notwithstanding (*impedimento canonico cessante*), at the altar of St. Nicholas in the chapel of the Blessed Mary of Beverley for the souls of Nicholas de Rise and Joan his wife when they shall die, and for the souls of William Rise, father of the said Nicholas, and of Joan his mother, also for the souls of Thomas Rise and Alice his wife, of Thomas Rise, junior, Adam Copandale, of Masters Richard de Thorn and John de Thorn, formerly canons of the Cathedral

---

[1] Tag for seal, but seal missing.

Church of York, of Hugh Totehill [Richard Thorn and Alice his wife, and Margaret Rowalde],[1] John de Warton and Dom. William de Cotyngham, chaplain, and the souls of all their benefactors and of all the faithful departed. The said Robert Smyth, and each of his successors, shall daily say *Placebo et Dirige* with commendation of the dead (*cum commendatione mortuorum*); and he shall be present at the canonical hours and the mass of the day in the choir of the chapel of the Blessed Mary aforesaid on all and singular Sundays and double feasts unless by any means impeded. He is to be bound, having touched the Holy Gospels on his induction (*in sua admissione*), to the same residence, personally and continually doing and carrying out there his office, as is promised. In like manner the said Dom. Robert Smyth, and each of his successors, shall swear that he will maintain all lands, meadows and tenements pertaining to the said chantry in the same state or better than he received them and will not alienate any part of the same for more than five years after the death of the same Nicholas, nor shall he alienate the books, chalice, vestments or any other ornaments to the same chantry pertaining, nor exchange them for worse or lend them to anyone (*alicui accomodabit*) under pain of deprivation of the said chantry. The said Nicholas wished and ordained that the presentation to the said chantry should pertain to him as well now on the first occasion as at any other time when it shall happen to fall vacant during his life, and in like manner to his wife Joan if she outlive him; further he ordained that after his death and the death of his wife, when the chantry shall be vacant the presentation shall pertain to the twelve rulers of the town of Beverley or to the mayor and more discreet part of them, and they within fifteen days of the time of the chantry becoming vacant shall present a suitable chaplain to the chapter of the collegiate church of the Blessed John of Beverley, and the said chaplain having taken the oath to maintain all the within-mentioned things let him be instituted and inducted into the same by the chapter. And if the twelve are negligent and do not do as is aforesaid within fifteen days, then the collation of the same chantry and the induction shall pertain to the chapter, and in like manner as often as the twelve default. And if the chapter fail to carry out the collation and induction then on every such occasion it shall devolve upon the archbishop of York who shall then be. . . . .[2] and the said archbishop of York is bound to confer the chantry on a suitable chaplain within fifteen days of this devolution. And in like manner for default of the said archbishop of York, the collation to the said chantry shall pertain to the dean and chapter of the cathedral church of York, in such manner, however, as not to prejudice the right of the chapter of Beverley of presenting, admitting or inducting a suitable chaplain to the

---

[1] These names have been inserted above the line.

[2] The manuscript is defective at this point.

chantry at any other time when it shall be vacant. If for any reason it should happen in future that there were not twelve rulers of the town of Beverley then the collation to the chantry shall pertain to the chapter of Beverley without any other presentation; and if the chapter of Beverley delay in the collation then that right shall pertain to the archbishop of York or the chapter of the cathedral church of York as above expressed, and so as often as the chapter of Beverley is negligent in this matter. If the chaplain of the said chantry is publicly defamed of incontinence or is a frequenter of common taverns, or shall commit any other crime by reason of which anyone holding a benefice might be deprived of it, he is at once to be deprived and removed by the chapter of Beverley, all appeal being set aside, saving always the right and jurisdiction of the archbishop of York in all things. In witness of which ordination tripartite, part of the document is to remain with the chapter of Beverley, part with Nicholas Rise and his assigns, and part with the twelve rulers of Beverley. Sealed[1] with the seal of the chapter of Beverley, that of Nicholas Rise and that of the commonalty of the town of Beverley. At Beverley.[2] (*Ibid.*, No. 151.)

46. Sept. 20, 1421, 9 Henry V. To all sons of Holy Mother Church seeing these letters tripartite, John atte Well, Thomas Skipwyth, Thomas Swanland, William Holm, Thomas Deen, and Richard Dodyng of Beverley, custodians of the fabric of the chapel of the Blessed Virgin Mary of Beverley, send greeting. Know that we, having had solemn and diligent discussion with several honourable parishioners of the said chapel, by our unanimous consent and with the assent of the same parishioners, have granted, in return for a certain sum of money which we have received from Isabel, late wife of John Withornewyke of Beverley, tanner, deceased, for the use and enlargement of the said chapel, to the said Isabel and her heirs, for ourselves and our successors, to pay yearly from the goods and rents of the said fabric 2s. 11d. for an obit for the souls of John Wythornewyke and Thomas his son deceased, and of Isabel after her death, and of all the faithful departed; the obit to be celebrated yearly in the choir of the chapel on the sixteenth day of February, or within the octave immediately preceding or succeeding, with due solemnity. The 2s. 11d. to be distributed as follows: to the vicar or chaplain celebrating mass 2d., to each of the eight other chaplains present 1d., to each of the four clerks 1d., to one thurifer (*turribulario*) 1d., to each of the two choristers ½d., for the offering at the mass 1d., for the light of four candles about the tomb of the said John, Isabel and Thomas and a decent covering for the tombs 7d., for the ringing of three of the greater bells, the greatest excepted, 8d.,

[1] Tags for three seals, but seals missing.

[2] *Dorso: Ista tercia pars ordinacionis Cantarie Sancti Nicholi in Capella beate Marie Beverlac' debet remanere Capitulo ecclesie Collegii beati Johannis Beverl' cui tradata.*

to the common bellringer (*campanatori*) of the town of Beverley for crying prayers (*deprecaturo*) through the town for the said souls, as is the custom, 3*d*. If it should happen that we or our successors should be deficient in the solemnization of the said obit or in the payment of the said 2*s*. 11*d*., according to the above manner and form, we grant that it shall be lawful for Isabel and her heirs, and after their decease for the chapter of the collegiate church of the Blessed John of Beverley, and the custodian of the fabric of the same church, to distrain on a messuage of the fabric of the said chapel in Beverley, lying within the North Bar (*infra barras boriales*), in width between the messuage of Richard de Lound on the south and the land of John Cave on the north, and in length from the highway on the west to the lands of the said Richard de Lound on the east, and on all other lands and tenements of the fabric of the said chapel when distraint cannot be made on that messuage, until 6*s*. 8*d*. is levied and received therefrom for each defect and omission. Further we grant that if on the day of the solemnization of the obit we fail to make the necessary payments or to celebrate the obit we shall be bound to pay on every such occasion 5*s*. to the said chapter and 5*s*. for the upkeep and repair of the fabric of the collegiate church. One part of the agreement to remain the property of Isabel, and the other that of the chapter: both these to be sealed[1] with the seals of the custodians of the fabric and with the common seal of the fabric; the third part to remain with the custodians bearing the seal of Isabel. At Beverley.[2] (*Ibid.*, No. 152.)

47. May 29, 1429, 7 Henry VI. Grant by John Barton de Wrawby, chapman, son and heir of John Barton of Beverley and Margaret his wife, both deceased, to John Bilton of Beverley, chaplain, and John Tasker of the same, their heirs and assigns, of a tenement with appurtenances in Beverley near the Cukstolepytt, which tenement is half a messuage, formerly in the possession of Richard Walkyngton *Wadiator*' and afterwards in the possession of Robert de Brune of Beverley, junior, and Joan his wife, the grantor's grandmother; it extends in length from the highway near the Cukstolepytt on the west to the land of William Holm, merchant, and Isabel, his wife, and the land of Katherine, sister of Isabel, formerly in the possession of the said Robert de Brune and afterwards in the possession of Thomas de Snayth on the east, and in width between the tenement of the said John Bilton, chaplain, which is the other half of the said messuage, on the south, and the tenement of William son of Adam Tyrwhitt, formerly in the possession of John de Routh, and the tenement of William Awne of York, formerly in the possession of John Humbrecolte, on the north. To hold of the chief lords of the fee

---

[1] Tags and seal missing.

[2] *Dorso: Ista tercia pars huius indenture debet remanere penes Capitulum Ecclesie Collegii beati Johannis Beuerlaci propter securitatem cui tradata.*

by the due and accustomed services. Warranty. Sealing clause.[1] Witnesses: John att Well, William Cokerell, Thomas Skypwith, John Bewme, Adam Ughtybrygg, Ralph Ebirston, Walter Dunhome of Beverley. At Beverley. (*Ibid.*, No. 71.)

48. Sept. 12, 1430, 9 Henry VI. Appointment by Henry Brounflete, knt., Walter Gude, Thomas Sprotley and Richard Yotyn, chaplains, of John de Portyngton and Edmund Portyngton, esqs., as their attorneys to deliver seisin to John de Portyngton, son of the aforesaid John and Margaret, his wife, and the heirs of the body of Margaret lawfully begotten, of all those lands and tenements, rents and services with appurtenances which the grantors had of the gift and feoffment of Joan Eyrmyn formerly wife of Richard [*or* Roger—*document defaced*] Ermyn in the vills of Beverley and Speton and elsewhere in co. York, which John de Portyngton, son of John, had of the gift and feoffment of the grantors as more fully appears in a charter made by them to the same John and Margaret, his wife. Sealing clause.[2] At Beverley. (*Ibid.*, No. 72.)

49. June 12, 18 Henry VI [1440]. Grant by Robert Skypse of Beverley to Edmund Portyngton, esq., and John Karr, chaplain, of a messuage and two gardens, with appurtenances, in Beverley, which the grantor lately had of the gift of John Ellerkar, sergeant-at-law, Thomas Santon, esq., and Cecily, widow of Robert Santon, esq.; which messuage lies in the street called Estgatte, stretching in length from the same street on the west to the common sewer on the east, and in width between the messuage formerly belonging to William Tyghler and a lane called Ferrourlane on the north, and a messuage formerly belonging to John Rede on the south; one of the gardens lies in Hayrerlane and is held of the Hospital of St. John the Baptist of Beverley, and the other also lies in Hayrerlane and formerly belonged to Walter Ferrour and is 31 rods long by the royal rod (*per virgam regiam*), and including the south wall is nine feet of a man's foot (*novem pedes hominis*) wide; to hold to them, their heirs and assigns, for ever of the chief lords of the fee. Warranty. Sealing clause. Witnesses: Roger Rolleston of Beverley, Thomas Everyngham of the same, esqs., Thomas Wylton of the same, Thomas Mayne of the same, William Spens of the same. At Beverley. (*Ibid.*, No. 73.)

50. [3]Oct. 22, 2 Edward [IV] [1462]. Letters Patent of Edward [IV]: General Pardon to Richard Tetnall of Beverley co. York, chaplain, otherwise called Richard Tetnall, the perpetual chaplain of the chantry of the gild of the Fraternity of Corpus Christi in the collegiate church of St. John of Beverley at the

---

[1] Tag and seal both missing.

[2] Seals: three of red wax; (1) oval, $\frac{9}{16}$ in. × $\frac{8}{16}$ in., in a lozenge the letter G; (2) diam. 1 in., on a small shield what appears to be a lion rampant double queued; (3) a head facing to sinister on a blob of wax.

[3] Document torn and illegible in parts.

altar of St. Nicholas, founded in the charnel house (*in charnello*) of the same church, for all transgressions and offences committed before 4 November last [*long list specified*] and pardon for the outlawry promulgated against him, on condition that he appears in the king's court to answer the charges made against him [*etc., etc.*]. It is provided that this pardon shall not apply to John Waleys late of Thornton co. Devon, esq., Roger Thorp late of London, esq., William Philipp' otherwise called William Ferrour late of London, esq., Edward Thorn[burgh] late of Carlile, *gentilman*, John Amyas late of Watton, co. York, *gentilman*, Nicholas Rigby late of Kyngeston super Thames, co. Surrey, yeoman, and Thomas Sergeauntson late of York, yeoman, or any other person or persons attainted of high treason by the authority of Parliament begun and held at Westminster the 4th of November last past, nor to any person or persons attainted by Parliament, nor to any rebels now existing in [Scotland or France] and adhering to the chief rebel and enemy, Henry, late *de facto* but not *de iure* king of England. Nor is it to apply to any [royal ministers] "who now are or late were," namely, to the Treasurer of Cales and of the royal household (*hospicii*) [*etc.*].[1] (*Ibid.*, No. 74.)

51. April 25, 1 Hen. [VII], [1486]. Letters Patent. General Pardon by Henry [VII] to the provost[2] and chapter of the collegiate church of St. John, Beverley, for all manner of transgressions [*etc.—long list specified*] committed by the said provost and chapter before Nov. 7 in the first year of his reign; also pardon for all fines, amercements, reliefs, scutages [*etc.*] due before Michaelmas 1484.

This pardon not to extend to any great accountants (*magnos computantes*) who now are or who late were, namely, the mayor and society of the Staple town of Cales or the mayor, constable and society of our aforesaid Staple, nor to any accountants (*computantes*) within the said town, the town and castle of Guysnes and the castle of Hammes and the Marches of the same [*etc., etc., applying to various royal officials*].[3] At York.[4] (*Ibid.*, No. 154.)

52. April 9, 5 Edward IV [1465]. Lease by John Cromwell, William Kyreton, Robert Wodd, John Chowe and Richard Smyth of Beverley, chaplains, to William Homerston of Beverley, yeoman, and Isabel, his wife, of a messuage or tenement in Beverley in a certain lane called Keldgate in which William Whyte, *parchementmakere*, lives, with a garden attached, which lies in length between the garden of John Kelke of Barton on the west and the grantors' tenement on the east; to hold for the term of the lives

---

[1] Tag for seal and seal missing.

[2] William Poteman, provost 1467–1493 (*Beverley Chapter Act Book*, ii, p. xcii).

[3] Seal and tag both missing.

[4] It is endorsed in an early seventeenth-century hand, " King Athelston Grants."

of William Homerston and Isabel, paying yearly 2s. in equal portions at Martinmas and Whitsuntide. Alternate seals. Witnesses: Alexander Lounde, Robert Sheffeld, esqs., Roger Kelke, esq., John Medilton, merchant, Robert Thomson, Thomas Haltreholme, William Whyte of Beverley, chaplains. (*Ibid.*, No. 75.)

53. April 17, 1472.[1] Indenture between William Potman, clerk, provost of the ' Collegiall ' church of St. John of Beverley and the chapter of the same, of the one part . . . . [William Rilston, gent., executor of] Henry Brounflete, knt., ' late lord Vessy ' of the second part, and us Thomas Halytreholme, William Rothemun, Thomas Wencelagh, John Crumwell, George Wryght, Thomas Kyrkman and Robert Wode, priests, the seven priests in the choir of the said 'collegiall' [church] . . . . John . . . . witnesses that whereas the late lord Vessy in his life and by his last will ordained among other things that six priests should be established in perpetuity to pray for his soul and the souls of those specified in his last will. To . . . . agreed and concluded between the party aforesaid and especially by us the seven priests, for us and our successors and their fellows in the future who shall be priests in the choir of the said ' collegiall ' church with the assent of the provost and chapter . . . . only to pray for the said souls in the ' collegiall ' church in manner and form ensuing, namely, that we the seven priests and our successors for the sum of [13s.] 4d. of lawful English money by the said executor to us given, shall daily for ever, the three days immediately preceding Easter excepted, find a priest [to sing] mass within the ' collegiall ' church, that is to say, each one of us to sing mass or cause it to be sung one whole week together by turns, starting with the oldest admitted, and so in order to the youngest admitted, 'which shall kepe ye last weke in order amongst us,' and after him the oldest to begin again . . . . with this clause *ut animam famuli tui famule tue et animas famulorum famularum, etc.*, with the principal collect 'under one conclusion dayly ' in his mass when he sings for the said souls, which mass so sung or said shall be called for ever the lord Vessy chantry in the said 'collegiall' church . . . . seven priests and our successors and fellows shall every Monday say a mass or memory of the Holy Ghost, Tuesday a mass or memory of Saint John of Beverley, and Friday a requiem mass or memory, the memories to be said at the same altar as the mass and immediately before or after the mass; also daily before or after the mass at the same altar if it be convenient, or at some other convenient place, he shall say kneeling in the church ' secrete wyse' for the souls of Sir Henry Brounflete, knt., Dame Alianore his wife, the souls of Sir Thomas Brounflete, knt., and Dame Margaret his wife and for all Christian souls, *De Profundis Clamavi*, saying the whole psalm with the parts and collects accustomed to be said

---

[1] In English. The document is badly torn and stained with the impressions of the seals.

for the souls of those who have passed from this earthly life; and if any of us the said seven priests or our successors or fellows who in time to come shall be priests in the said choir shall be otherwise beneficed or have any salary so that he may not carry out the duty in his own person, he shall find at his own cost another of the said priests, if any one is so disposed, or else some other suitable priest, to carry out his duty; also we the seven priests shall every year at the altar of Our Lady within the ' collegiall ' church solemnly ' do an obite ' with note for the soul of the said lord Vessy in this form, namely, ... day of January within two days before or two days after, ' at afternone ' *placebo* and *dirige* with nine lections and at the day next following at the same altar a requiem mass with deacon and subdeacon, and in the [middle] of the cross aisle before the image of Our Lady at the ' Rood owk ' . . . . and covered with a black cloth having a white cross ' ordeyned ' for the same with four tapers of wax, every taper weighing two pounds, to be set about the same 'herce' upon four candlesticks ordained for the same, burning at the times of the said *placebo* and *dirige* and requiem mass [there shall be provided] . . . . the sacristan of the ' collegiall ' church and his successors yearly for the same wax 16*d.* ' yf they so wole be contented,' otherwise the 16*d.* to be distributed among the poor; and the common bellman of the town of Beverley . . . . shall announce through the said town, as is the custom, on the day that the *placebo* and *dirige* shall be done, the *obit* for the soul of the said late lord Vessy at the costs of us the said [priests] . . . . who are to pay the bellman yearly for his labours 2*d.*; and the bells in the north steeple of the '' collegiall ' church are to be rung both to and at the *dirige* and requiem mass, the sacristan's clerks being paid yearly for their labours in ringing [12*d.*], otherwise the 12*d.* to be distributed among the poor; at which [service] we the seven priests shall be present upon pain of forfeiture of 3*s.* 4*d.* to be paid to our steward and to be disposed of for our common expenses . . . . we seven priests or our successors and all others who shall be of our habit (*abite*) and fellowship, to the intent that our promised grants and charges and every of them shall be more openly known and more clearly had in remembrance and mind, in our or their proper persons shall [on the] translation of St. John of Beverley next after the making of this deed indented in the chapter house of the ' collegiall ' church, come before the canon or canons resident (*chanons residencers*) if any at that time be present, or in their absence before the auditor of the said [chapter] . . . . their power, and there in the presence of the canon or canons or of the auditor and show that part of this deed which remains with us and read it and declare that this is our yearly and perpetual charge; and we the seven priests shall make labour and instance that the said chapter shall make a new act . . . . that every priest that in time to come shall be admitted of our fellowship and habit shall upon admission in the chapter house have the said part of the deed read and declared to him and he shall be bound on his oath to observe and fulfil all the premises; to observe which, we, the seven priests now bind ourselves and successors to the provost and chapter and to the said William Rilston, binding also us and our successors that if they or any of them through obstinacy or malice are remiss so that any of the duties be unperformed they shall pay for every such default to William Rilston during his life and after his death to the provost and chapter and their successors and the successors of either of them 40s., and after the death of William Rilston this money to be divided equally between the provost and chapter; and if after such a default William Rilston in his lifetime, and the provost and chapter after his death, be not paid at the first asking they shall have power [to enter and distrain] as well within our mansion beside the Bedern of Beverley as within any other lands [*etc.*] of which we are seised until they shall be fully recompensed for the said 40s.; and now we the seven priests bind ourselves and our successors by these presents to the said [William Rilston] that we shall put ourselves in .... within the space of four years next after the making of these presents to purchase lands and tenements to .... whereof the issues and revenues which shall yearly be sufficient to support .... and every one of them aforesaid; to all which promises, agreements [*etc.*] to be performed by us the seven priests, we the provost and chapter give our assent and approve and confirm the same, and will in no wise that the said ordinances and agreements .... article or clause concerning them and their successors specified and contained in an ordinance made by Thomas Arundel sometime archbishop of York made in the said ' collegiall ' church in these words *nostre tamen intencionis non ex. . . . quin tres officiarii et septem persone libere possint recipere annualia.* In witness of which to one part of this tripartite deed to be delivered to William Rilston, the said seven priests and [the chapter] have set their seals,[1] to the second part to be delivered to the provost and chapter the seven priests and William Rilston have set their several seals, and to the third part remaining with the seven priests and their successors the said chapter has set its common seal and William Rilston his seal. In the chapter house at Beverley. (*Ibid.*, No. 153.)

Birdsall.

54.   May 17, 18 Edward IV [1478].   Copy of a grant by John Kyldayll, son and heir of Robert Kyldayll late of Garton, to Edmund Twhaytts, Thomas Wylson, chaplain, and Robert

---

[1] Seals: two, one of dark brown wax, diam. *c.* 2 in., badly broken; device appears to be a church; legend S: ARCHIE in strong well-formed Lombardic letters all that remains; the other, part of an oval seal of reddish brown wax; device a bird facing dexter; legend blurred and not deciphered.

Parkynson, of a messuage and a derelict messuage (*messuagium vastum*) with 2 crofts and 3½ bovates of land in the vill and territory of Birdsaull, which lately belonged to Robert Kyldayll, the grantor's father; to hold these lands and tenements of the chief lords of the fee. Warranty. Witnesses: John de Sancto Quintino, Edmund Skerne, John Jaklyn. Sealing clause. (*Ibid.*, No. 157.)

Bramley (Leeds).

55. St. Gregory, 1262 [March 12, 1262–3]. Bond. Peter de Ferseley and Alice, his wife, hold themselves bound to the abbot and monks of St. Mary of Kyrkestall, to appear before the King's justices at their next coming to Yorkshire, to secure to the abbot and monks the lands, tenements and goods which they [Peter and Alice] had sold or given to them. This they swear by touch of the Gospels (*sacrosanctis*), and promise to perform the covenant faithfully and without fraud. Sealing clause. (*Bramley MSS.*, No. 1.)

56. Grant by Adam son of Peter de Ferselay to Adam son of Peter Full....s of Ferselay and Clarice, the grantor's daughter, of that toft and croft which he had of the gift of his mother in the vill of Bramelay; to hold to them and their heirs, freely [*etc.*], of the chief lords of the fee; should they die without legitimate heirs, reversion to the grantor. Warranty. Sealing clause. Witnesses: Sir William de Weston, William de Alta ripa, Hugh de Wodehalle, Elias de Bramelay, Henry de Armelay. (*Ibid.*, No. 2.)

57. July, 1265. Indenture whereby Adam son of Norays de Bramelay releases to his lords, the abbot and monks of Kyrkestall, the timber of the common woods of Bramelay, which pertains to him and his heirs, for lighting their buildings, saving only to him and his heirs the rights and customs laid down in his charter of feoffment; and he agrees that no contention or controversy shall ever arise between him and his lords in this matter. Alternate seals.[1] Witnesses: Mag. Warner de Pontefracto, Adam de Beston, Ralph son of Robert of the same, Ralph Hedne, Robert de Wyrkelay, Peter de Ferseley, Thomas son of Matilda de Bramelay. (*Ibid.*, No. 3.)

58. Grant by Adam son of Norays de Bramelay to Alan de Berdesai, of a bovate of land in the territory of Bramelay with appurtenances which Roger son of Maurice once held; to hold to him and his heirs and assigns, in fee and hereditarily with all liberties pertaining to the land, within the vill of Bramelay and without, paying yearly to the grantor a pair of white gloves during the octave of Whit Sunday for all services except forinsec service. Warranty. Sealing clause. Witnesses: Robert de Wirkelay,[2] Ralph de Eden, Thomas de Fernlay, Alexander de Ledes,[3]

[1] Seal: fragment of green wax.
[2] Wortley.
[3] See note on Alexander de Leeds in *The Coucher Book of Kirkstall Abbey*, p. 303*n*.

William Frantenant, Thomas son of Matilda, John de Bercroft, Jordan de Wudehal. (*Ibid.*, No. 4.)

59. Agreement between Adam son of Norays de Bramelaye and William son of William Cokeman, whereby Adam demises to William 2 acres of land in Bramelaye, adjacent to the land which Adam demised to Thomas Cokeman, William's brother, for the term of 8 years. Warranty. Sealing clause. Witnesses: Richard de la Haye, John de Alta ripa, Ralph Heden, Thomas Sampson, Robert son of Peter, Robert Cokeman. (*Ibid.*, No. 5.)

60. Quitclaim by Thomas, called *le Strenger*, of Norton, and Isabel de Bramelay, his wife, to Matilda, daughter of Alan de Berdesay, for a sum of money, of all right in a toft and a croft in Bramelay, lying between the tofts once belonging to Roger son of William and Ralph de Morewik; also of an assart called Martin's assart; to hold to her and her heirs of the chief lords of the fee with all liberties [*etc.*]. Sealing clause.[1] Witnesses: Thomas Sampson of Farnelay, Hugh his son, Henry de Mayingham, Jordan de la Wodehall, William son of Roger de Podissay, William *ad portam* of the same, Simon de Culcotes, John son of Allater, Robert son of Simon, Roger son of William de Bramlay, William de Bercroft, Adam son of Peter, Elias son of Francis of the same. (*Ibid.*, No. 6.)

61. Quitclaim by William le Tyburner and Isobel, his wife, Richard le Charter and Matilda, his wife, to Elias de Alwodeley and Mary, his wife, their heirs and assigns, of all right in 2 messuages with a croft adjoining and a bovate and an assart in Bramlay, which messuages lie between the toft of Richard Penne on one side and the toft of William Nagtegale on the other, and the bovate of land once belonged to William Mancurnays, and the assart is called Esterode; to hold to Elias and Mary and their heirs and assigns, of the chief lords of the fee, with all easements [*etc.*], within the vill of Bramlay and without. Warranty. Sealing clause.[2] Witnesses: Sir Hugh de Swylington, Sir Alexander de Led', knts., Walter de Grimston, William de Wyrkeley, John Morman of the same, William de Bercroft of Bramley, Roger son of William of the same, Robert son of Thomas of the same, John de Rotheley. (*Ibid.*, No. 7.)

62. Octave of St. Hilary, 20 Edward, son of Henry [Jan. 20, 1291–2]. Final concord at Westminster before John de Metyngham, Robert de Hertforde, Elias de Bekyngham, and William de Giselham, justices, between Elias de Alwodeleye, and Sara, his wife, of the one part, and Hugh son of Henry de Thorparches and Matilda, his wife, of the other part, concerning 2 messuages and a bovate and $14\frac{1}{2}$ acres of land with appurtenances in Bramleye; whereby it was agreed that Hugh and Matilda shall recognise

---

[1] Two seals: (1) missing; (2) brownish wax, broken.

[2] Tongues for five seals, all missing.

that the land rightly belonged to Elias, as he and Sara had once received it as gift from Hugh and Matilda; to hold to Elias and Sara and the heirs of Elias, of the chief lords of the fee, in perpetuity. Warranty. And for this recognition Elias and Sara shall give to Hugh and Matilda a red sparrowhawk (*sparuarium sorum*). (*Ibid.*, No. 8.)

63. Martinmas [Nov. 11], 1315. Indenture whereby the abbot and convent of St. Mary of Kyrkestall demise to John de Sallay the toft and croft and rood of arable land on the east side of the vill of Bramlay, and the 2 bovates of land which they had in the vill of Bramlay by the demise of William de Burcroft of Bramlay, for the term of 15 years next following; to hold with all liberties and easements on payment of 6s. of silver yearly to the abbot and convent. John to yield the land and buildings in good condition at the end of the term, and should he die within the period, reversion to the abbot and convent. Alternate seals.[1] At Kyrkestall. (*Ibid.*, No. 9.)

64. Friday, the morrow of St. Vincent the Martyr [Jan. 23], 1343[-4]. Grant by Sara de Bramley to John her son of 2 messuages with a croft adjacent in Bramlay, which lie between the messuage which Thomas Sarrator held of the house of Kyrkestall on the east and the toft which Thomas de Shelf, senior, held of Kyrkestall on the west; also one bovate in the fields of Bramlay with an assart called le Estrode in the same vill; to hold with all appurtenances to John, his heirs and assigns, of the chief lords of the fee. Warranty. Sealing clause.[2] Witnesses: Henry de Plumpton, William de Lepton, William son of Roger, Robert de Bercroft, Elias son of Thomas. At Bramlay. (*Ibid.*, No. 10.)

65. 10 Kal. June [May 23], 1344. Grant by John, son of Sara de Bramley, to the abbot and convent of Kyrkestall of the 2 messuages and croft [*as in the preceding deed*], which he lately had of the grant of Sara, his mother. Witnesses: John Scott of Calverlay, Walter de Haukesworth, John Chaumberlayn of Neuton, Thomas le Wayt of Ledes, John Passelewe of the same. At Bramlay. (*Ibid.*, No. 11.)

66. Monday after the Circumcision [Jan. 4], 1377[-8]. Quitclaim by Robert Passelew to the abbot and convent of St. Mary of Kyrkestall and their successors of all right in all the lands, woods, pastures, and fishings in . . . .[3] of the abbot and convent in the vill of Bramlay. Warranty. Sealing clause.[4] At Kyrkestall. (*Ibid.*, No. 12.)

67. Feb. 9, 13 Henry VI [1434-5]. Lease by John de Lepton, son and heir of William de Lepton of Wyrklay esq., to William

[1] Seal: fragment of the abbot's seal in yellow wax.

[2] Seal: dark green wax, broken. Leg. ....OMALEY.

[3] Document blurred.

[4] Seal: red wax, chipped, diam. 1 in.; in a cusped border, a shield of arms—a fess between three mullets; ..LLUM..TI PAS.LEW.

Scargyll esq., senior, and John Kylkenny esq., their heirs and assigns, of all the lands, tenements, rents, services and reversions, with appurtenances in Bramlay; to hold of the chief lords of the fee, paying yearly to the lessor for the 99 years next following 13s. 4d. at Whitsuntide and Martinmas in equal portions, and after the term of 99 years, 40s. yearly in the same manner; and if the rent of 13s. 4d. be in arrears for 40 days, power to the lessor to enter and distrain until satisfaction be made, and if the rent of 40s. be in arrears in whole or in part, power to enter and retain, this charter notwithstanding. Warranty. Sealing clause.[1] Witnesses: John Langton, knt., William Myrfeld, Robert Maulyuerer, Brian Beston, William Scotte, esqs. At Bramlay. (*Ibid.*, No. 13.)

68. Sept. 20, 1451. Quitclaim by Thomas Lepton, esq., son and heir of John de Lepton, to William Scargyll, John Kilkenny now being deceased, of all the lands, tenements, rents and services [*as in the preceding deed*]. Sealing clause. Witnesses: Walter Calverley, esq., William Bradford, William Passelew, William Clyffe, Thomas Turbage. At Bramlay. (*Ibid.*, No. 14.)

69. Nov. 1, 30 Henry VI [1451]. Demise by William Scargill, esq., senior, to William, the abbot, and the monks of St. Mary of Kyrkestall and the convent of the same, of all lands, tenements, rents, reversions and services with appurtenances which he recently had and held jointly with John Kylkenny, now deceased, of the gift and feoffment of John Lepton, son and heir of William Lepton esq., in Bramlay; to hold to the abbot and convent of the chief lords of the fee. Sealing clause. Witnesses: Walter Calverley esq., William Scargill, junior, William Calverley, junior, esqs., William Bradford, William Passelew. (*Ibid.*, No. 15.)

Brandsburton.

70. Saturday in Easter week [April 2], 1334. Quitclaim by Henry le Vavasour, son and heir of Adam le Vavasour of Esk, to Alice Sourdeual of Esk and Robert, her son, and to the heirs of Robert, of all right in a messuage, 5 tofts and 4 bovates of arable land with appurtenances in the vill and territory of Brandesburton, and in a piece of pasture which abuts on the water of Hull in such a way that the dyke is included, also in all the messuages, tofts, lands and pastures which Amandus Sourdeual had of the gift and feoffment of Adam le Vavasour, the grantor's father; also quitclaims all right in the homage and service to the lord, Herbert de Sancto Quintino, arising from a toft and 3 bovates of land in Brandesburton, and in the homage and all the service of Isobel, daughter of John le Barne, in respect of a toft and 4 bovates of land there, also of John, heir of John Bernard and Juliana, his wife, from a toft and 2 bovates of land, also of Robert de la More, from a toft and a bovate of land, also of Beatrice,

---

[1] Seal: red wax, undeciphered.

daughter and heir of Walter de Bristhill, from a toft and a bovate of land there; also quitclaims an annual rent of 2*d*. which a certain Hugh de Berswyk and Isobel, his wife, once held in Brandesburton; also a bovate of land with appurtenances in Esk, called Caue Oxgong, and 6 acres of meadow lying in le Newkere en le Oxfrith of the vill of Esk, which Amandus had of the gift and grant of Robert de Melton; also 4 acres of meadow lying in le Polefen, which Amandus had in Esk of the gift of William Northewod of Beverley; also 4 acres of meadow lying in le Neuker of the vill of Esk, which Amandus had of Adam le Vavasour, and which abuts on the water of Hull on the west, and on le Aldeker on the east, and in breadth between the meadow of Richard de Hebbeden on the south, and on the meadow of Henry le Vavasour on the north; also 2 acres in the meadows, lying in length between the meadow of Henry le Vavasour on the west and le Aldeker on the east; also 2 acres of meadow lying in le Neuker of Esk in length between the meadow of Richard de Helbeden on the north and Scurthdyk on the south, and in breadth between the meadow of William de Stavely on one side and the meadow of Richard de Hebbeden on the other; also an annual rent of 12*d*. from a toft and a croft which Ingram de Lesset once held in Esk; also 3 acres and a rood of meadow lying in le Oxfurth in Esk, and in length between le Scurthdyk on the north and le Oxfurth on the south, and in breadth between the meadow of Richard de Helbeden on the west, and the meadow of William Bard on the east; also quitclaims all lands, tenements, rents, services and lordships which Alice and Robert hold and which formerly belonged to Adam le Vavasour in the vills of Brandesburton and Esk. Warranty. Sealing clause.[1] Witnesses: William de Tweng, John de Hothum, senior, knts., John Sourdeual of Bernigholm, Amandus de Frothingham, Patrick de Langdale, Elias de Beleby, John son of Thomas de Esk, Adam de Berswyk of the same, Adam Scot of the same, John son of Matilda. At Esk. (*Y.A.S.*, M[D] 120, No. 5.)

71. Saturday in Easter week [April 2], 1334. Quitclaim by Henry le Vavasour, son and heir of Adam le Vavasour, to Alice Sourdeual of Esk, and Robert, her son, and the heirs of Robert, of all right in all the lands, tenements, meadows, pastures, turbaries, rents and services and lordships, which Alice and Robert hold in the vills of Brandesburton and Esk, which formerly belonged to Adam le Vavasour. Warranty. Sealing clause. Witnesses: [*same as to the preceding deed*]. At Esk. (*Ibid.*, No. 4.)

72. Tuesday after St. Michael, 21 Edward III [Oct. 2, 1347]. Indenture[2] by which the lands of Peter de Sourdeuall in Esk, Brandesburton and Routh are divided between Richard de Aldefeld and Alice, his wife, and Robert de Sourdeuall, namely,

---

[1] Seal: white wax, diam. ½ in.; blurred; ...IVE.
[2] In French.

C

half the capital messuage with the enclosure (*ofuenam*) as it is bounded and fenced, and a bovate of land which belonged to John, son of Emmot, and a toft which Henry, son of Walter, held, and a toft which Roger the carpenter (*le carpentre*) held, and a toft which John le Mulevere held, and a toft which Alice de la Grene held, and a toft which Isobel Buntyng held, a toft which Richard de Hundesle held, and half of a toft and an acre which Hugh de Lyndelow held, and half of a mill and a rent of 2s. from a toft which Ingram Blome held, and 2d. (*douces darres*) rent from a toft which Tyllot holds, and 14 acres of meadow and 8 acres of moor with appurtenances in Esk, and 4 marks, 3s. 1½d. (*meale*) with appurtenances in Brandesburton, and 3s. 4d. rent and appurtenances in Routh; to hold to Richard and Alice for the life of Alice; and the other half of the capital messuage with the enclosure as it is fenced and bounded, and a bovate and a half of land called Caue Oxgang which William son of Gilbert holds, and a toft which Ralph, son of Walter, holds, and a toft which Geoffrey de Burton holds, and a toft which Hugh Berier holds, and a toft which John Kyteson holds, and a toft which Beatrice Vauasour holds, and a toft which Ingram Blome holds, and half a toft which Walter le Halleman holds, and half a mill and half of a toft and an acre of land which Hugh de Lyndelow holds, and 4 acres of meadow and 3 acres of moor with appurtenances in the vill of Esk, and 4 marks, 3s. 1½d. rent in Brandesburton, and 3s. 4d. rent in Routh; to hold to Robert and his lawful heirs. Alternate seals[1]. Witnesses: John Sourdeualle of Benyngholme, William de la Wodehalle, Amandus de Frothyngham, Patrick de Langdale, Henry Vauysour, John Vauysour, Adam de Berswyk. At Esk. (*Ibid.*, No. 6.)

73. Ascension Day [May 26], 1373. Lease by Robert de la More and Denise (*Dyonissam*), his wife, to Dom. Stephen de Beforde, chaplain, his heirs and assigns, of a toft with appurtenances in the vill and territory of Brandesburton, which toft lies between the tenement of William de Sutton on one side and the common way of the vill of Brandesburton on the other; to hold freely, quietly and in peace, paying yearly to Robert and Denise 28d. of silver in equal portions at Whitsuntide and Martinmas, for all secular services, actions and demands. Warranty. Alternate seals. Witnesses : John de Sancto Quintino, knt., Robert Wytyk, William de Brysthyll, William de Gemellyng, Adam Gybon. At Brandesburton.[2] (*Archer-Houblon MSS.*, No. 159.)

74. Friday, April 10, 1377. Grant by Stephen de Beford, chaplain, living (*manens*) in Brandesburton, to Dom. Thomas

---

[1] Seals: two of red wax; (1) diam. 7/10 in., a fess between three lions rampant, each holding a cross; Leg. JE SUS SEL DE IMOV...; (2) Vesica-shaped, 1 in. × ½ in. Virgin, crowned, holding a Child; beneath, the head and shoulders of a praying figure; Leg. PIA.TE PCOR MARIA MIS....

[2] Seal missing. Endorsed: Brandsburton 1 Toft White Rent xxid. at Whitsontide and Martinmas. This in a later hand.

Glede, vicar of the church of Skipse, Thomas Selow of Beforth, Dom. John de Dyghton, chaplain, and John Scott of Bonnewyk, of his toft and croft which lie in length and breadth in the vill and territory of Brandesburton, which he had of the gift and feoffment of Robert de la More and Denise his wife; to hold of the chief lords of the fee. Warranty. Sealing clause.[1] Witnesses: John de Sancto Quintino, knt., Robert de la More, Robert Lorymer, Robert Wytyk. At Brandesburton. (*Ibid.*, No. 160.)

75. Monday after St. Luke the Evangelist [Oct. 16], 1391. Grant by Thomas Glede, vicar of the church of Skipse, John de Dyghton and John Scott, chaplains, to Dom. Stephen Brese, chaplain, and Isabel, his servant, of a messuage with appurtenances in Brandesburton which the grantors had of the gift and feoffment of Stephen in the vill of Brandesburton; to hold to Stephen and Isabel, their heirs and assigns, freely and in peace of the chief lords of the fee. Sealing clause.[2] Witnesses: Robert de le More, Dom. Thomas de Sancto Martino, rector of the church of Brandesburton, William de Gemelyng, Robert Smyth, Henry Skryuen. At Brandesburton. (*Ibid.*, No. 161.)

76. Friday before the Purification of the B.V.M. [Jan. 30], 1394. Grant by Thomas Gled, vicar of the church of Skipse, and William Day of Brandesburton, chaplain, to John Walker of Brandesburton and Isabel his wife, of the whole of that messuage with appurtenances which the grantors had of the gift and feoffment of Dom. Stephen de Beford, chaplain; to hold to John and Isabel, and the heirs of their bodies lawfully begotten, of the chief lords of the fee, with remainder to the heirs and assigns of the said John and Isabel or the heirs of the survivor. Witnesses: Robert de le More, John de Redeness, Amandus Well.[3] (*Ibid.*, No. 162.)

77. The Annunciation of the B.V.M., 3 Henry IV [March 25, 1402]. Grant by Robert Smyth of Brandesburton to Robert de la More, lord of la Moretoune (*domino de la Moretoune*), his heirs and assigns, of a plot of ground (*placeam*) and a bovate of a d with appurtenances lying in the vill and territory of Brandesburton, which plot of ground and bovate the grantor formerly had of the gift and feoffment of John de Garthes of Brandesburton; to hold to Robert de la More, his heirs and assigns, for ever. Warranty. Sealing clause.[4] Witnesses: William de Merton, Nicholas de Preston, John Laurenson, John Parcor, John Warner. At Brandesburton.[5] (*Ibid.*, No. 163.)

[1] Seal: red wax, diam. 1¼ in.; under a plain crocketed canopy a standing figure of a crowned Virgin and a smaller figure holding a cross. INNOC....

[2] Tags for three seals, one of which remains, similar to that to preceding deed.

[3] Seals: two, green wax; (1) oval, 1 in. × ¾ in. approx., chipped, within a circle a letter R; (2), oval, badly chipped; a bird, facing to the sinister.

[4] Seal: red wax, small, round, a letter T.

[5] Endorsed: una placea, An oxgang of land Brandsburton.

78.   All Souls Day [Nov. 2], 1409, 11 Henry IV.   Grant by
Henry Brynkyll of Beverley, mason, and Isabel his wife, formerly
wife of John Walker of Brandesburton, to Margaret de Hoton of
Brandesburton, widow, and John de Hoton, chaplain, her son, of
a message with appurtenances in Brandesburton which formerly
belonged to Dom. Stephen Brese otherwise called Beford, chaplain,
which lies between the tenement formerly belonging to William
de Sutton on one side and the common way on the other; to hold
of the chief lords of that fee by the due and accustomed services.
Warranty. Sealing clause.[1] Witnesses: John Mounceux, Robert
de Burton, chaplain, Thomas de Gemelyng, William de Marton,
John Myton of Brandesburton.   At Brandesburton.[2]   (*Ibid.*,
No. 164.)

79.   Dec. 17, 1413, 1 Henry V.   Grant by Marmaduke del
More of Midelton, co. York, son and heir of John del More, of the
same, and of Agnes his wife, to John Hoton of Brandesburton,
chaplain, and Margaret de Hoton, his mother, of a toft with
appurtenances in Brandesburton in a street called Croupellane of
the fee of St. John of Beverley, which lies in width between the
land formerly of William de Sutton on the east and the land of
Sir Henry Fitzhugh, lord of Brandesburton, on the west, and in
length from the said street on the north to the common sewer
(*communem seweram*) on the south; to hold of the chief lords of
the fee.   Warranty.   Sealing clause.[3]   Witnesses: Sir John de
Routh, John Mounceux, John Lauranceson.   At Brandesburton.
(*Ibid.*, No. 165.)

80.   Wednesday after the Conception of the B.V.M.,
7 Henry V [Dec. 13, 1419]. Grant by John de Hoton of Brandesburton, chaplain, to Edmund de Kyrketon,[4] rector of the parish
church of Brandesburton in Holdernes, of a messuage with
appurtenances in Brandesburton which formerly belonged to Dom.
Stephen Brese, otherwise called Beford, chaplain, which lies
between the tenement formerly belonging to William de Sutton on
one side and the common way on the other. This tenement he,
with his mother Margaret de Hoton, lately had of the gift and
feoffment of Henry Brynkyll of Beverley, mason, and Isabel, his
wife, late wife of John Walker of Brandesburton; to hold freely,
quietly and in peace of the chief lords of the fee by the due and

---

[1] Seals: two, olive green wax; (1) diam. ⅞ in., chipped, a shield of arms,
not deciphered, * SI ROBTI ..OV.V.L.; (2) diam. ⅞ in., a letter H between
two branches of foliage.

[2] Endorsed: Bransburton A Messuage wth bounder 10./

[3] Seal: red wax, diam. *c.* 1 in.; in a cusped border a shield of arms on
a chevron between three birds, a crescent; above the shield is apparently
a tree; legend, SI[G] ....MARMEDUC : MORE

[4] Also, same date, appointment by Edmund de Kyrketon of Roger
Bitterlay, carpenter, as his attorney to receive seisin of the same. Seal:
red wax, diam. 1¼ in.; in a six-ended figure, a trident. Endorsed in a later hand,
A letter of Attorney to take liverie and seisin of one messuage. (*Ibid.*, No. 167.)

accustomed services. Warranty. Sealing clause.[1] Witnesses: Sir John Routh, knt., George More, Thomas de Gymlyn, William Boteler, John Louson. At Brandesburton. (*Ibid.*, No. 166.)

81. Jan. 29, 7 Henry V [1419–20]. Grant[2] by Edmund de Kyrketon, rector of the parish church of Brandesburton, to John Grenakreys, mercer of London, of a messuage [*as in the preceding deed*]. Warranty. Sealing clause. Witnesses: John de Routh, knt., George del More, William Buttiller. At Brandesburton.[3] (*Ibid.*, No. 168.)

82. Feb. 5, 7 Henry V [1419–20]. Appointment by John Grenakreys, mercer (*mercerus*) of London, of Roger Bytterlay as his attorney to deliver seisin and full possession to Alice Grenakreys, his mother, of a messuage with appurtenances in Brandesburton, according to the form of a certain charter made by him to his mother. Sealing clause.[4] (*Ibid.*, No. 171.)

83. March 12, 1 Henry VI [1422–3]. Quitclaim by Master Edmund Kyrketon, rector of the church of Brandesburton, to John de Wencelagh of Arnall[5] in Holdernes of all actions real and personal, charges, quarrels and demands which he has or might have in future against him by reason of any debt, contract, transgression, agreement, obligation, receipt, account or any other cause from the beginning of the world to the day of the making of this agreement. Sealing clause.[6] (*Ibid.*, No. 172.)

84. April 5, 8 Henry VI [1430]. Demise by Thomas Gemlyng and John Ouste to John Smyth and Margaret his wife, of a messuage and a bovate of land with appurtenances in the vill and territory of Brandesburton, which they [the grantors] lately had of the gift and feoffment of John Smyth; to hold for the term of their lives and of the lifetime of the survivor, with remainder to Thomas Smyth, son of the said John Smyth, his heirs and assigns for ever. Sealing clause.[7] Witnesses: John Wencelagh, William Bristhill, Thomas Dalton, chaplain.[8] (*Ibid.*, No. 173.)

85. Dec. 24, 12 Henry VI [1433]. An indenture[9] made between William, lord Fitzhugh, and John Wencelagh the younger,

[1] Seal: red wax, a letter I.

[2] Same date. Appointment of Roger Bitterlay as his attorney to deliver seisin; also appointment by John Grenakreys of John Ripon of Molseby (Moreby ?) to receive seisin. (*Ibid.*, No. 169.)

[3] Endorsed in a later hand: one messuage, T,14.

[4] Seal: small fragment of red wax attached to tongue cut from the bottom of the deed. Endorsed: A lettre of Attorney to deliver seizen bransburton.

[5] Arnold.

[6] Seal: red wax, diam. 1¼ in.; in a six-sided figure, a trident.

[7] Seals: two, pendent on tags from the bottom of the deed, (1) red wax, round, chipped, the letters I C through which passes an arrow, above the letters, apparently a crown; (2) on a blob of red wax the letter T surmounted by a crude form of crown.

[8] Endorsed in a later hand: one messuage with one oxgang of land.

[9] In English.

to the effect that John is retained for the term of his life *to be of
counsaill with* the said lord Fitzhugh and his heirs in the faculty
of law against all manner of men except those that are kinsmen
and allies of the said John.   He shall do such service, *after his
comyng in the sayde faculte*, as the said lord shall reasonably com-
mand, receiving yearly at Martinmas for his fee 13s. 4d. during
the life of his father and after his father's death he shall have
in the name of his fee a messuage, a croft, and four oxgangs of
land in the town and fields of Brandesburton in Holdernes for
the term of his life, according to the form and effect of an indenture
made to him and his father.   Alternate seals.[1] Given at Rauenswath.[2] (*Ibid.*, No. 175.)

86.   Dec. 24, 12 Henry VI [1433]. Grant[3] by William, lord
Fitzhugh, to John Wencelagh of Brandesburton in Holdernes, of
a messuage, a croft and 4 bovates of land with appurtenances
which John Parcour formerly held in the vill and territory of
Brandesburton; to hold for the term of his life with remainder
to John, son of John Wencelagh for the term of his life. Warranty.
Alternate seals.[4] Witnesses: John Conestable of Halsham, Robert
Haytfeld of Haytfeld, William Mounceux of Lecette,[5] John Roos
of Routh, William Bristhill of Bristhill. (*Ibid.*, No. 174.)

87.   April 4, 20 Henry VI [1442]. Demise by William, lord
Fitzhugh and Margery his wife and John Wencelagh to Maurice
Berkley, knt., John Constable of Halsham, James Strangways,
junior, John Eppelby, rector of the church of Rumaldkirk, Robert
Shirwynd, rector of the church of Wath, William Crayke, rector
of the church of Tanfeld, Nicholas Mispryngton, citizen of York,
William Catryk and John Catryk, of a messuage, a garden, a toft
and 4 bovates of land, with appurtenances, which John Parcour
formerly held in Brandesburton in Holdernes, which messuage,
garden and toft lie between the tenement of lord Fitzhugh, in
the tenure of Thomas Shipehird, on the south, and the free tenement of Brian de Holme on the north; also demises to the same
Maurice [*etc.*] another toft in the same vill abutting as well on part
of the same messuage as on part of the said free tenement of Brian
de Holme on the west, and lying between the common way which

[1] Seal: small blob of red wax; a helm from which emerges the head and
neck of a dragon; probably a signet or *secretum.*

[2] Endorsed: That John Wenslay retained in Counsaile for Willm. Lo.
Fitzhugh and his fee covenanted, viz. xiiis. ivd. per annum, and afterwards
Messuage croft 4 oxgangs in Bransbreton.

[3] Appointment of William Bristill and John Ouster to deliver seisin.
Same date, same seal. (*Ibid.*, No. 175.)

[4] Seal: red wax, diam. 2 ins. (broken); a shield couchée, Quarterly (1) and
(4), three chevronels interlaced in base and chief, (2) and (3), on a field vair
a fess. Crest, a helm surmounted by a coronet from which issues a dragon's
head. On each side of the shield a badge, the dexter bearing three chevronels
a chief vair, the sinister an eagle displayed. Leg. SIGILLŪ': WILLI: DNI:
FITZHUGH ET DE MARMYOUN.

[5] Lissett.

leads from the same messuage towards the church on the south, and a lane which leads from the free tenement of Brian de Holme to the said common way on the north and east of the said toft; to hold all the said messuages, gardens [*etc.*] to Maurice, John Constable [*etc.*] for ever.

William, lord Fitzhugh, Margery and John Wencelagh appoint William Bristhill, William Buk, chaplain, and William Dorant as their attorneys to deliver to Maurice, John Constable [*etc.*] full and peaceful seisin and possession of all the said messuage, garden, 2 tofts and 4 bovates of land, with appurtenances, in the form aforesaid. Alternate seals.[1] Witnesses: Thomas Metham, knt., John Melton of Swyne, William Twyer of Gaunsted, Robert Hattefeld of Hattefeld, William Mounceux of Barneston, Thomas Constable of Catfos, John Ros of Routh, esqs. At Rauenswath. (*Ibid.*, No. 177.)

88. Morrow of the Ascension, 20 Henry VI [May 11, 1442]. Final Concord[2] made at Westminster between Maurice Barkley, knt., John Constable of Halsham, knt., James Strangways, junior, John Eppelby, rector of the church of Rumaldkirk, Robert Shirwynd, rector of the church of Wath, William Crayke, rector of the church of Tanfeld, Nicholas Mispryngton citizen of York, William Catryk and John Catryk, claimants, and William Fitzhugh, knt., Margery his wife, and John Wenselagh, deforciants; concerning a messuage, 2 tofts, a garden and 4 bovates of land with appurtenances in Brandesburton; to hold to Maurice Barkley, John Constable [*etc.*] and the heirs of the same John Eppelby of the chief lords of the fee by the services which pertain to that tenement. Warranty by the said William Fitzhugh, Margery, and John Wenselagh against all men. Maurice Barkley, John Constable [*etc.*] pay 100 marks of silver. (*Ibid.*, No. 178.)

89. May 20, 13 Edward IV [1473]. Indenture by which William Wencelagh son and heir of John Wencelagh late of Brandesburton in Holdernes, deceased, grants to Walter Wencelagh, his brother, all the lands and tenements, rents, reversions and services, meadows, pastures and pasture rights with appurtenances in the vills and territories of Rolleston and Southorpp near Hornese in Holdernes, which descended to the grantor by right of inheritance on the death of his father John Wencelagh; to hold all the said lands [*etc.*] to Walter Wencelagh for the term of his life, of the chief lords of the fee by the due and accustomed services. Warranty. Sealing clause.[3] Witnesses: Martin de la

---

[1] Tags for three seals, but only one seal remains: blob of red wax; a gem, a pelican in her piety; DIEU AIDE. Clear impression left by the mount of the gem.

[2] Two parts of this Final Concord have survived. Appointment by Lord Fitzhugh of William Brysthill, William Buk, and William Durant as his attorneys to take seisin of the messuage [*etc.*], dated Aug. 1 [1442]. Seal of Lord Fitzhugh. (*Ibid.*, No. 181.)

[3] Small fragment of a small seal of red wax,

See of Barneston, Robert Twyer of Gaunsted, John Hedon of Marton, esqs. At Rolleston. (*Ibid.*, No. 186.)

90. March 4, 15 Edward IV [1474–5]. Grant by William Ellerkar of Ellerkar and Thomas Ellerkar of Moretowne to William Wencelagh and Elizabeth, his wife, of all their lands and tenements, rents, services, meadows, feedings, pastures, moors, marshes, ways, paths, waters, ponds, stew ponds (*viuarias*), and fisheries, with all appurtenances and easements, which the grantors lately had of the gift and feoffment of the same William Wencelagh in the vills and demesnes of Acclom near Kyrkham and Brandesburton; also grants the reversion of all those lands, tenements, rents and services, with appurtenances, which Cecily Wencelagh, widow, holds for the term of her life, in Brandesburton, with reversion of the same to William and Thomas Ellerkar, by the grant and confirmation of William Wencelagh, after the death of Cecily, in accordance with a charter made to them [William and Thomas Ellerkar] by William de Wencelagh at Brandesburton March 1, 14 Edward IV [1474–5]; to hold the lands, tenements [*etc.*] and the reversion after the death of Cecily to William Wencelagh and Elizabeth his wife, their heirs and assigns, of the chief lords of the fees by the due and accustomed services.

William Ellerker appoints Thomas Ellerkar to deliver, for him and in his name, to William Wencelagh and Elizabeth, his wife, full and peaceful seisin of all and singular the said lands [*etc.*], and of the said reversion. Sealing clause.[1] Witnesses: Walter Wencelagh, Robert Avis, and John Melton of Brandesburton. At Brandesburton. (*Ibid.*, No. 183.)

91. Aug. 1, 17 Edward IV [1477]. Release by Edward Holme son and heir of John Holme of Bilton, esq., to William Wencelagh of Brandesburton and his heirs, of all right, title and claim which he has or may have in all lands and tenements, rents and services, meadows, feedings and pastures, turbaries, and in digging and carting turves, with all appurtenances, in the vill and territory of Brandesburton; further he quitclaims to William Wencelagh all manner of actions, as well real as personal, which he has or may have against him. This release not to extend to an annual rent of 6s. 8d. payable by William Wencelagh to the said Edward Holme and Isabel, his mother, for the term of their lives and the lifetime of the survivor, according to a charter of William Wencelagh. Sealing clause.[2] (*Ibid.*, No. 184.)

92. Sept. 23, 22 Edward IV [1482]. Release by Martin del See of Barneston in Holdernesse, knt., to William Ellerker of Ellerker and Thomas Ellerker of Moretown of all right and claim

[1] Seals: two, of red wax; (1) blob of wax, device not clear, possibly a bird; (2) blob of wax, a barrel and a ladder.

[2] Seal: red wax, apparently a merchant's mark. Endorsed: Bransburton, releas 3./; Brandsburton and Seaton Ros: for releases made of lands there by the Holmes dated this.

which he had or may have in all those lands and tenements which he, with Robert Twyer and William Wencelagh deceased, had of the gift and feoffment of Isabel Holme, late wife of John Holme of Bilton, and Edward Holme, son and heir of the said John and Isabel, in the vill and territory of Brandesburton. Sealing clause.[1] (*Ibid.*, No. 185.)

93. Oct. 3, 22 Edward IV [1482]. Demise by William Ellerkar of Ellerkar and Thomas Ellerkar of Moretown, to Elizabeth Wencelagh, widow, late wife of William Wencelagh, of all the lands and tenements, pastures and feedings, rents and services, moors, marshes, ways, paths, waters, ponds, stew ponds, and fish ponds, with all appurtenances and easements, which the demisors lately had of the gift and feoffment of William Wencelagh in the vills and territories of Brandesburton and Acclom iuxta Kyrkham; to hold all the said lands and tenements [*etc.*] to Elizabeth for the term of her life with remainder to the heirs of William Wencelagh; to hold to him his heirs and assigns for ever, of the chief lords of the fee by the due and accustomed services.

William Ellerkar and Thomas Ellerkar appoint Robert Askwyth as their attorney to deliver seisin. Sealing clause. Witnesses: Thomas Byrstyll of Byrstill, gent., John Whitehed, Robert Dande, William Smyth, George Cowper. At Brandesburton. (*Ibid.*, No. 187.)

94. Feb. 26, 22 Edward IV [1482–3]. Grant by Richard, lord Fitzhugh Marmyon and Santquyntyn to Thomas Ellerker, esq., and Elizabeth Wenslawgh, widow, for a certain sum of money paid to him, of the custody of all lands, tenements, rents, services and possessions, and other hereditaments with their appurtenances, which belonged to William Wenslawgh, gent., deceased, who held of the grantor by military service on the day of his death; which lands after the death of the said William came into the grantor's hands by reason of the fact that his son and heir, John Wenslawgh, was under age, and are still in his hands; also grants to the same Thomas Ellerker and Elizabeth custody of John Wenslawgh with his marriage, which is to be without disparagement (*absque disparagacione*), from the time of the death of his father until he reaches full age, with the profits of all his lands [*etc.*]. If the said John should die under age leaving an heir under age, then Thomas Ellerker and Elizabeth to have custody of all and singular the lands and tenements [*etc.*] of the said heir, with his marriage, which is to be without disparagement, from the time of John's death until the heir comes of age; and so from heir to heir (*et sic de herede in heredem*) until some heir of the said William

[1] Seal: blob of red wax, a small shield of arms, probably two bars dancetty; legend not deciphered; a signet.

Endorsed in a later hand: Will. Wensley Enfeoffs Ellerker of the lands in the deed marked with 2 as is supposed by the deed marked with 4 which recites such a deed 5 and this release is made thereupon.

Wenslawgh reaches lawful age, paying no rent or other payment to the grantor or his heirs (*absque aliquo compoto seu aliquo alio inde michi vel heredibus meis reddendo*). Sealing clause.[1] (*Ibid.*, No. 188.)

95. March 4, 15 Henry VII [1499–1500].[2] Lease by Thomas Hillyard of Catwyk, esq., and Elizabeth his wife, and John Wensley of Beverley, gent., son and heir of the said Elizabeth, to Richard Northus of Wassand, yeoman, of their messuage in Brandesburton with the croft thereto annexed, and another croft in the same town called Holme Garth with 5 oxgangs of arable land late in the tenure of . . .[3] long, with all the commodities and easements belonging to the messuage within the said town and fields; also another messuage with 4 oxgangs of land within the said town and fields, with a garth and orchard lately in the tenure of John Skynner, with all the meadows, pastures, commons and ways pertaining; to hold the said premises to Richard and his assigns from Martinmas next after the date of this indenture for twenty-one years, paying to Thomas and Elizabeth or their assigns yearly 5 marks, and to the said John [Wensley] 4 marks yearly, in equal portions at Whitsuntide and Martinmas, the first payment to be made at Whitsuntide 1501. Richard to be responsible for the repair of thatch and earth wall on the premises. The lessors and their heirs to be responsible for the repair and maintenance of all timber in the premises. Warranty. Sealing clause. (*Ibid.*, No. 189.)

96. May 20, 3 Henry VIII [1511]. Grant to uses by John Wensley of Beverley, gent., to John White, merchant, Robert White, mercer, Thomas Wensley, mercer, John Willymote, draper, and Robert Myreskewe, husbandman, of a capital messuage in Brandsburton with another messuage there in the tenure of Robert Myreskew, a cottage there late in the tenure of Robert Cice, a cottage there in the tenure of William Roger, another cottage there in the tenure of William Rosse, another cottage there in the tenure of Elizabeth Martyn, and a messuage there in the tenure of John Hornby, and a cottage in Bristyll late in the tenure of Ralph Leek, and all and singular the grantor's lands and tenements, rents and services, with appurtenances in the vill and fields of Mappilton, Reston, Seton, Rowston, Southorpe, Collome,[4] and Aclame in the county of York; to hold to the grantees, their heirs and assigns for ever for the use of the grantor and his heirs according to the intention to be set out in his last will, as is declared in a certain writing attached to the present charter. Warranty.

He appoints as his attorney Thomas Northouse to enter the premises and to take and deliver peaceful seisin of the same to

---

[1] Seal: small blob of red wax; device not deciphered, probably impression of a small signet ring.

[2] In English.   [3] Gap in deed.   [4] Cowlam.

the grantees. Sealing clause.[1] Witnesses: Sir Gilbert Staynton, Robert Merskowe, Robert Storesman, John Herryson, William Wright, Laurence Gibson, William Lightfote, William Gibson. (*Ibid.*, No. 191.)

97. A deed of Entail to Feoffees in Trust.[2] The feoffees within the feoffment to the Bill annexed to be feoffees to the use of John Wensley for the term of his life and after his death to stand feoffees to the use of Christopher Wensley, younger son of the said John Wensley for the term of fourteen years next after the date of the feoffment. During this time the feoffees shall with the rent from the lands and tenements repair and maintain the same, the residue to be given to Christopher. At the end of the fourteen years the feoffees to stand feoffed to the use of William Wensley, son and heir of John Wensley, and his heirs for ever. Should the said Christopher [or William][3] die within the said fourteen years then the feoffees are to dispose of all profits, rents and revenues derived yearly from the lands and tenements as follows: to the daughter of Thomas Wensley £20 to be paid in piece; to Elizabeth Martyn £20 to be paid in piece; to Joan and Isabel the daughters of the said Elizabeth £20 to be divided equally between them; to Nicholas, Hugh, Robert, Eleanor and Elizabeth, the children of Walter Rudeston, £25 to be divided equally between them; to Annah [*sic*] Rudeston, the daughter of the said Walter, £10; £20 to be given for a suit of copes (*A sutie of Copyes*) for Saint Mary's Church in Beverley; for the building and making of the vestry (*revestr'*) in the church of Brandesburton £6 13s. 4d.; for building and making up again the steeple of Saint Mary's church at Beverley,[4] if it be taken down, £10, and if it is not taken down the money to be disposed for the health of the soul of the said John Wensley. Should it happen that either the said William or Christopher live only part of the fourteen years, and within the said years should die, then the feoffees shall dispose of the profits of the lands and tenements in the years after the death of the said John Wensley and Christopher Wensley according to their discretion and in accordance with the intent above written. (*Ibid.*, No. 190.)

98. July 10, 1521. The will of John Wensley of Beverley, gent. He commends his soul to God and to the intercession of the Blessed Virgin Mary and to the prayers of all saints of Holy Church. In primis: he leaves his body to be buried in the church or chapel of Blessed Mary of Beverley or in some other place to be decided by him. Item: 13*li.* 6s. 8d. to be distributed for the

---

[1] Seal: This and the next document are attached by one tag bearing a blob of bright red wax; device not deciphered.

[2] The document is endorsed with this title, and is in English.

[3] Hole in the deed.

[4] In 1520 the tower of St. Mary's fell, necessitating the rebuilding of a large portion of the church. See *Y.A.J.*, xxv, 417.

good of his soul on the day of his burial, namely for one trental[1] to be celebrated 10s., to each priest present at his exequies and mass 4d., to each clerk 2d., to each boy having a surplice 1d., the remainder to be given to the poor from house to house according to necessity. Item: 7li. to be disposed of on the seventh day after his burial in like manner as above. Item: 10li. to the fabric of the church of Blessed Mary of Beverley. Item: 60s. for a stone to be placed over his tomb. Item: to the fabric of the church of Brandsburton 20s., a doublet (diplon') de lezcremesyn satyn and a jacket de blak velwett to make a vestment. Item: 10s. to the fabric of St. Peter, York. Item: 4li. 13s. 4d. to an honest priest to celebrate for his soul for a year. Item: to his son William Wensley a gilt standing cup (cifum) with a cover, two gilt saltcellars with covers, two goblets of parcel gilt with covers, a gown furred with tawny fur, an agate (hakett) and a gold ring called a hoop weighing one and three quarter ounces, also a gold cross, a pouch of gold with a ruby in it and all the implements in his house on the day of the making of this will, nothing excepted other than half of lez Napry, namely, cloths, linen, hand-towels, etc.; and of those goods which belonged to his wife [the testator's] after the death of Thomas Newark, he wishes she should have as her portion such things as were formerly chosen. Item: to each of the houses of friars in Beverley 10s. and to each of the houses of friars in Kingston-upon-Hull 5s. Item: to each of the houses for the poor in Beverley 2s. Item: to William Wensley his son 2 good sheets (linthiamina bona) containing three widths (bredis) and (four) bolsters (servicalia) of the same cloth garneshed with black rybban, also a bed cover, seven spoons (cocliaria) with apostles on their ends and six spoons with Wodwoshes[2] on their ends. Item: to his wife 5li. Item: to William his son 40li., and if he should die before he reaches the age of twenty-one it is his will that his son Christopher Wensley should have all the goods which his brother William would have had. Item: to his son Christopher certain lands in Brandsburton, Rouston, Mappleton, Reston, Southorp, Collum and Acclam for the space of three years after his death, as more fully appears in a charter of feoffment made to John Whyte, Robert Whyte, Thomas Wensley, John Wylymote, Robert Myarscowe. Item: to his son Christopher 28li. to be received from divers lands of Ralph Ellarcar in Beverley in two annual payments of 14li. as by a lease (lece) made by the said Ralph for a certain sum of money. Item: to his son Christopher all his tenements in Atwyk for the space of ten years as more plainly appears by a charter of feoffment made to Robert Whyte and others. Item: to John Whyte farmer 20s. that he shall be a good uncle to his sons. The rest of his goods he leaves to Christopher

---

[1] Trental, an office for the dead lasting thirty days and consisting of as many masses.

[2] Woodwose (of obscure origin), a figure of such a being (i.e. a wild man of the woods), as a decoration, a heraldic bearing or supporter, etc. (O.E.D.).

Wensley, his son, and if he dies before he reaches the age of twenty-one or marries (*traxerit matrimonium*) then his son William Wensley is to have all the goods which his brother Christopher should have had; and if he should die before he reaches full age or before marriage then all these goods which they should have had shall be dispersed to relieve the necessities of his friends and to the fabric of the churches of the Blessed Mary of Beverley and Brandsburton, and for improving the roads and other good works according to the discretion of his executors. He appoints John Fyssher, doctor of theology and bishop of Rochester, the supervisor of his will and his sons and the goods left to them until they come of age or marry. Appoints as his executors William Wensley, Christopher Wensley, Thomas Wensley, Robert Fyssher, and he leaves to Robert Fyssher 40s. [?] that he will be a good uncle to his sons. He leaves Thomas Wensley his brother 6*li.* 13s. 4*d.* that he will be a special uncle to his sons and that he will gather in entirely all his debts to the use and profit of his sons. Sealing clause.[1] Witnesses: Roger Garrad, clerk, Robert Whyte, Christopher Hudsun, Robert Ravfeld and others.
(*Ibid.*, No. 192*a*.)   By me John Wensley.

Brodsworth.

99. Grant by Robert *ad fontem* son of John *ad fontem* to Master William de Seton, his heirs and assigns, of a certain plot of land which lies in length and breadth between the land which Robert son of Reginald holds of Sir Edmund Darel, knt., on the west, and the land which Thomas de Hoton holds of Sir William Darel, knt., on the east, and which abuts on the beck (*le beck*) on the south and on the hill (*montem*) called Bakehoushille on the north, and contains in length 8 perches of which each perch contains 20 feet, and in width 32 feet; to hold with all appurtenances, liberties and easements, of the chief lords of the fee. William de Seton, his heirs and assigns to be allowed to enclose the whole of this plot of land and to hold it in severalty without contradiction of the grantor and his heirs. Warranty. Sealing clause. Witnesses: Robert Haryngel of Hoton Paynel, William Kyrkeby of the same, Thomas de Treton of the same, Thomas Baruyle of Billham, Robert son of Reginald de Broddesworth, Richard de Pikeburgne,[2] junior, Henry de Birthwayte of the same.[3]
(*Ibid.*, No. 2.)

100. April 19, 19 Henry VI [1440]. Appointment by William Darell' of Wiltshire, Henry Willesthorpe, clerk, William Darell'

---

[1] The tag and seal are both missing.
[2] Pigburn, par. Brodsworth.
[3] Endorsed: Robertus *ad fontem* Adlyngflete. But this seems a mistake. The witnesses all suggest the neighbourhood of Brodsworth, of which Marmaduke Darel held a moiety in 1284–85, and where William Darel held an interest in 1316 (*Feudal Aids*, vi, 5, 199).

of Mowgrene and Robert Crosse, gent., of John Etton, Richard Askham and John Kendale as attorneys to deliver seisin to George Darell', son and heir of Edmund Darell', knt., and Margaret, daughter of William Plumpton, knt., of their manor of Broddesworth, with appurtenances in co. York, in accordance with their charter. Sealing clause.[1] At Broddesworth. (*Y.A.S.*, M^D 182, No. 1*a*.)

Broughton=in=Craven.

101. Monday after SS. Philip and James, 10 Edward II [2 May, 1317]. Release by Thomas son of Thomas de Multon' and his heirs to William son of Richard de Essheton' and his heirs of all right in all the lands and tenements, both in demesnes and services of free men and villeins (*bondorum*) which William was holding in the vill of Broghton' in Crauen', and which Richard de Essheton, William's father, had of the gift of John de Essheton'; saving to Thomas and his heirs the services from the said lands and tenements due to the manor of Skipton' on the day of this writing, when the said manor should fall to his hands or those of his heirs. Witnesses: dom. John de Landa, prior of Boulton' in Crauen', William Fauuel, Henry de Marton', William Deseert, Robert de Egglesfeld, William son of William de Skipton', Robert son of Richard de Bradelay.[2] At London'. (*Duke of Devonshire, Bolton Abbey Estate MSS.*)

Burnsall.

102. Sunday before the Annunciation of the B.V.M., 28 Edward III [23 March, 1353–4]. Grant by Walter son of Elias Styringg' of Thorpe to Richard de Frekilton', his heirs and assigns, of all his lands and tenements which had descended to him after the death of Walter [*sic*] Styringg' his father in Brinsall' and Thorp'; and release of all right in a third part of the tenements which Richard held of the demise of Alice widow of William son of Agnes, and which she had held in dower of the grantor's inheritance. Warranty. Witnesses: John de Malghum, John le Vauasour, William Glasebrok, Thomas Osmond, and Elias de Rilleston. At Boulton'.[3] (*Duke of Devonshire, Bolton Abbey Estate MSS.*)

Burythorpe.

103. Nov. 11, 22 Henry VI [1432]. Grant by Robert Lorymer, rector of the church of Berythorp to Ralph Bygod esq., of a toft with a croft adjacent and 3 acres of land and half an acre of arable land with appurtenances in the vill and territory of Berythorp, which toft and croft lie near the church on the

---

[1] Seals: two, of red wax on tongues cut from the document; (1) a dog, sejant; (2) an animal?; both to the dexter.

[2] Tag for seal missing.

[3] Seal: red wax, round, diam. ¾ in.; not heraldic.

west side of the vill, and the 3½ acres lie scattered in the fields of Berythorp, all of which the grantor had of the gift of Robert Wylton of Esthorp; to hold to Ralph, his heirs and assigns, of the chief lords of the fee. Warranty. Sealing clause. Witnesses: William Naulton, Robert Naulton, William Kyrk, Robert Leuenyng, Robert Cotum. At Berythorp. (*Y.A.S.*, M^D 120, No. 14.)

Camblesfortb (Dray)

104. Oct. 4, 15 Henry VII [1499]. Grant by William Towton' of Camylsforthe and Agnes, his wife, to William Caldecott' of Carleton, of a toft with buildings lying in Camylsforthe between the land of Ralph Babthorpe on the east and the land of Mary de Carleton towards the south, and on the common way towards the north; to hold to William, his heirs and assigns, of the chief lord of the fee. Warranty. Sealing clause.[1] Witnesses: John Sland of Carleton, Henry Frerr and Thomas Medelay of Camyls-forthe. At Carleton. (*Y.A.S.*, M^D 182, No. 1*b*.)

Cawtborne (Wl.R.)

105. Grant by Robert, son of Luke de Calthorn' to Richard de Calthorn, of half that assart in the territory of Calthorn, called Huerod, which Robert [*sic*], the grantor's father, once shared with Hugh, son of Agnes de Calthorn; to hold with appurtenances, of the chief lords of the fee. Warranty. Sealing clause. Witnesses: Robert de Barneby, William de Ethewaldeleye of the same, Richard de Chaumpenays of the same, William son of Adam son of Marre, Richard de Mickelthwayt, John de Northcroft, Roger son of Lettice (*Letie*), of Calthorn'. (*Farnley Hall MSS.*, No. 27.)

106. Sunday after St. Lucy the Virgin [Dec. 8], 1390. Grant by John Taili of Peneston, to John Addy of Calthorn, junior, of all his lands and tenements with appurtenances in the vills and lordships of Calthorn and Holan Swayne, also the rever-sion of the lands and tenements which Alice Taili holds within the same lordships as her dower after the death of Adam Taili, her husband, also the reversion of the lands and tenements which Agnes Catell of Crydeling holds in the said lordships as her dower after the death of her husband, Richard de Elmehirst; to hold to John Addy, his heirs and assigns, freely [*etc.*], of the chief lords of the fee. Warranty. Sealing clause.[2] Witnesses: Robert de Barmesby of Calthorn, Robert Chedill', John de Crawschagh of the same, Thomas del Apilyherd of Thurleston, William Russell of the same. At Calthorn. (*Ibid.*, No. 28.)

---

[1] Red wax, undeciphered.

[2] Seal: brown wax, shield of arms, undeciphered.

107. Oct. 1, 1438. Grant by John Addy of Calthorn to John Addy, his son, of all the lands and tenements, pastures and grazings which he has in the vills of Calthorn and Holandswayne; to hold of the chief lords of the fee. Sealing clause.[1] Witnesses: John de Barmby, John de Kereforth, John Methelay of Calthorn, Thomas Mokeson of Holandswayne, John Galbargh of the same. At Calthorn. (*Ibid.*, No. 29.)

Cononley.

108. Grant by Peter son of John del Grene of Cunedlay to the B.M. of Boueltun and the canons, of two acres of land, half a rood and a plot, namely one acre which Adam son of Ysoda had held of Peter del Grene, lying together on Langeflath in Suinwath, a plot of land called le Rane between the said land and the other road extending towards Gluseburne and Cunedlay, and another acre in the green assart on the west side of Suinwath; in free and perpetual alms without any secular demand. Warranty against all men. Witnesses: William de Pharenhill', Robert and Adam [?] his brothers (*fratribus de eadem*), Henry son of Ambrose de Cunedlay, William Reuel, Robert Cuuel, William his son.[2] (*Duke of Devonshire, Bolton Abbey Estate MSS.*)

109. Martinmas, 1305. Agreement[3] between brother John de Landa, prior of Boulton' in Crauen', and the convent, on the one part, and Adam de [?] Coling on the other, by which the former demised at farm to the latter a messuage and two bovates of land in Conedelay, which John Spire had formerly held; to hold to him and his heirs of the said priory for a term of twelve years, rendering yearly 10s. sterling, half at Whitsuntide and half at Martinmas, and leaving the premises in as good state or better at the end of the term. Warranty. Witnesses, Robert de Farnhil, Alexander de Esteburn, Henry Crocbayn, Thomas Reuel, Adam Pedefer.[4] (*Ibid.*)

Cowick.

110. Friday, St. Luke [Oct. 22], 1333. Grant by Henry le Barker of Couwik to Alexander, son of Thomas de Crideling', and Agnes, his wife, of a butt of land with a certain workshop upon it, lying in the field of Couwik, between the land which is called Ermegarent Land on the west, and the land once of Daniel Manbridd on the east, and abutting on a tenement of the same Alexander and Agnes at the southern end, and on the land once of John the Smith (*Le Ferour*) of Snaythe at the northern end;

---

[1] Seal: dark brown wax, broken.

[2] Tag for seal, missing.

[3] Cirograph. In a damaged condition.

[4] Fragment of seal of white wax.

to hold to Alexander and Agnes, their heirs and assigns, in perpetuity of the chief lord of the fee. Warranty. Sealing clause. Witnesses: John son of Thomas, clerk of Snaythe, William, his brother, William Mons of Couwik, John *under the hill* of the same, John son of John de Mora of the same. At Cowick. (*Y.A.S.*, M^D 153, No. 1.)

111. Tuesday, the Exaltation of the Holy Cross [Sept. 14], 1344. Appointment by Nicholas de Mar, chaplain, of Richard son of Richard del Hill' of Snayth as attorney to take seisin of a messuage with houses built thereon in Cowyk, and of all the lands, tenements, rents and moors with appurtenances, in which he, Nicholas, was enfeoffed by the gift of William Mons of Couwyk, and Agnes his wife in accordance with their charter of feoffment. Sealing clause. At Couwyk. (*Y.A.S.*, M^D 182, No. 1.)

112. Sunday after the Purification of the B.V.M. [Feb. 5], 1346[-7]. Grant by John son of Henry de Byrne and Margaret, his wife, to Adam Tot' of Cowyk and Emmotta, his wife, their heirs and assigns, of a certain plot of ground and a toft with buildings upon it in Cowyk near Wrymore, lying between a toft once belonging to Agnes Lambe on the east and a toft once of Thomas Dede on the west, and containing in breadth a perch and a half and 5 rods and in length 5 perches; to hold to Adam and Emmotta, their heirs and assigns, of the chief lord of the fee by the due and accustomed services, namely, 3*d.* yearly to the convent of Selby at the two terms, i.e., Whitsuntide and Martinmas, for all services, suit of court and demands. Warranty. Sealing clause.[1] Witnesses: Alexander de Cridelyng, Richard son of William de Snayth', Thomas Godard, John *sub monte*, John *del more*. At Cowyk. (*Ibid.*, No. 2.)

113. Monday after Epiphany [Jan. 10], 1351[-2]. Grant by Thomas Metham *le piere*, knt., to John de Neuton' and Joan, his wife, of a messuage and 5½ acres of land with appurtenances in Couwyk, which once belonged to Thomas son of William de Couwyk, of which the messuage lies between the holding of the said John de Neuton' on the east and that which a certain Matilda, daughter of John Jakson', now holds on the west; and the said land lies respectively in 6½ selions of which 5 lie between the land of the said John on the east and the land of John son of John le Walker of Snayth on the west, and adjoins the said messuage at the southern extremity (*in capite australi*); and one selion stretches from the end of the same 5 selions as far as the hedge of the field of Couwyk towards the north, and lies between the land which belonged to Thomas Camyn on the east and the land which belonged to Adam Cardinal on the west; and the said half

---

[1] Seals: (1) oval, white wax, undeciphered, (2) oval, green wax, a device; JOHANEM.

D

selion adjoins the land of John de Neuton' towards the north and lies between the land which Matilda now holds on the east and the land of John son of Peter de Couwyk on the west; which messuage and 5½ acres of land the grantor had of the gift and quitclaim of John son of Margaret de Bouncroft, junior; to hold to John and Joan and the heirs of John, of the chief lord of the fee. Warranty. Sealing clause.[1] Witnesses: Nicholas Roscelyn, Richard son of John de Snayth, Robert son of William de Snayth, John of the moor (de mora) of Couwyk, Thomas Godard, John son of William de Couwyk, Henry son of Joyce de Couwyk, William son of William de Redenesse of Rouclif. At Couwyk. (Ibid., No. 3.)

114. Monday after St. Hilary [Jan. 6], 1368[-9]. Indenture recites that whereas Adam Smyth' of Couwyk having granted to William Shephird of the same an acre of land with appurtenances in Couwyk, as described in the charter of feoffment to William, now William agrees on behalf of himself and his heirs, that if Adam pays to him or his executors at the close of the five years next following 40s. sterling, then the charter of feoffment shall be invalid, but if payment be not made, then the said acre shall remain in the possession of William, until the sum is forthcoming, without obstruction from Adam or his heirs; and similarly Adam shall, during the stated term, render to the lord of the fee the due and accustomed services, and also if William does not enjoy possession for the stated term, then Adam agrees that he shall have an acre belonging to Adam, which lies adjacent to the aforesaid acre, until satisfaction is made to William concerning the said terms. Alternate seals.[2] At Couwyk. (Y.A.S., M^D 153, No. 2.)

115. Dec. 9, 19 Richard II [1395]. Indenture by which John Daunay leases to John son of Robert de Hek of Cowyk all his moor called Wilby Mor or Dandsone Mor, adjacent to the moor recently belonging to Henry Cardinalle of Cowyk in Inkylsmor; to hold to John, his heirs and assigns in perpetuity, paying to the grantor yearly 2d. at Easter and Michaelmas, and doing all suits of court for the grantor and his heirs yearly at Snaith, from the next court held there after the Feast of St. Lawrence. Warranty. Alternate seals.[3] Witnesses: John Frer, Robert Forman', William Bate, John Scot, Thomas de Cowyk, John de Gledowe. At Cowyk. (Ibid., No. 3.)

[1] Seal: brown wax, diam. ½ in., broken, possibly a mailed fist.

[2] Seal: pale brown wax, on tongue cut from bottom of deed; blurred, but apparently a mounted figure to the sinister; legend undeciphered.

[3] Seal: red wax, diam. ¾ in.; device blurred but apparently a cross and dots.

116. Dec. 16, 19 Richard II [1395]. Indenture by which John Daunay leases to William Gate of Cowyk and Isolde, his wife, 3 acres of land in the east field of Cowyk, of which one and a half acres lie between the land of John Jepok on the west and the land of Matilda Denny on the east, and abut on the hedge (*sepe*) of the meadow towards the north, and on the broad way leading to Cowyk towards the south; and the other one and a half acres lie between the land recently belonging to Henry Cardinalle on the east and the land of Robert Gybson' towards the west, and abut on Rouclifgat to the south, and on the hedge of the meadow on the north; to hold to William and Isolde, their heirs and assigns, paying to the lessor yearly 2*d.* at Easter and Michaelmas, in equal portions. Warranty. Alternate seals.[1] Witnesses: John Lynlay, John Frer, Thomas de Cowyk, John Scot, Robert Forman', John Underhille. At Cowyk. (*Ibid.*, No. 4.)

117. Michaelmas [Sept. 29], 1398. Lease by Robert Gibson' of Cowyk near Snayth to William Turpyn and Alice, his wife, their heirs and assigns, of a tenement in Cowyk lying between the tenement formerly of Henry Cardinall on one side, and the toft late of John Daunay on the other, with a fourth part of a bovate of land, meadow and moor, with appurtenances, of the fee called Gramoryse; to hold to William and Alice, their heirs and assigns, of the chief lords of that fee, from Michaelmas 1398 for 51 years, saving the terms of the then tenants of certain parcels, namely, to Thomas de Cowyk and Thomas de Crulle, their dwelling house in the buildings of the said tenement, a parcel of meadow and the right for one man to dig for two days [yearly ?] on the moor during the term aforesaid, if the said Robert and Agnes should live so long, as appears in their indenture from Robert and Agnes, after whose death William and Alice, his wife, shall hold the tenement and the fourth part of the bovate during the term aforesaid, in their entirety, as they have taken them, without any contradiction of any of the heirs of the said Robert, and if William and Alice, his wife, or their heirs, erect any buildings, within their term, on the tenement, it shall be lawful for them or their assigns to remove them within the said term or receive the true value of the same from Robert or his heirs. Warranty. Alternate seals. Witnesses: John de Lynlay, Adam Olyne, Henry de Horden, John Deye, John Rudde. At Cowyk. (*Y.A.S.*, M[D] 182, No. 4.)

118. Monday after the Apostles SS. Peter and Paul [July 2], 1403, 4 Henry IV. Grant by John Walkar living in the east of the vill of Snayth near the house formerly belonging to Adam

---

[1] Seal: red wax, small gem with man's head to the dexter.

Manbrid', to Thomas de Cowyk, his heirs and assigns, of a selion of land lying in the field of Cowyk between the land of Henry Horden on the west, which formerly belonged to William Gybson, and the land of [Lawrence ?][1] Rud' on the east and abutting on the tenement of Thomas on the south, and on le Crosgate leading [to the tenement ?][1] of John Scot' as far as the cross on the north, and containing two perches in breadth; to hold of the chief lord of the fee. Warranty. Sealing clause. Witnesses: John Daunay, John Lyngley, Thomas de Crull', John Smyth, senior, William Jollam, Henry Horden. At Snayth. (*Ibid.*, No. 5.)

119. Feb. 20, 1426[-7]. Indenture by which John Daunay, senior, grants to William, his son, his croft in Couwyk called Jocecroft with appurtenances; to hold to William for the term of 51 years after the grantor's death if William shall live so long; after William's death remainder to the grantor and his heirs; to hold the same according to the customs of the soke of Snaythe. Sealing clause.[2] Witnesses: William Lynneley of Couwyk, John Thornhille of Snaythe, Thomas Maunselle of the same, Simon Thornton of the same, John Rudde of Couwyk. (*Y.A.S.*, M[D] 153, No. 5.)

120. March 28 in the year from the beginning of the reign of Henry VI 49, and from the reattainment of royal power the first [1471]. Grant by William Henryson of Cowyk and Beatrice, his wife, to John Dawney of Cowyk, esq., his heirs and assigns, of a toft with buildings thereon in Cowyk, with the whole length and breadth as it lies between the messuage formerly of John Etenward, chaplain, on the west, and the messuage formerly of William Lynneley, called Emycetoft, on the east, and abutting upon the garden of John Etenward on the north and on the highway on the south; also 3 acres of land lying in the east field of Cowyk of which 2 acres lie together between the land of John Cowper on the east, and the land of Thomas Foster on the west, and abut on the hedge of the north meadow of Snayth on the north, and on the highway leading to Snayth on the south, and the other acre of land lies between the land of Henry Awkbarrowe on the east, and the land of the king on the west, and abuts on the toft of Richard Story on the south and the land called lez Wroo on the north; to hold of the chief lords of the fee. Warranty. Sealing clause.[3] Witnesses: John Cartwryght of Cowyk, Nicholas Rudde of the same, John Scott .... At Cowyk. (*Y.A.S.*, M[D] 182, No. 6.)

[1] Hole in document.

[2] Seal: red wax, diam. 1 in., a heart-shaped shield of arms in a cusped border, bearing the Dawnay arms, on a bend three annulets; ✠ SIGILLUM JOHIS . . . .

[3] Seals: (1) small fragment of red wax; (2) small blob of red wax, the etter I.

121. July 22, 3 Richard III [1485]. Indenture[1] by which John Dawney of Cowyk within the soke of Snaith, esq., grants to John Scotte of Cowyk, esq., his heirs and assigns, 5 roods of arable land lying in the territory of Cowyk, between the land of the grantor and John Gledow on the west, and the land of John Gledow on the east, and abutting on a toft of the said John Dawney on the south, and on the road leading from Snaith to Turnebrig' on the north; in exchange for 5 roods of land belonging to John Scotte lying in the same territory between the land formerly of John Cowyk on the east, and the land of William Lyghtesyll on the west, and abutting on the land of the grantor on the north, and on a barn (*orium*) formerly of John Cowyk on the south; to hold of the chief lords of the fee. Should the grantor, his heirs or assigns, re-enter the 5 roods it shall be lawful for John Scotte, his heirs or assigns, to re-enter the 5 roods given in exchange. Warranty. Alternate seals. Witnesses: John Rither of Cowyk, John Gledow of the same, John Cartwright of the same. At Cowyk. (*Ibid.*, No. 7.)

122. Feb. 5, 18 Henry VII [1502–3]. Grant by John Mascald' of Haymylen and Katherine, his wife, to Thomas Kyddall of Cowyk, of a toft there and 8 mowings (*falciculos*) of meadow with appurtenances in le Southfeld, within the lordship of Snayth, which toft lies in Cowyk between the toft formerly of John Mylner on the south, and the toft called Fylcok toft on the north, and abuts on the common pasture on the east and on a lane (*venella*) formerly of Henry Haceby on the west; and one mowing of meadow lies in le Southfeld between the meadow of John Ossett on the east, and the meadow of John Mylner on the west; and another mowing of meadow lies there near Depsyk, between the meadow of William Celer on the east, and the meadow of John Mylner on the west, and abuts on the middle of the water (*super medium aque*) of Wentt on the south and on le Hyghtdyk on the north; and 3 mowings of meadow lie there between the meadow of John Cowyk on the east, and the meadow called Peshedthyng on the west, and abut on the middle of the water of Wentt on the south and on le Gott on the north; and another 3 mowings of meadow lie there near le Depsyk between the meadow of John Cowyk on the east and the meadow called Peshedthyng on the west, and abut on the middle of the water of Wentt on the south, and on le Hyghtdyk on the north; also grants to Thomas, his heirs and assigns, half a bovate of moor in Ynclysmore, lying between the moor of John Cowyk on the north, and the moor of John Mylner on the south; to hold of the chief lord of the fee. Warranty. John and Katherine appoint John Rude of Cowyk

---

[1] Also counterpart of this indenture. (*Ibid.*, No. 7a.)

as their attorney to deliver seisin to Thomas Kyddall. Sealing clause. Witnesses: John Scott, Henry Mod'by, Gregory Giffard of Cowyk. At Cowyk. (*Ibid.*, No. 8.)

Crakeball.

123.   Grant[1] by John Darelle and Joan, his wife, to Edmund Darelle, knt., of a tenement and a bovate of land with appurtenances in the vill and territory of Crakall' which lies between the land of the dean and chapter of the church of St. Peter of York on one side, and the land of Peter Multon', esq., on the other, which tenement the grantors recently had of the gift and feoffment of Marmaduke Darelle, esq., for the term of their lives or for the lifetime of the survivor; to hold to Edmund for the term of the grantors' lives or while one of them lives, of the chief lords of the fee. Warranty. Sealing clause. Witnesses: John Grene, Thomas Malby, William Darelle, Richard Elyston, Robert Mason, chaplain. (*Ibid.*, No. 9.)

Croom.

124.   Oct. 20, 1402, 4 Henry IV. Grant by Thomas Carter, vicar of the church of Wyuerthorp, and William Warde of Lokynton to William Wyuerthorp of Wyuerthorp and Margaret, his wife, daughter of William Driffeld of Sledmer, of a messuage and 8 bovates of land with appurtenances in Crome iuxta Sledemer, which the grantors had of the gift and feoffment of the said William Wyuerthorp; to hold to William and Margaret of the chief lords of the fee. Sealing clause. At Crome. (*Y.A.S.*, M[D] 120, No. 13.)

Dale.

125.   Thursday before the Conversion of St. Paul [Jan. 23], 1325[-6]. Appointment by Thomas Salcoc of Robert Talpe of Cessay as his attorney to deliver seisin to Thomas, son of Marmaduke de Arelle, of 2 crofts with other lands and tenements with appurtenances in the vill and territory of Dale, as contained in the charter of feoffment. Sealing clause. At Salkoc.[2] (*Y.A.S.*, M[D] 182, No. 53.)

Dalton (Topcliffe)

126.   Sunday after St. Michael the Archangel [Oct. 3], 1316, 10 Edward II. Grant by Alice daughter of Richard de Decima of Dalton iuxta Toppeclyffe, to William Blaufrount of Dalton and Helewise, his wife, of a toft and a croft with appurtenances in the vill and territory of Dalton, which lies between the toft of

[1] Contemporary copy or draft of original deed; not executed.
[2] Sawcock.

Dom. Thomas de Gristwayt, chaplain, on the east, and the toft of William son of William son of Richard on the west, which toft and croft the grantor's father gave to Beatrice, the grantor's elder sister, and to the grantor after Beatrice's death, and she is now dead; to hold to William and Helewise and the heirs and assigns of William, of the lord of the fee. Warranty. Sealing clause. Witnesses: John de Kilvington, Dom. Thomas de Gristwayt, chaplain, John Byuyll', Richard son of Ranulph, Robert de Neuby, Robert de Toppeclyff, Edmund *ad fontem*, William son of the clerk. At Dalton. (*Ibid.*, No. 10.)

127. Sunday, the morrow of the Exaltation of the Holy Cross [Sept. 15], 1325. Quitclaim by Beatrice, daughter of Richard del Tende of Dalton' iuxta Toppeclive, in her widowhood, to William Blaufrend' and his heirs, of all right which she has in an annual rent of 2s. customarily received from William for a toft and croft in the vill and territory of Dalton. Warranty. Sealing clause. Witnesses: Robert de Neuby, Edmund *ad fontem*, Robert son of William the clerk. At Dalton. (*Y.A.S.*, M^D 153, No. 6.)

128. Friday before St. Peter in cathedra, 23 Edward III [Feb. 20, 1348-9]. Grant by Marmaduke Darell to Dom. Thomas, the chaplain, dwelling in Crekal, of two parts of a messuage with a croft and two parts of a toft and croft and 5 acres, and two parts of a rood of land, and an acre and two parts of an acre of meadow with appurtenances in the vill and territory of Dalton near Topclif; to hold to Thomas, his heirs and assigns, of the chief lords of the fee. Sealing clause. Witnesses: John de Malton, John de Neweby, William Dalton, Richard de Crekal, Lawrence Croft. At Elvedmer.[1] (*Y.A.S.*, M^D 182, No. 11.)

129. Mar. 24, 1348[-9]. Grant by Dom. Thomas, the chaplain, to Marmaduke Darell of the lands [*as in the preceding deed*], for the term of his life, and after his death to Thomas, his son, for life, with remainder to the heirs and assigns of Marmaduke. Witnesses: [*as before*]. (*Ibid.*, No. 12.)

130. Wednesday after St. Ambrose the Bishop, 38 Edward III [April 10, 1364]. Indenture by which Marmaduke Darelle grants and sells to William Attewelle of Dalton the marriage portion of William, son and heir of William Darelle on his marriage with Agnes, daughter of William Attewelle, also custody of all lands, tenements, rents and services which William, son of William Darelle had by inheritance from his father in Dalton near Toppeclif, Iselbek and Letteby[2]; to hold to William Attewelle, his heirs

---

[1] Elmire.
[2] Leckby (Cundall).

and assigns, until the attainment of lawful age by William, son
of William Darelle; and should it happen that Agnes die before
William reaches lawful age, then William Attewelle, his heirs and
assigns, may give William in marriage wheresoever they wish,
without disparagement, and they may hold all the lands, tenements, etc., until the coming of age of William; and should it
happen that William die under age, the grantor wills that William
Attewelle, his heirs and assigns, should hold all the lands [etc.],
as William, son of William Darelle would have held them had he
lived until attaining lawful age.   Warranty.   Alternate seals.[1]
At Cessay.   (Ibid., No. 13.)

131.   Monday after All Saints, 43 Edward III [Nov. 5, 1369].
Grant by Emma, daughter of William atte Well to John.Darell'
of Ceszay and John de Bellerby, their heirs and assigns, of all
the grantor's lands and tenements with appurtenances in Dalton
iuxta Topclif, Catton and Heton; to hold of the lords of the fees.
Warranty.   Sealing clause.[2]   Witnesses: William Darelle, Henry
de Bellerby, Thomas de Neusam, John de Thorp', John son of
Robert de Dalton.   At Dalton.[3]   (Ibid., No. 14.)

132.   Tuesday after Martinmas, 43 Edward III [Nov. 13,
1369].   Indenture[4] between William, son of Marmaduke Darelle
of the one part and Anneis [sic], widow of William son of William
Darelle of Dalton and Henry Bellerby of the other part, witnessing
that William, son of Marmaduke grants to Anneis a third part of
all the lands, tenements, rents, services of all free tenants, with
appurtenances in Dalton, which belonged to the said William,
son of William Darelle, recently her husband; to hold as the
dower for the term of her life; also grants to Anneis and Henry,
their heirs and assigns, two parts of the said lands, etc., to hold
for the term of 4 years next following the date of these presents,
paying yearly to the grantor or his heirs a rose at the Nativity
of St. John for all services; also grants that if Anneis be delivered
of a child who is the heir of the said William, then Anneis and
Henry shall hold all the two parts until the coming of age of the
child; further grants that if the child die before attaining lawful
age then Anneis shall hold a fourth part of the two parts for the
term of her life to the increase of her estate, paying to the grantor

[1] Seal: round, white wax, diam. $\frac{7}{10}$ in.; very blurred, but probably
small armorial shield surrounded by a legend.

[2] Seal: fragment of round seal of red wax, badly broken, not deciphered:
surface of seal defaced by punchings with a blunt-ended instrument.

[3] Endorsed in an early hand in English: "all my lands and tenements
in Dalton, Catton and Heton."

[4] In French, also counterpart, with seal missing, and endorsed:
"Dower assigned in Dalton."

or his heirs a rose at the feast aforesaid for all services. Alternate seals.[1] At Ceszay. (*Ibid.*, No. 15.)

133. Purification of the B.V.M. [Feb. 2], 1375[-6]. Release[2] and quitclaim by Hugh Kae of Dalton to Emma and Agnes, daughters and heirs of William Acthebeld of Dalton, of all right and claim in an annual rent of 8*d.* from lands and tenements which are called Dalby's lands (*terre de Dalby*). Sealing clause. Witnesses: Sir Robert de Rowclif', knt., John Darel, William de le Rywer, John de Thorpe, John son of Robert de Dalton, John Forest of the same. At Dalton iuxta Topeclif. (*Ibid.*, No. 16.)

134. Feb. 20, 8 Henry V [1420-21]. Release and quitclaim by John de Toppeclyffe, son of Walter de Toppeclyffe of Markharh in co. Notyngham to Robert Grene of Neuby, his heirs and assigns, of all right and claim in a messuage with a bovate of land and appurtenances within the vill and territory of Dalton. Warranty. Sealing clause. Witnesses: Marmaduke Darelle of Ceszay, Henry Maunselle, Thomas de Malton', Richard Jonson' of Dalton, Thomas Kaa. At Dalton.[3] (*Ibid.*, No. 18.)

135. Oct. 20, 2 Henry VI [1423]. Grant by Margaret, widow of Richard Grene of Danby to John Grene, her eldest son, and Jane, daughter of Robert de Plumpton, knt., his wife, of her manor of Dalton, with all rents, services, commodities and easements, as well within the vill of Dalton as without; to hold to John and Jane and to the heirs of his body lawfully begotten. Reversion to the grantor if John dies without heirs. Warranty. Sealing clause. Witnesses: William Tempest, knt., Roger Ward, knt., Marmaduke Darelle, William Lassels, Richard Jacson. At Dalton. (*Ibid.*, No. 19.)

Danby.

136. Nativity of St. John the Baptist, 1[4] Richard II [June 24, 1397]. Grant by Robert son of Robert Stevenson of Thorp to Thomas Lowysson of Daneby, his heirs and assigns, of a messuage with houses and buildings, and a bovate of land and appurtenances in the vill and territory of Danby, lying together within these boundaries, namely, between the land once belonging to William son of Henry and le Newbryg and between Arnethorpmer and Sykecum de Suwardholm; to hold to Thomas of the chief lord of the fee all the lands within and without the vill of Danby,

---

[1] Seal: white wax, diam. $\frac{7}{10}$ in., I.H.S. surmounted by a cross and a spray of leaves.

[2] In French.

[3] Endorsed in a later hand in English: "Dalton, the deede of John Topclif of Markham to Robert Grene of Newbie, the viij of King Henrie Vth."

[4] Probably 21.

near and far, wherever situated, and with common pasture where-
ever the free tenants of Danby have right of pasture, except for
the heirs of Matthew de Slaphow in Fryop; and there shall be
pannage for pigs on the common; rendering yearly to the chief
lord of the fee 7s. of silver in equal portions at Whitsuntide and
Martinmas for all secular services, suits and demands [etc.], and
he shall grind his own corn grown on the said lands at the mill
at Danby to the twentieth measure. Warranty. Sealing clause.[1]
Witnesses: Thomas de Etton,[2] William de Fulthorp, ... ayce,
William del Dale, John Hudson, William junior. At the said
messuage. (Ibid., No. 19a.)

Rortb Duffielb.

137. Sunday after Pope Gregory, 7 Richard [II] [March 13,
1384-5]. Grant by John de Menthorp' of Northduffeld to Thomas
Daunay, of all his meadow lying in Crukelede in the pastures of
Northduffeld, namely, 2½ acres of meadow with appurtenances;
to hold to Thomas, his heirs and assigns, of the chief lords of the
fee. Warranty. Sealing clause.[3] Witnesses: Robert de Merston',
Nicholas Wright, Richard Ibson, John Baker, Adam Blaunchard.
At Northduffeld. (Ibid., No. 20.)

South Duffielb.

138. Thursday after St. Ambrose the Bishop [April 7], 1345.
Indenture by which Richard de Amcotes grants to Isabel le
Poulter of Southduffeld a messuage, 8 butts adjacent and 2 acres
of land in le Gayres in Southduffeld; to hold to Isabel for the
term of her life, paying yearly to Richard or his heirs 10s. 6d. in
equal portions at Whitsuntide and Martinmas; should the rent
be in arrears wholly or in part, power to Richard or his heirs to
enter and distrain; Isabel agrees to maintain the lands without
waste or destruction during her lifetime. Warranty. Alternate
seals.[4] Witnesses: Robert de Hathelsey, William de Hathelsay,
John de Sadyngton, John de Surflet, Thomas Paynson. At
Southduffeld. (Farnley Hall MSS., No. 43.)

139. St. Leonard, 36 Henry VI [Nov. 6, 1457]. Quitclaim
by William Laton of Southduffeld in the parish of Hemyngburgh,
gentilman, to John Sandesby and Isabel, his wife, of Bouthorp
in the same parish, of all right which he has in a wood lying in

---

[1] Seal: white wax, broken.

[2] He became Master forester of Danby in 1388 (Cal. Pat. Rolls, 1388-92,
p. 197) and died in 1401 (Y.A.J., xix, 112).

[3] Seal: brown wax, diam. ₁⁸₆ in.; a figure, probably an angel, with two
heads of corn on the dexter side and holding a lily; legend undeciphered.

[4] Seal of white wax, undeciphered.

the field and territory of Southduffeld, between a certain ditch belonging to William on the east, and 2 acres of land belonging to John Sandesby on the west; to hold to John and Isabel, with appurtenances, from the bank of the ditch towards the west as far as the grantees' 2 acres in the east. Sealing clause. Witnesses: Robert Portyngton, esq., Thomas Hagthorp, Richard Hagthorp of Brakenholme, gents., John Bedell of Clyff, John Rowden of Hemyngburgh. At Southduffeld. (*Ibid.*, No. 45.)

Eastborpe (E.R.)

140. Grant by Sybil,[1] widow of William de Coleby in her lawful widowhood, to William Danyel and Lucy, his wife, of a bovate and a half of land with appurtenances in the demesne lands of Estorp, which land accrued to her after the death of Sybil Foliot and which lies between the land of Nicholas de Percy on one side and the land of John de Ekton on the other in the demesne land of Estorp; to hold in meadows, grazings, pastures, moors and commons and all other liberties and easements, freely, peacefully as is held all the remainder of the demesne land of the same vill, to the said William and Lucy, their heirs and assigns, of the grantor and her heirs and assigns in perpetuity, and performing to the grantor and her heirs for free seisin whatever scutage is due from the demesne lands of the fee in the same vill, namely, that proportion of service which pertains to the forinsec service of a bovate and a half of land in the same fee, for all services, customs and suits of court, aids and all other demands; so that William and Lucy and their heirs and assigns shall be freely seised of the said tenement, quit in perpetuity of wards, marriages, reliefs and all other demands. Warranty. Sealing clause.[2] Witnesses: Sirs John de Ekton, Geoffrey Aguilun, Richard de Tweng, James de Feuile [?], knts., Brian de Killingwik, John de Cresak, Roger de Caue, Laurence de Etton, John de Finner, William de Cresak, William Abel, John Submonitor', Walter Francis. (*Y.A.S.*, M⁰ 239, No. 1.)
Dorso: *Estorp de Dominico. una bovata terra.*

141. St. Peter in cathedra, 9 Edward son of Henry [Feb. 22, 1280–81]. Grant by Sybil, widow of William de Colleby, to William Sturmy and Joan, his wife, of all the service which was due to her from Sir William Danyell, knt., for a tenement which he held of her in the vill of Esthorp'; also grant and quitclaim of all right in all the lands and tenements which she inherited after the death of Avice, her sister, as well in lordships as in wards,

---

[1] Daughter of Roger Maleverer, lord of the manor of Whixley (*Early Yorks. Charters*, ii, 76, and *Glover's Visitation*, ed. Foster, p. 266).

[2] Seal: white wax, oval, ⁷⁄₁₀ × ½ in.; floral spray; ✠S.SIBILLE.DE. COLBI.

homages, etc., also quitclaim of 3 roods of meadow in Everingham with appurtenances, with all lands, rents and possessions within and without the same vill; also the services of a chaplain in the chapel of Esthorp for the celebration of the divine offices; to hold of the chief lords of the fee, freely etc., as held by her sister; and paying to the grantor, her heirs and assigns, half a pound of wax at the Nativity of the B.V.M. in the chapel of Esthorp for all secular services, suits and demands. Warranty. Sealing clause. Witnesses: Sirs ˙ Thomas de Lutton', Robert Salueyn, Thomas de Houeton, knts., Thomas de Arreynes, Mag. Richard de Bruneby, William de Arreynes, Robert Vyele of Schupton,[1] Hugh de Coluyle, William de Wodehus, clerk. At Thorp'. (*Ibid.*, No. 2.)

Dorso: *Car' Sibillie de colby de omnibus terris et serviciis suis in Esthorp'*.

142.   Grant by Sybil, widow of William de Coleby, to William Sturmy of Lounesburg' and Joan, his wife, of all the land in Esthorp and all the pasture in Everingham which descended to her by hereditary right after the death of her sister, Avice; also the capital messuage and all other liberties and easements, with wards, reliefs, escheats and the services of free tenants, villeins and their lands, sequel and chattels, also tofts, crofts, meadows, grazings, pastures, ways, paths, waters, enclosures, rents, mills, ponds and appurtenances thereof (*attachiamentis stagnorum*), all of which the grantor held by law or ought to hold, without reservation; to hold to William and Joan, their heirs and assigns, of the chief lords of the fee, in fee and hereditarily, freely, peacefully, etc., in perpetuity, performing to the chief lords of the fee the due and accustomed services and paying to the grantor and her heirs and assigns half a pound of wax at the Nativity of the B.V.M. in the chapel at Esthorp for all secular services, suits, exactions and demands. Warranty. Sealing clause.[2] Witnesses: Sirs Robert Saluayn, Thomas de Lutton, Thomas de Houeton, knts., Mag. Richard de Bruneby, Thomas de Araynes, John de Fanecurt, Robert le Veyl de Schupton, Hugh de Colevile of Gothemundeham, Stephen his brother, William de Prestona. (*Ibid.*, No. 3.)

143.   Grant by Sybil, widow of William de Coleby, to William Sturmy of Lounesburg' and Joan, his wife, of all that land in Esthorp and all that meadow with appurtenances in Everingham which came to her by hereditary right after the death of Avice, her sister, with all appurtenances, namely a messuage, 2 tofts, 2 half tofts, 10 bovates and a half of land and a third part of

---

[1] Shipton.
[2] Seal: as to No. 140.

a bovate and 2 acres and a piece of land called le Haggard and all that part of a mill which Avice held in Esthorp, also the path to the pond and free entry and exit pertaining to the same mill in perpetuity; also the customary services of Sir John de Eketon, Sir William Danyel, Peter de Mounceus, the prioress of Wylberfose, John Dagny, Juliana de Clyf, Henry Page, of 2 bovates of land which the Hospitallers hold, and of Roger Kyde, and of their heirs; also all the villeins, male and female and their sequel and chattels, also all other customs, liberties and easements which pertain to the said tenements within and without the vill of Esthorp; to hold to William and Joan, their heirs and assigns, of the chief lords of the fee, in fee and hereditarily, performing to them the due and accustomed services and paying yearly to the grantor, her heirs and assigns, half a pound of wax at the Nativity of the B.V.M. in the chapel of Esthorp for all services. Warranty. Sealing clause.[1] Witnesses: Mag. Richard de Brunneby, John de Fanecourt, Thomas Darayns, Robert de Veyl of Scupeton, Hugh le Coleuile of Godmundham, Stephen his brother, Geoffrey de Hosgoteby, William Darayns. (*Ibid.*, No. 4.)

144.   Grant and quitclaim by William de Royeresfeld to William Sturmi and Joan, his wife, and the heirs and assigns of William, of all right in his manor and lands in the vill and territory of Estorp, with all appurtenances which he had of the gift of Sybil de Colebi, without reservation, namely, 10½ bovates of land, a third part of a bovate and a piece of land called le Aggarat, and all that part of a mill which Avice le Percy once held in Estorp, also the services of [*as described in preceding deed*]: to hold of the chief lord of the fee by the due and accustomed services and paying yearly to the grantor and his heirs ½*d.* at the Nativity. Sealing clause.[2] Witnesses: Sir Robert Saluayn, Sir Thomas de Lutton, Sir Thomas de Houeton, Mag. Richard de Brunneby, John de Fanecurt, Robert Vetere, Robert le Fraunkelain, Hugh de Coleuille of Gudmundham, Stephen his brother, Robert Roland. (*Ibid.*, No. 5.)

145.   Grant by Elias de la Mar' son of Adam de Bleynleueny to William son of Richard Sturmy of Lonnesburg' and his heirs or to whomsoever he may wish to sell or assign it, of all that land with appurtenances, without any reservation, namely, 4 selions in the territory of Hestorp lying between the common pasture of Lonnesburg' which is called le Slekht and the land which Peter ad Fontem of Hestorp holds, and which extends in length from the path of Scupton' as far as Heldayles, all of which Thomas Ingehuer the grantor's ancestor had of the gift of Henry

---

[1] Seal: green wax, as to No. 140.
[2] Seal: broken, a floral device; ✠ NOVILIS . . . . IMO.

son of Ralph and William the steward, and John Playn' in accordance with the charter of the said Henry, William and John and the grantor, which lands are in the possession of the said William; to hold to William son of Richard, his heirs and assigns, of the grantor and his heirs, and of the heirs of the said Henry, William and John, of the chief lords of the fee, freely [etc.], as held by Elias of the same lords, paying yearly to the heirs and assigns of the said Henry, William and John, 3d. at the Nativity of the B.V.M. in the autumn for all services, exactions, customs and demands, and to the grantor and his heirs and assigns a clove gilly-flower at the Nativity for all services and demands. Warranty. Sealing clause.[1] Witnesses: John de Feugers of Hestorp, Gilbert de Neubald of the same, Robert Sene [of] Stuptun, Richard de Wytewel of the same, Bartholomew Tyrel of Godmundham, Hugh de Colwyl of the same, Robert le franklyn of Wycton, Walter the [?] cook (*le cu'*) of the same, Thomas de Hofton, Mag. Richard de Bruneby, Thomas de Hundegayt of the same. (*Ibid.*, No. 6.)

146. Grant[2] by Walter son of Amyas de Estorpe to John his son, his heirs and assigns, of a toft in the vill of Esthorpe with appurtenances which lies between the toft which Dame Alice, widow of Sir John de Ecketon, once held, on one side, and the toft which Jurdan de Newbald once held of the same Dame Alice on the other; also a bovate of land with appurtenances in the territory of the same vill which lies adjacent towards the south next to that bovate which Juliana wife of Roger Kyde sold to John de Ecketon, with all liberties and easements pertaining to the aforesaid lands, except for 2½ acres which Sir John, son and heir of Sir John de Ecketon, William Sturmy and Sir William Danyel hold; to hold to John, his heirs and assigns, of the chief lords of the fee, freely and in peace, and paying yearly to the prior of Watton 6d. at Whitsuntide for the said toft for all services, and to the churches of Lonnesburgh and Guthmundham 15d. yearly in equal portions at Whitsuntide and Martinmas, and 3d. at Easter for synodal dues (*senagio*). Warranty. Sealing clause. Witnesses: Dom. William, rector of the church of Lounesburgh, John Roland of Guthmundham, Richard Biset, John de Holm', Richard the clerk of Wyghton. (*Ibid.*, No. 7.)

147. Monday after SS. Peter and Paul [July 2], 1352. Indenture witnessing that whereas John son of Richard Sturmy of Wyghton had recently granted and demised to Richard de Derlton of Wyghton 2 bovates and an acre of land with appurtenances in Esthorp, to hold to him and his heirs from Martinmas

---

[1] Seal: black wax, vesica-shaped, undeciphered; ✠ SIG . . . . LERIO.
[2] Copy of original deed, not executed.

next for 18 years in return for a sum of money received, without any further [payment], and also demised an annual rent of 20s. from his lands and tenements in Wyghton, payable at Whitsuntide and Martinmas in equal portions, as more fully appears in the charters granting the same; now Richard grants for himself and his heirs that if he and they may peacefully hold and enjoy all the said lands ·without disturbance, claims or ejection during the said term, as is more fully described in the charter of demise, then during the said term the charter relating to the annual rent is to be of no effect to anyone into whose hands it may fall in the future, but otherwise to remain in full force. Alternate seals. At Wyghton. (*Ibid.*, No. 8.)

148. Feb. 20, 14 Henry IV [1412–3]. Appointment by John Brakkele, vicar of the parish church of Wolaston, and William Heriot, chaplain, of Richard Norfolke and Robert Daubeney of North Caue, co. York, as their attorneys to deliver seisin and possession to Edward Brouneflete, son of Thomas Brounflete, knt., and Katherine, his wife, daughter of William Kyngesman and Elizabeth, his wife, of the manor of Esthorp, with all appurtenances, tenements, rents, services in the vills of Esthorp, Lounesburgh, Touthorp, Keblyngcotes, Eueryngham and Northcaue, co. York, according to their charter to the said Edward and Katherine. Sealing clause.[1] (*Ibid.*, No. 9.)

Egbrougb.

149. June 1, 1352. Grant by William, son and heir of Roger de Preston', to Richard de Snayth, his heirs and assigns, of two tofts in the vill of Eggbrough, 3 acres of meadow lying in Bailycroft and half an acre of meadow lying in le Flaske, a croft called Wadworthcroft abutting on the field of Heck and a croft called le Claycroft; grant in like manner to the same Richard, his heirs and assigns, of a bovate of land in the same vill with 14 doles of meadow lying in the east meadows and 4 doles of meadow in the west meadows of Eggbrough; to hold of the chief lord of the fee by the due and accustomed services, namely 2d. yearly. Warranty. Sealing clause.[2] Witnesses: John de Shirwode, Henry his brother, John de Laisyngcroft then dwelling in Rowale, Robert Alayn of Hethensale, John Howelet of the same, William son of Matilda of Eggbrough. At Eggburgh. (*Y.A.S.*, M⁰ 182, No. 21.)

---

[1] Seals: tongues for two seals cut from base of deed, one remains; red wax, diam. 1 in.; in a cusped border and beneath a canopy, two figures facing, the sinister an angel; possibly the Annunciation. S'IOHANIS . . E . . HEM.

[2] Seal: white wax, diam. 1 in., on a heater-shaped shield a lion rampant: W . . LELMI PRESTON.

Escrick.

150. Thursday before St. Margaret the Virgin [July 15], 1294, 22 Edward son of Henry. Grant[1] by William de Lasceles son of William de Lasceles of Escryk, to William de Grymmesby of York, and Matilda, his wife, of his capital messuage and all his land in the vill and territory of Escryk, with all appurtenances; to hold to William and Matilda and the heirs and assigns of William of the chief lords of the fee, with all meadows, grazings, pastures, houses, gardens, woods, hedges, dykes, spinneys, fields, wastes, moors, marshes, turbaries, fishings, waterways, lands sown, closes, escheats and all other commodities and easements pertaining to the messuage and land, within and without the vill and territory of Escryk, whether near or far, high or low, as held by the grantor and his ancestors. Warranty. Sealing clause.[2] At Escryk. Witnesses: Sirs Roger de Lasceles, William de Sancto Quintino, Paul de Lilling, knts., Simon de Stoteuill', steward of the Liberty of St. Mary of York, William son of Peter de Thorneton', sergeant (*seruiente*) of the same Liberty, Thomas de Selby, citizen of York, Hugh de Selby of Escryk, Reginald de Vescy, Adam de Aula of Fulford, William called the skinner (*dicto skynner*) of the same, Roger de Dighton, John son of Ralph de Clyfton, Richard called the baker (*dicto pistore*) of the same, Adam de Popelton, clerk, Robert de Dernington, clerk, John his son, clerk. (*Y.A.S.*, M⁰ 114, No. 1.)

151. June 30, 1322. Grant by William de Selleby, son of Thomas de Selleby of York, to Simon de Semerer, of his assart called Uggelker in the territory of Escrik, co. York, which lies in length between the wood of Kelkefeld and the land which belonged to William de Grymmesby, and in breadth between the park of the abbot of Blessed Mary of York and the waste of Stiuelingfleet; to hold to Simon, his heirs and assigns, of William and his heirs, paying to the chief lords of the fee the accustomed services. Warranty. Sealing clause. Witnesses: Henry de Moreby, Walter de Henley, Richard de Fishergate, John de Fishergate, John Russell'. At York. (*Ibid.*, No. 2.)

152. Monday, St. Nicholas, 13 Edward III [Dec. 6, 1339]. Appointment[3] by Dame Avice, widow of Robert Conestable esq., of Halsham, of her clerk, John de Syglesthorn' as her attorney to deliver seisin to John Bardolf esq., lord of Wyrmegeye[4] and Dame Elizabeth, his wife (*compaigne*) and the heirs of Dame

---

[1] Also two copies in a slightly later hand.

[2] Seal: dark brown wax, pointed oval, $\frac{8}{16}$ × $1\frac{2}{16}$ ins., possibly a bird to the sinister along the major axis: WILLI . DE . LASELIS.

[3] In French.

[4] Wormegay, Norfolk.

Elizabeth, of 3 messuages (*mees*), 2 bovates and 10½ acres of land and the fourth part of a windmill, and the fourth part of a water mill (*eweret*), with appurtenances in Escryk, according to her charter to them. Sealing clause.[1] At Escryk. (*Ibid.*, No. 3.)

153. Whitsunday [May 27], 1341. Indenture[2] by which William de Lindlawe of Beverley, merchant, leases to Dom. Simon de Monkton, rector of the church of Eskryke and William Godefray of Walkyngton, his servant, all the lands, tenements, rents and services which he has in the vill and territory of Eskryke; to hold of William, his heirs and assigns from Whit Sunday, 1341 for the full term of 6 years following, paying to William, his heirs and assigns, 40s. at the two terms, namely, Martinmas and Whitsuntide in equal portions. Warranty. Alternate seals.[3] Witnesses: Richard de Louth of Beverley, Robert Jolyf of the same, William Walkyngton of the same, John Lassels of Eskryke, Henry Laurence of the same. At Beverley. (*Ibid.*, No. 4.)

154. Monday after the octave of the Trinity, 15 Edward III [June 11, 1341]. Indenture[4] by which William Marmyoun of Ryseby, knt., grants to William de Lyndlawe of Beverley, merchant, his manor of Eskeryk, co. York, with appurtenances, liberties and easements on condition that William, his heirs or assigns shall pay to the grantor or to his attorney having this indenture on the feast of St. Michael next following, at Eskeryk, 55 marks[5]; to hold of the chief lords of the fee. Power to the grantor to re-enter and hold the manor if the payment is not made. Warranty. Alternate seals. Witnesses: Ralph de Lassels, knt., Henry de Morby, John de Lassels, Henry Laurenc', Walter de Poynton, John Toundu, William de Walkynton. At Eskeryk. (*Ibid.*, No. 5.)

155. Monday after Whitsunday, 18 Edward III [May 24, 1344.] Grant by William de Lyndelawe of Beverley to John de Bentelay, his heirs and assigns, of an annual rent of 40*li.* from his lands and tenements in the vill and territory of Escryk payable at Martinmas and Whitsuntide in equal portions. Power to John to enter and distrain should the rent be in arrears in part or in

[1] Seal: red wax, ₁₀⁶ × 1 in.; shield of arms, Constable impaling Lascelles. ✠ . . . GILL' AVICE . . . CONESTABEL.

[2] Quitclaim by the same to the same of all right in the lands, etc., dated Sept. 28, 1342. Same witnesses. Same seal as to deed. (*Ibid.*, No. 6.)

[3] Seal: red wax, diam. ₁₀⁶ in., pseudo armorial, a fess between two crosses and the letter W. ✠ S. WILLELMI DE LINDLAWE.

[4] Also counterpart, with fragment of seal of red wax; also quitclaim, same date, same witnesses. (*Ibid.*, No. 7.)

[5] Acknowledgement of this payment dated Saturday, Sept. 29, 1341, and witnessed by Ralph de Lasceles, knt., Henry Laurence of Eskeryk, John Tundu of Beverley. Seal: red wax, armorial, a lion rampant. (*Ibid.*, No. 8.)

E

whole at any of the terms, until satisfaction be obtained. Sealing clause.[1] Witnesses: Richard of London', Thomas de Humbercroft, Peter de Clay. At Beverley. (*Ibid.*, No. 10.)

156. May 14, 17 Edward III [1345]. Indenture by which William de Seleby of Eskrik leases to William son of Henry le Wright of Qweldrik,[2] his heirs and assigns, his piece of land with appurtenances in the vill and territory of Eskrik, as it is enclosed and which lies in breadth between the land of the abbot and convent of Fountains on the east, and the lessor's land on the west, and in length from the land of William de Lyndlawe on the north, which is called le Wraa, and the land also of William de Lyndlawe which is called Brokhirst on the south; also with free entry and exit through the lessor's land to the extent of 20 feet, from the highway leading from Eskrik to Qweldrik as far as the said piece of land; also leases the right to drive cattle and oxen back and fore (*chaceam et rechaceam*) across the lessor's *ranam*[3] lying on the east side of the said entry and exit; to hold to William, his heirs and assigns of the chief lords of the fee, paying yearly to the lessor, his heirs or assigns for the first 20 years a rose at the Nativity of St. John the Baptist if demanded, and thereafter at Martinmas and Whitsuntide 40s. in equal portions. Power to re-enter and take possession if the rent be in arrears at any of the terms for longer than 15 days, and this charter to be no longer valid. Warranty. Alternate seals.[4] Witnesses: Sir Ralph de Lascels of Eskrik, knt., Henry Laurenz of the same, John Lascels, Henry de Moreby, Robert Moregraue of Qweldrik, John Mordok, William de Estoft. At Eskrik. (*Ibid.*, No. 9.)

157. Tuesday after the Translation of St. Thomas the Martyr, 19 Edward III [July 12, 1345]. Grant by William de Lyndelawe of Beverley, merchant, to John de Bentelay of all lands, tenements, rents and services which he has in the vill and territory of Escrik in the county of York; to hold with all liberties and easements to John, his heirs and assigns, of the chief lords of the fee. Warranty. Sealing clause.[5] Witnesses: Sir John de Meaux, Sir William de Meleton', knts., William de Houton', Richard Sturmy of Esthorpe, Robert Danyel, Richard de London, Thomas de Humbercroft of Beverley, Peter de Clay. At Benteley. (*Ibid.*, No. 11.)

158. Tuesday after the Translation of St. Thomas, 19 Edward III [July 12, 1345]. Indenture between William de Lyndelawe of Beverley, merchant, and John de Bentelay, wit-

---

[1] Seal: fragment of seal of red wax.
[2] Wheldrake.
[3] Possibly *rain*, a division between lands, an unploughed balk (*O.E.D.*).
[4] Seal: small, white wax, blurred.
[5] Seal: as to No. 150.

nessing that whereas William has enfeoffed John of all the lands, tenements, rents and services which he had in the vill of Escryk as described in his charter to John, now John concedes that if William shall pay to Nicholas Trank of Northampton 40*li.*—20*li.* at Martinmas next following and 20*li.* at Easter—and if he also pays an indemnity of 80*li.* to Nicholas on John's behalf, as ordered to be made in acknowledgement of a debt in accordance with a statute merchant before the mayor and clerk of London, and if he also pays an indemnity to Thomas de Ketryngham and John de Randworth' before the marshals of the king's bench, then the aforesaid charter shall be no longer valid, but otherwise to remain in force. Alternate seals.[1] At Bentelay. (*Ibid.*, No. 12.)

159. Wednesday after the Circumcision [Jan. 3], 1346[–7]. Quitclaim by William de Lyndelawe of Beverley, merchant, to John de Neuton of Snayth, his heirs and assigns, of all right in all the lands and tenements with appurtenances which John had of his gift and feoffment in the vill and territory of Escrik. Warranty. Sealing clause.[2] Witnesses: William de Remyngton', John de Esthorpe of York, clerk, Thomas Humbercroft, William de Ryse of Beverley. At York at the house of St. Leonard. (*Ibid.*, No. 13.)

160. Tuesday after St. Hilary [Jan. 16], 20 Edward III, 1346[–7]. Quitclaim by John son of Geoffrey de Bentelay to John de Neuton of Snayth', of all right in all the lands and tenements with appurtenances and in any rents therefrom, which he had of the gift and feoffment of William de Lyndelawe of Beverley, in Eskrik near Queldrik. Warranty. Sealing clause.[3] Witnesses: Sirs Ralph de Lascelles and Edmund Dauereygnes, knts., Dom. Simon de Munketon, priest of the church of Escryk, William de Meryngton, John de Flete of Bubwith, John de Lascels of Eskryk, William de Rimyngton', John de Esthorpe of York. Within York Castle. (*Ibid.*, No. 14.)

161. Friday after St. Matthew [Sept. 25], 23 Edward III, 1349. Grant by Joan, daughter and heir of Richard Brette of Overfulford, in her virginity, to John de Barton' of Naburn, and Alice, his wife, of a messuage, lands and tenements with all appurtenances, namely, meadows, grazings, pastures, waters, ways, woods, moors, paths, marshes, etc., which she has in the vill and territory of Eskryk, which once belonged to William de Grymysby and Joan, his wife; to hold to John and Alice and the heirs and assigns of John, of the chief lords of the fee. Warranty. Sealing

---

[1] Seal: as to No. 153.

[2] Seal: red wax, broken; as to No. 153.

[3] Seal: red wax, diam. ⁸⁄₁₆ in.; a shield of arms (blurred) in a circle within a cusped and pointed border. . . . . VERITE DE . . .

clause.[1] Witnesses: Sir Ralph de Lascels, knt., Henry de Moreby, William de Morby, John de Lascels, Henry Laurence, William de Groue, John Russel of Naburn'. At Eskryk. (*Ibid.*, No. 15.)

162. Saturday after St. James the Apostle [July 29], 1351, 25 Edward III. Indenture between Ralph de Lascels, knt., and Roger Lascels, his son and heir of the one part, and John de Neuton, tenant of the messuage and 2 acres of land with appurtenances in Escrik which once belonged to William de Marmyoun, knt., of the other, concerning the right to take a reasonable supply of timber for *housebote & haybote* from the woods of Escrik, an appurtenance of that messuage and land, whereby strife and controversy have now arisen; now this indenture witnesses that John made a claim by writ of novel disseisin before William Basset and his fellow justices at the assizes lately held in co. York, against Roger de Lascels and Walter, his brother, Ralph de Lascels, knt. and Isabel, his wife, John Bardolf, knt. and Elizabeth, his wife, Nicholas Dammory, knt., John Rausseruaunt de Lascels, Robert Carter, John son of William de Selby, Hugh Souter, John Blode and William Jakes of Ellerton, clerk, concerning his free holding in Escrik, whereby he accused Roger and others of having deprived him of his reasonable supply of wood from the 1000 acres of woodland in Escrik, namely, his *housebote & haybote* for building, fencing (*includens*) and burning, also as much as he needed for other necessities, and which was due to him from the messuage without inspection or authorisation from the forester there; nevertheless, John, for the sake of peace and amity between himself and Ralph and Roger in the future now agrees and desires that he will, during the lives of Ralph and Roger, take the supply of wood according to the approval of the forester if he will take part in the collection thereof, but if he is not willing, then John, his heirs and assigns may take whatever wood is needful notwithstanding his presence; and Ralph and Roger agree to take into consideration those losses which John sustained when deprived of his supply of timber, and to perform whatever is just, as when the messuage was in the seisin and possession of William de Marmyoun, from time past memory up to the time when William and the tenants of the land took the said *housebote & haybote* appertaining to the messuage with approval of the forester; moreover they agree that John, his heirs and assigns may have in perpetuity from the woods of Escrik whatever timber was allowed to William without hindrance from them, their heirs or any in their name. Alternate seals.[2] Witnesses: Sir Thomas

---

[1] Seal. red wax, diam. $\frac{8}{10}$ in., two interlocking squares, enclosing a design of 6 leaves joined at centre; letters in the angles of the squares undeciphered.

[2] Seals: (1) missing; (2) brown wax, oval, $\frac{6}{10} \times \frac{8}{10}$ in., female figure to the sinister; SPES MEA IN . . . .

Ughtred, Sir Thomas Metham, knts., William de Plumpton, knight of the shire of York, John Shireburn of York, Hamo de Hessay of York, William de Meryngton, John Lascels of Escryk, William de Moreby, John de Barton of Naburn, John de Selby of Escryk. At York. (*Ibid.*, No. 16.)

163. Sunday after St. Laurence the Apostle [*sic*], 30 Edward III [Aug. 14, 1356]. Lease by John de Selby of Escryk, to Henry son of William de Qweldryk, of a close called le Brynkar in the territory of Eskryke; to hold to Henry, his heirs and assigns, of the chief lords of the fee, paying yearly to John and his heirs a red rose at the Nativity of St. John the Baptist if demanded. Warranty. Sealing clause. Witnesses: John Lascels of Escryk, John Laurance, John Neuton, Robert Margraue, Robert Amy, John Amy. At Escryke. (*Ibid.*, No. 17.)

164. March 12, 37 Edward III [1362-3]. Appointment by Joan de Neuton' of John de Lascels, senior, and John de Lascels, junior, as her attorneys to deliver seisin to Thomas Daunay and Elizabeth, his wife, of a third part of a messuage, 200 acres of land and 10 acres of meadow with appurtenances in Escryk, which she holds in dower of the inheritance of the said Elizabeth, according to her charter to them; they shall also deliver to Thomas and Elizabeth two parts of all the lands and tenements which belonged to John de Neuton', once her husband, in the same vill, to hold in custody until the attainment of legal age by Alice and Isobel, the two [other] daughters and heirs of John. Sealing clause.[1] At Escrik. (*Ibid.*, No. 18.)

165. Sunday before Christmas, 38 Edward III [Dec. 22, 1364]. Grant by Joan, widow of William de Ulveston, to Thomas Daunay, of a messuage and a carucate in the vill of Escryk, which once belonged to John de Grymmesby; to hold to Thomas and his heirs of the chief lords of the fee. Warranty. At Escryk.[2] (*Ibid.*, No. 20.)

166. Tuesday after Christmas, 38 Edward III [Dec. 31, 1364]. Indenture between Thomas Dawenay of the one part and Joan, widow of Thomas de Ulueston of the other, witnessing that whereas they are bound to each other in 60*li.* to be paid at York at the Purification of the B.V.M. next following, now Joan agrees for herself, her heirs and assigns, that if Thomas renders satisfaction to her in respect of damages and expenses should judgement go against her at an assize, by reason of her entry into a messuage with appurtenances in Escrik; also if Thomas releases (*exoneret*) all the lands, tenements, rents, and services which Joan holds in

---

[1] Seal: red wax, diam. ½ in.; Virgin and Child beneath a gothic canopy.

[2] Seal: red wax, diam. ₁₆/₁₀ in.; small shield (blurred) in a cusped border; SIGILL' : JOHANNIS| : BRET.

the county of York, on the day of the making of a certain statute-merchant in respect of 40*li*. owed by Joan to a certain John de Barton', and if satisfaction be made to her for her reasonable expenses on the occasion of the release and of the execution of the aforesaid statute; and Thomas for his part concedes that if he and his heirs are able to enjoy the tenement in Escrik which he had of the gift and feoffment of Joan; and if Joan and her heirs act according to his advice in all matters touching the tenement, and neither Joan nor her heirs make any entry, suit of feoffment, or release in respect of a tenement in Walmegate in York, which John de Barton' had of the gift of Joan, without the advice of Thomas; and in case Thomas should surrender the tenement in Escrik, because of any action (*assisam*), or otherwise, against (*versus*) the tenants of the said tenement, and should Joan and her heirs prosecute Thomas for the carrying out [?] (*ordinacionem*) and cost of the same, by a writ while he is under age, and if, the tenants having recovered their debts, he should be enfeoffed of the tenements, to hold to him and his heirs; then the obligations of Thomas and Joan to each other to be null and void, otherwise to remain in full strength.[1] Alternate seals. At Escrick. (*Ibid.*, No. 29.)

167. Tuesday after Christmas, 38 Edward III [Dec. 31, 1364]. Indenture[2] between Thomas Dawenay and Joan, widow of William de Ulueston, witnessing that whereas Thomas is bound to Joan in 7 marks to be paid at the Purification of the B.V.M. next following, and Joan is bound to Thomas in 5 marks to be paid to him or his attorney at the same time; now Thomas agrees that if he and his assigns may enjoy in perpetuity a messuage and a carucate of land with appurtenances in Escrik which he had of the gift and feoffment of Joan, then the bond to be invalid; and Joan agrees that if Thomas or his heirs or assigns should be ejected from the tenement, or should release it by any legal action (*assisam judicum*) or by any deception or fraud, so that neither he nor his heirs are able peacefully to enjoy it, as laid down in Joan's charter to him, then the bond to be invalid. Alternate seals. At Escrik. (*Ibid.*, No. 21.)

168. Friday after Gregory the Pope, 42 Edward III [March 10, 1367–8]. Quitclaim by Robert de Bossale to Thomas Daunay of a messuage and a carucate of land with appurtenances in Eskrik, which once belonged to William de Grymesby. Sealing clause.[3] At Eskrik. (*Ibid.*, No. 22.)

---

[1] This is somewhat complicated and there seems to have been a previous action relating to the tenement in question.

[2] Also counterpart of indenture.

[3] Seal: brown wax, diam. $\frac{6}{10}$ in.; an animal, possibly a stoat, curled up in a circular border of twisted branches.

169. Monday in the third week of Lent, 42 Edward III [March 13, 1367–8]. Quitclaim by William son of John de Barton' of Naburn to Thomas Daunay of a messuage and a carucate of land with appurtenances in Eskrik, which once belonged to John de Barton', the grantor's father. Warranty. Sealing clause.[1] At Eskrik. (*Ibid.*, No. 23.)

170. Jan. 10, 44 Edward III [1370–1]. Indenture by which John, rector of the church of Escryk, John son of John Lascels of Escryk, and Thomas de Kyrkeby, chaplain, grant to Thomas Daunay and Elizabeth, his wife, all their lands, tenements, rents and services with all appurtenances, which they had of the gift and feoffment of Thomas and Elizabeth by a fine[2] in the king's court, in the vills of Escryk, Camelesford and Carleton iuxta Snaith, namely, all those lands, tenements etc., which belonged to John de Neuton', father of Elizabeth; to hold to Thomas and Elizabeth for their lives, with remainder to John, their son and lawful heir and his lawful heir, and in default of issue remainder to Thomas, his brother and his heirs, and should he die without heirs to his brother Ralph and his heirs, failing which, remainder to the right heirs of Thomas and Elizabeth, and should they die without heirs, to Joan, widow of John de Neuton' and her heirs in perpetuity; to hold of the chief lords of the fee, under the following condition, that Thomas and Elizabeth be allowed waste in the said tenements should it please them, without hindrance or obstruction, also to Elizabeth, after Thomas's death, should she survive him. Alternate seals.[3] Witnesses: Ralph Lascels and Roger Lascels, knts., John de Lascels, senior, John Lawrence, John Mergrayue. At Escryk. (*Ibid.*, No. 24.)

171. Dec. 26, 44 Edward III [1370]. Indenture[4] between the prioress and convent of Nun Appelton of the one part, and John, rector of the church of Escrik, John son of John Lascels of Escrik and Thomas de Kirkeby, chaplain, of the other, witnessing that as John, John and Thomas having granted to the prioress and convent and their successors an annual rent of 40 pence, from lands and tenements . . . .[5] they had of the gift of Thomas Daunay and Elizabeth, his wife, in the vills of Escrik,

[1] Seal: white wax, blurred.

[2] See *Yorks. Fines*, 1347–77, p. 150.

[3] Seals: (1) brown, $\frac{8}{10}$ in. diam.; armorial shield (blurred), pendant from a spray of leaves between two birds facing. Leg. undeciphered; (2) Brown, diam. 1 in.; a female figure holding a shield (blurred) standing beneath a canopy. Leg. IOHIS LASCELS; (3) Brown, diam. $\frac{8}{10}$ in.; in a cusped border a shield of arms a bend. Leg. IOHANNIS DE.

[4] Copy of original deed. In French.

[5] Hole in deed.

Camelsford, [Carleton juxta] Snayth, by a fine[1] in the king's court, received at the two terms, namely Whitsuntide and Martin‑mas, in equal portions; to hold to the prioress and convent and their successors from Whitsuntide next following for the term of 80 years for the . . . .[2] and profit of Dame Alice de Neuton; now the prioress and convent wish and grant for themselves and their successors that the said . . . .[2] [rent] . . . . the life of Joan, widow of John de Neuton; they also grant that should Alice die during the term of 80 years then the said rent shall remain for ever to John, John and Thomas and their heirs and assigns holding the said lands and tenements. Alternate seals. (*Ibid.*, No. 25.)

172. Saturday after the Assumption of the B.V.M., 11 Richard II [17 Aug. 1387]. Grant[3] by Thomas Daunay of Escrik to John Daunay, his son, and Helen, daughter of John Barden of York, of all the lands and tenements with appurten‑ances which he has in the vill and territory of Menthorp', with all the meadows by the water of Derwent which he has in the same vill; also grant of a messuage and 26 acres of land with appur‑tenances in meadows, woods, moors, turbaries, pastures, etc., in the vill and territory of Escrik, which he had of the gift and feoffment of Joan, widow of William de Ulleston of York; to hold to John and Helen, and their heirs lawfully begotten, of the chief lords of the fee, with reversion in default of issue to the grantor and his heirs in perpetuity. Warranty. Sealing clause. Witnesses: Gerard Saluayne, Thomas FitzHenry, knts., Ralph Lascels, William Pawmes, Nicholas Northfolk, William Woderawe, John Morgane, Richard de Garton. At Escrik. (*Ibid.*, No. 26.)

173. Jan. 12, 14 Richard II [1390–1]. Indenture[4] by which Elizabeth Daunay[5] daughter and heir of John de Neuton of Snayth, in her widowhood, grants to Mag. John de Neuton, rector of the parish of Tichenisch in co. Northampton, Nicholas Northfolk of Naburn, William Roselyn of Cottenays and John Daunay of Escrik, all right in all the lands, tenements, rents, services, woods, meadows, moors, pastures, grazings, fishings, turbaries, estovers,

[1] See *Yorks. Fines*, 1347–77, p. 150.

[2] Holes in deed.

[3] Copy of original deed.

[4] Demise of the lands to Elizabeth Daunay by the grantees dated Feb. 1, 1390–1, and witnessed by Thomas Fitzhenry, knt., Walter Lascels, Ralph Lascels, Thomas Saltmarsh, junior, Adam de Wyntworth in addition to the above witnesses. Seals: six, of red wax; (1) diam. 1 in., female figure in a border of twisted branches, probably St. Catherine; SIGILL'M JOHIS DE NEUTON; (2) a dwarf with two ears of corn facing to the dexter; (3) a castle, leg. un‑deciphered; (4) a lozenge surrounded by sprays of flowers; (5) blurred; (6) as to No. 173. (*Ibid.*, No. 28.)

[5] See *Cal. Close Rolls*, 1389–1392, p. 232, for orders to the Escheator of Yorkshire concerning the lands in Snaith, etc., held by Elizabeth Daunay.

dues, rights and easements with all appurtenances and reversions which she has in the vills of Escrik, Camelesford and Carlton iuxta Snayth; to hold of the chief lords of the fee; also grants to John, Nicholas, William and Nicholas Rosselyn, brother of William and John Daunay, all the lands, tenements, etc., which she has or may have by inheritance within the vill of Snayth after the death of her father, John de Neuton; to hold to them, of the chief lords of the fee, on condition that they will enfeoff her in the following manner with all the afore-mentioned lands with appurtenances in the said soke, in the county of York or elsewhere when any of them shall be requested by her, and thereafter they shall have full and peaceful seisin according to a charter, and shall hold the lands, etc., by attorneyship (*per attornamentum*); to hold of Elizabeth and her male heirs by Thomas Daunay, her husband, with remainder after her death to those same male heirs; and should she die without male heirs, remainder to their lawful heirs, and failing lawful heirs, remainder to Joan de Neuton, mother of the grantor, in perpetuity. Seals to the four parts of the indenture.[1] Witnesses: William de Skipwith, lord of Skipwith, John Berden, Henry Wyman, John Brathwait, citizens of York, John Lascels of Escrik, William Garton of Menthorp , John de Snayth, John del Hall' of Whittelay. (*Ibid.*, No. 27.)

174. July 10, 16 Richard II [1392]. Release by Henry de Percy, Earl of Northumberland, Brian de Stapelton, Robert Twyer, John de Hotham' and Thomas Coluill', knts., and their heirs, to Sir Thomas Ughtred, knt., his heirs and assigns, of all right in a fourth part of all the lands, tenements, rents and services both of freemen and villeins, of the manor of Escryk iuxta Queldryk, between the Ouse and Derwent, and in a fourth part of the advowson of the church of Escryk, with all appurtenances, rights, easements in woods, plains, meadows, moors, waterways, and paths pertaining to the lands and tenements of the manor, which they lately had of the gift and feoffment of Dom. Peter de Auburnwyk, rector of the church of Munkton' *super moram*, and Dom. William Farnam, chaplain, as more fully described in their charter of feoffment to Sir Thomas Ughtred. Warranty. Sealing clause. At the manor of Kexby. (*Ibid.*, No. 29.)

175. Jan. 11, 17 Richard II [1393–4]. Grant by William Henrison of Queldryk to John son of Thomas Daunay of Escrik of all his land called le Bryntkar in the territory of Escrik; to hold to John, his heirs and assigns, of the chief lords of the fee. Warranty. Sealing clause.[2] Witnesses: Sir Thomas de Ughtred, Thomas Fitzhenry, Gerard Saluayn', knts., William Skypwyth,

---

[1] Seal: red wax, diam. $\frac{1}{2}$ in.; blurred, possibly a kneeling figure beneath a canopy.

[2] Seal: red wax; small gem, man's head to the dexter.

Ralph Lascels, Francis Paumes, Nicholas Norfolk, John Margraue, William Wodrawe, John Cotflat. At Escrik. (*Ibid.*, No. 30.)

176. Jan. 11, 17 Richard II [1393–4]. Grant by William Henryson, son of Henry Wilkynson, son of William, son of Henry le Wryght of Queldryk to Mag. John de Neuton, treasurer (*thesauario*) of the Cathedral Church of Blessed Peter of York, John . . . .[1] Millington, and Nicholas Norffolk of Naburn, William Rosselyn [of Cottanaye and Nicholas his brother], Sir John Pygot [knt.], John Pigot his brother, John Daunay [son of Thomas Daunay] of Escryk, and the heirs of John Daunay, of all his land in the territory . . . of Escryk, called . . . . Bryntkarr, lying on the north above the land of John Daunay . . . . called le Wr . . . ., and the southern part abuts on John Daunay's land called . . . .; to hold to the grantees with all appurtenances in the same manner as held by the grantor, of the chief lords of the fee. Sealing clause.[2] Witnesses: Sir Thomas Ughtred, Thomas Fitzhenry, knts., John Lascels, William de Skypwyth, John Margraue, Ralph Lascels, William Wodrawe, John Cotflat, Robert Chapman, Robert Souman'. At Escryk. (*Ibid.*, No. 31.)

177. Jan. 13, 17 Richard II [1393–4]. Quitclaim by John son of John de Selby, son of William de Selby of Escryk, to John Daunay son and heir of Thomas Daunay of Escryk, his heirs and assigns, of all the land in the territory of Escryk called le Bryntkar, with all rights, easements, etc. Warranty. Sealing clause.[3] (*Ibid.*, No. 32.)

178. May 22, 19 Richard II, 1396. Grant by John Daunay son of Thomas Daunay of Escryk to John Brune and Thomas Souter of Qweldryk of 20 acres of land with appurtenances within the lordship of Escryk called Bryndkerr, which lies between the grantor's land on the south and north and the land of the abbot and convent of Fountains on the east, and the land of the nunnery of Thykheued'[4] on the west; to hold to John and Thomas, their heirs and assigns, freely [*etc.*], of the chief lords of the fee. Warranty. Sealing clause.[5] Witnesses: John Morgraue, John Lascy, William son of Henry, Thomas Porter, John Skorton. At Escryk. (*Ibid.*, No. 33.)

179. May 23, 1396, 19 Richard II. Indenture by which John Daunay son of Thomas Daunay of Escryk witnesses that whereas he has granted to John Brune and Thomas Souter of

[1] Deed badly stained.

[2] Seal: red wax, diam. ½ in.; a squirrel; leg. blurred.

[3] Seal: red wax, diam. ⁴⁄₁₀ in.; letter I between two sprigs of leaves.

[4] Thicket, where was a small Benedictine nunnery.

[5] Seal: red wax, diam. ½ in.; two heads facing, the dexter bearded and with a coronet.

Qweldryk 20 acres of land [*described in previous deed*], now John Brune and Thomas Souter agree that if John or any other in his name shall pay to Thomas, his heirs, executors or attorney, 6*li*. 6*s*. 8*d*. at Whitsuntide, 1406, then their charter of feoffment shall be null and void. Alternate seals. At Escryk. (*Ibid.*, No. 34.)

180. July 1, 3 Henry IV [1402]. Appointment by Thomas de Hornby and William de Sandford, vicar of the church of Gyllyng, of Robert de Chatherton and Thomas Prestwode as attorneys to deliver seisin to Edmund son of Edmund de Sandford, knt., of their manor of Escrik with appurtenances in co. York, and of the advowson of the church of Escrik in accordance with their charter. Sealing clause. (*Ibid.*, No. 35.)

181. Monday before St. Andrew [Nov. 27], 1402. Grant by Elizabeth Daunay widow of Thomas Daunay of Escryk to Thomas Thurkell of York, William Roselyn of Cotnes, and Nicholas Northfolk of Naburn for (*per*) John Daunay her son, of her manor of Escryk which she lately had of John de Neuton, with the land and buildings and a messuage built upon called Grymesby, there; to hold freely [*etc.*] of the chief lords of the fee. Warranty. Sealing clause. Witnesses: Thomas Daunay, Adam Totte of Carleton and John Lonesdale. At Escryk. (*Ibid.*, No. 36.)

182. April 23, 8 Henry IV [1407]. Appointment by William de Hekilton, rector of the church of Sprotburgh, of John Swaynby and John de Selby to deliver seisin to Roger Morton, chaplain, John Murdon and Robert Chatirton, of the manor of Escryk[1] with appurtenances in co. York, also the advowson of the church of the same manor, in accordance with their charter. Sealing clause.[2] At Eskeryk. (*Ibid.*, No. 37.)

183. Aug. 4, 9 Henry IV [1408]. Quitclaim[3] by Elizabeth, widow of Thomas Daunay of Escryk to John, Lord Darcy, Robert de Waterton, William Rosselyn and John Daunay, her son, their heirs and assigns, of all right in a tenement with buildings, crofts and appurtenances in the west part of the vill of Escryk, which Thomas, her husband, recently gave to the said John, her son and Ellen, lately his wife, as dowry. Warranty. Sealing clause. (*Ibid.*, No. 39.)

184. Quitclaim by Elizabeth, widow of Thomas Daunay of Escryk, and daughter and heir of John de Neuton of Snayth to Sir John Darcy, lord de Menyll', Robert de Waterton esq.,

---

[1] On Feb. 26, 1407[-8] Roger de Morton, Robert Chaterton of Thorp Salvayn', and John Mordon of Laghton quitclaimed the same to Edmund de Sandeford, lord of Thorp Salvayn'. (*Ibid.*, No. 38.)

[2] Seal: red wax, diam. $\frac{8}{10}$ in.; in a cusped border a shield of arms, a chevron between three fishes. Leg. undeciphered.

[3] Also quitclaim by the same to the same, dated Oct. 4, 1408, of 26 acres of land in the demesne of Escryck, called Ugilkar. (*Ibid.*, No. 39a.)

Nicholas Rosselyn and John Daunay, her son and heir, for 21*li.* 5*s.* paid to her, of all right in all lands, meadows, woods, moors and pastures, and in all profits thereto pertaining, which lately belonged to John de Neuton or Thomas Daunay in the lordship and vill of Escryk. Warranty, on condition that John Daunay on behalf of the grantor and her heirs shall pay to Elizabeth [*sic*], her mother for the ten years next following the Feast of St. Martin 1409, 10*s.* . . . .[1] at the four terms in the soke of Snayth, namely, St. Andrew, Easter, the Nativity of St. John the Baptist and St. Michael in equal portions, and if the rent is in arrears at any of the terms for three weeks, power to enter and distrain until satisfaction be made, and if it is in arrears for one year power to enter and hold against the grantor and her heirs for the term of her life; appoints John de Snayth as attorney to deliver seisin. Alternate seals. Witnesses: John son of John de Snayth, John de Harple and Thomas de Yrby. (*Ibid.*, No. 40.)

185. Easter Day, 10 Henry IV [April 7, 1409]. Grant by Edmund Sandeford, lord of Thorp Salvayn, to Roger de Morton', John Mordon' of Laghton', and Robert de Chatyrton, of a fourth part of the land and tenements, rents and services, both of freemen and villeins, of the lordship of Eskeryk iuxta Queldryk between Ouse and Derwent, also a fourth part of the advowson of the church of Eskeryk, and half a windmill pertaining to the same lordship, with all appurtenances, liberties, rights and easements, in plains, woods, pastures, moors, waters, ways, paths [*etc.*]; to hold to them, their heirs and assigns, of the chief lords of the fee. Warranty. Sealing clause. Witnesses: Thomas Ughtrede, William de Skypyth, Nicholas de Northfolk, Ralph Lassell', John Lassell'. At Eskeryk. (*Ibid.*, No. 41.)

ffarnley (Leeds).

186. [2]Since controversy has arisen between Sir Geoffrey de Nevill and Thomas Sampson concerning the latter's supply of wood from the woods belonging to Sir Geoffrey in Farneleye, it has been amicably settled between them that Sir Geoffrey grants for himself and his heirs, to Thomas, 30 cartloads of wood, except oak, ash (*fraxino*), maple (*arable*), *grand querilu,*[3] crab apples (*pomerio silvestris*), and the great white thorn (*alba spina magna*), which Thomas and his heirs may receive for burning or fencing, from the woods outside the manor, which belong to the grantor in Farneleye, each year, in accordance with the view of the foresters there serving the grantor or his heirs; these to be taken at the four terms in the following manner, namely, at Michaelmas,

---

[1] Document stained and blurred.

[2] Copy of original deed, in a considerably later hand.

[3] Possibly some species of oak.

8 cartloads; at the Nativity, 8; at the Purification, 6; and in the month of April, 8; and they shall be carted from the woods by the Invention of the Cross. Sir Geoffrey also grants to Thomas timber from the woods for the maintenance and repair of his house in Farneley, and for the construction of a new dwelling in the same vill should it by chance be destroyed by fire; to have and to hold to Thomas, according to the view of the foresters or bailiffs, in perpetuity. And for this concession, Thomas and his heirs quitclaim all right to a larger supply of wood, or to the right to take it in any other way than that agreed to above. Alternate seals. Witnesses: Sir Bernard de Nevill', Sir Alan de Suctoran [?], Adam de Beston, Ralph de Hedon, John de Alta ripa, Robert de Wirkeleyne, Thomas de Beverill'. (*Bramley MSS.*, No. 16.)

187. Wednesday after St. Peter ad vincula, 17 Edward son of Edward [Aug. 3, 1323]. Grant by Edmund de Nevyll to Richard Samson of Farnelay and Anabel, his wife, of all the lands which he had of the gift of Richard in Farnelay; to hold to them and their lawfully begotten heirs, paying yearly to Edmund and his heirs a rose at the Nativity of St. John; and should Richard and Anabel die without heirs, reversion to the grantor and his heirs. Warranty. Sealing clause.[1] Witnesses: Sir William de Beeston, knt., William de Wyrkelay, Adam, the clerk of Gyldosum, John Le..re de Podesay, William de Alwaldlay, Adam de Lepton, William, the clerk of Farnelay. At Farnelay. (*Ibid.*, No. 17.)

188. Nov. 16, ... Henry V. Indenture[2] by which Robert Clerk of Ledes and Thomas del Rodes grant to Thomas Sampson of Farnelay all the lands and tenements with appurtenances in the vill and territory of Farnelay, which they had of the gift and feoffment of Thomas, with a room called Maltechaumbre . . . . within the dwelling house of the said tenement, which they had conditionally granted to William, Thomas's son, and Agnes, Robert's daughter . . . . in such a way that if the said Thomas and William do not wish to live together . . . . And should it happen that William and Agnes die without legitimate heirs, remainder to Thomas and his right heirs; to hold of the chief lords of the fee in perpetuity. Sealing clause. Witnesses: Robert de Hopton, Richard de Beston, William de Lepton, John de Lepton, William Wyllers. At Farnelay. (*Ibid.*, No. 18.)

189. Jan. 31, 11 Henry VII [1496–7]. Demise by John Lepton and James Musgraue to Robert Sampson and Joan, his wife, of all the messuages, lands, tenements, fields, grazings, pastures, rents and services with appurtenances in Farneley, which they had of the gift and feoffment of Robert; to hold to Robert

---

[1] Seal: fragment of an armorial seal of yellow wax.

[2] Deed faded and indecipherable in places.

and Joan and their lawfully begotten heirs, of the chief lords of the fee; and should they die without heirs, remainder to the right heirs of Robert. Sealing clause.[1] Witnesses: Thomas Musgraue of Armelay, John Lepton, *taylour*, John Musgraue of Wirkeley. (*Ibid.*, No. 19.)

ffarnley (®tley).

190. Quitclaim by Gilbert son of Henry Campe of Farnelay, to Paul Ketel of Ottelay, his heirs and assigns, of all right in an annual rent of 4*d.* from 2 acres of land lying in the fields of Farnelay in the place called Suet Milke Riddinge. Warranty. Sealing clause.[2] Witnesses: William Faukus of Neual, William son of Henry de Farnelay, William son of William son of Beatrice of the same, Paul son of Ede de Ottelay, Henry Bonenfaunt, Roger de Aberford, William, the clerk, son of Maug'i. (*Farnley Hall MSS.*, No. 1.)

191. Grant by William son of Henry de Fernelay to William Somerscales, of a toft and a croft with appurtenances in the vill and territory of Fernelay, which is situated in a place called Knyxtecroft; to hold with all liberties and easements, paying yearly to the lessor 2*d.* in equal portions at Whitsuntide and Martinmas for all services [*etc.*], except forinsec service. Sealing clause.[3] Witnesses: Fulk (*Falcasco*) de Lindelay, William son of William de Fernelay, Simon Godebarn, Henry Camp of the same, Robert Gafayre of Lelay,[4] Thomas de Northewode, Simon son of Jordan de Fernelay, Gilbert son of Paul de Cayli. (*Ibid.*, No. 2.)

192. Grant by Robert Gafayre of Lelay to Alan son of Robert de Farnlay, of a certain piece of land which he has in the fields of Farnley in the place called Wateridding between Smithel and the water of Werf[5]; to hold to Alan, his heirs and assigns, of the grantor, paying yearly 2*d.* in equal portions at Whitsuntide and Martinmas. Warranty. Sealing clause. Witnesses: Sir Richard de Luterington, William de Otteley, his bailiff, Henry son of Thomas de Farnley, William son of Beatrice of the same, Henry de Stokeld, Paul de Farnlay. (*Ibid.*, No. 3.)

193. Release by William son of Adam de Elstanboyem to Constance de Essold, and Beatrice, her daughter, and their heirs and assigns, of all right which he has in all that tenement which once belonged to Adam Elstanboyem, his father, in that place called Elstanboyem in the vill and territory of Fernelay. Warranty.

---

[1] Seals: two blobs of red wax.

[2] Seal: green wax, vesica-shaped, broken; a fleur-de-lis; S' GIL . . . AMP DE F'.

[3] Seal: green wax, diam. ½ in.; a dragon [?] to the dexter; leg. undeciphered.

[4] Leathley.

[5] Wharfe.

Sealing clause. Witnesses: Sir Richard de Goldesburgh, Sir Mauger le Wauesur, knts., Walter de Midelton, William de Castelay, Henry Scotenay, William son of Henry de Fernelay, Robert Gafayre, William Faukes, Henry Bonenfaunt. (*Ibid.*, No. 4.)

194. Grant by Constance de Esscholt to Richard de Wiginton and Beatrice, her daughter, of a messuage with land, meadow and wood with appurtenances lying in length and breadth between their boundaries (*suas diuisas*) at Elstanbothem in the vill and territory of Farneley; to hold to them, and their heirs lawfully begotten, with all liberties and easements, of the chief lords of the fee, paying yearly to the grantor a rose at the Nativity of St. John the Baptist for all services. Warranty. Should they die without lawful heirs, reversion to the grantor. Sealing clause. Witnesses: Lawrence de Arthington, William son of Elias de Casteley, William son of Hugh of the same. Walter de Burghelay, William de Farneley, Robert de Fosse. (*Ibid.*, No. 5.)

195. Release by Agnes, sister and heir of William son of Henry de Fernelay, in her lawful power, to William son of William de Castelay, of all right in a toft and a croft and 2 acres of land in the vill and territory of Fernelay iuxta Ottelay, which William, son of Henry, gave to Cecily, his servant, for the term of her life; also quitclaim to William, his heirs and assigns, of all the lands, tenements, rents and services which William, son of Henry, demised to William de Castelay, father of the same William son of William de Castelay. Sealing clause.[1] Witnesses: William de Mohaud, James, his brother, Lawrence de Castelay, Walter Gafair, Gilbert, the clerk of Fernelay, William, the clerk of the same. (*Ibid.*, No. 6.)

196. Sunday before St. Margaret the Virgin, 23 Edward son of Henry [July 17, 1295]. Grant by Simon, called Godebarn, of Ferneley to William son of Paul de Ottelay, clerk, his heirs and assigns, of 1*d.* and a clove gillyflower rent from 2 acres of land with appurtenances in the field of Ferneley, which Paul, son of Ede, holds of the grantor in fee; with all wards, escheats, homages, reliefs, marriages and fealties pertaining to the lands, in perpetuity. Sealing clause. Witnesses: Henry de Scoteney of Ferneley, Walter de Middelton, William Faukes of Newall, William son of Henry de Ferneley, William Malebranche of the same, William de Casteley, Simon son of Jordan de Ferneley, Henry de Bonenfant of Otteley. At Otteley. (*Ibid.*, No. 7.)

197. Sunday after Martinmas [Nov. 15], 1321. Grant by William Doberell' of Fernelay to John son of William de Fernelay, of half a rood of land lying in the field of Fernelay in the place called Hesilhit, between the land of Thomas Fullon on the east, and the land of Robert de Fosse on the west; also half a rood

---

[1] Seal: red wax, small gem.

there, lying between the land of Richard de Lyndelay on the east
and the land of William de Fernelay, clerk, on the west; to hold to
John, his heirs and assigns, of the chief lords of the fee. Warranty.
Sealing clause. Witnesses: Richard de Wygington, William de
Fernelay, William of the same, clerk, Robert de Fosse of the
same, William de Ottelay, clerk. At Fernelay. (*Ibid.*, No. 8.)

198. Tuesday after the Annunciation of the B.V.M. [Mar. 27],
1330. Release by William de la Mor of Farnelei to Geoffrey de
Wyginton, his heirs and assigns, of all right in a messuage of land
and meadow extending from the vill of Farnelei to the water of
Walkesburne. Warranty. Sealing clause. Witnesses: William de
Mohaut of Letheley, Adam de Dunwelle of the same, Henry son
of John de Farnelei, Gilbert the clerk of the same, William the
clerk. At Letheley. (*Ibid.*, No. 9.)

199. Sunday after the Assumption of the B.V.M., 5 Edward
III [Aug. 17, 1331]. Grant and confirmation by Matilda, daughter
of William son of Stephen de Fernelay, to John son of William
the clerk of Fernelay, of her piece of land called Kerkeenge in
the vill of Fernelay, and 1*d*. rent from an acre of land in the same
vill in a place called Stanelcroft, which she receives from Richard
de Kexelay at Whitsuntide; also ½*d*. rent from an acre of land
in a place called Hellerschae which she receives from William de
la Brod at the Nativity; to hold to John, his heirs and assigns,
of the chief lords of the fee. Warranty. Sealing clause.[1] Witnesses: William de Mohaude, James, his brother, William de
Lyndelay, William de la Grene, Simon, his brother, William
Goday. At Fernelay. (*Ibid.*, No. 10.)

200. Sunday after the Nativity of the B.V.M. [Sept. 12],
1344. Grant by Henry Cournays of Fernelay and Alice his wife,
to Henry son of Robert son of Hugh de Fernelay, his heirs and
assigns, of a messuage and all that land and meadow, pasture
and wood with appurtenances in the vill and territory of Fernelay,
which they had by reasonable legal division after the death of
Henry, son of John, the father of Alice; with the exception of
3 roods of land with appurtenances which they had previously
granted to Lawrence Bonenfant of Ottlay in the place called
Thorfynryddang, in the field of Fernelay; to hold with all easements [*etc.*], within and without the vill of Fernelay, to Henry,
his heirs and assigns, of the chief lords of the fee, paying yearly
to the chaplain of the chapel of Blessed Mary of Ottelay, who,
for the time being, celebrates the divine office there, 12*d*. of silver
at Whitsuntide and Martinmas in equal portions, similarly 12*d*.
to the chaplain of St. Helen at Fernelay. Warranty. Sealing
clause. Witnesses: Patrick de Marton, William de Lyndelay,
William de Mohaud, Richard de Wygyngton, Thomas de Oisford,

---

[1] Seal: brown wax, diam. ½ in.; a four-footed animal to the dexter;
legend undeciphered.

trumpeter (*Trompour*), Richard Faukes, William del Grene of Fernelay, Simon, his brother, Thomas son of Simon. At Fernelay. (*Ibid.*, No. 11.)

201. Thursday, the Nativity of the B.V.M. [Sept. 8], 1356. Release by John de Castelay to John de Wyginton, of all right in the manor of Fernelay iuxta Ottelay, with appurtenances, and in the lordship and services thereto pertaining; to hold of the chief lords of the fee. Sealing clause.[1] At Fernelay. (*Ibid.*, No. 12.)

202. Friday, St. Thomas the Apostle called Didymus [Dec. 21, 1358]. Grant by Hugh Courneys of Lyndelay to Thomas, his son, his heirs and assigns, of a toft and a croft and 6 acres of land and meadow with appurtenances in the vill and territory of Farnelay, in the place called Elfstanebothem, which he had by hereditary right, from his brother, Henry; to hold to Thomas, freely [*etc.*], of the chief lords of the fee. Warranty. Sealing clause. Witnesses: John de Wyginton, Thomas de Marton, Richard Faukes, William son of Paul del Grene, Simon, his brother. At Farnley. (*Ibid.*, No. 13.)

203. Sunday before the Nativity of St. John the Baptist, 4 Richard II [1380].[2] Grant by Thomas Huetson of Farnley to Laurence, his son, his heirs and assigns, of lands [*as in the preceding deed*]. Sealing clause.[3] Witnesses: Robert de Lyndelay, Richard Faukes, John Faukes, William Faukes, William Symson, Henry Wilkynson, John Henreson. At Farnelay. (*Ibid.*, No. 14.)

204. Oct. 6, 15 Richard II [1391]. Grant by William son of Simon Pavson of Farnelay, and Joan, his wife, to Dom. Robert de Newall, chaplain, and William Warde, of all the lands, tenements, rents and services with appurtenances in the vill and territory of Farnelay; to hold to them, their heirs and assigns in perpetuity, of the chief lords of the fee. Warranty. Sealing clause. Witnesses: Robert de Lyndlay, Lawrence de Lyndlay, Percival de Lyndlay, John de Burlay, John de Farnelay. At Farnelay. (*Ibid.*, No. 16.)

205. Sunday after the Assumption of the B.V.M., 7 Henry V [Aug. 19, 1419]. Grant by John Williamson to John Weskew and John Bekewith of Kenynghall[4] of 2 messuages which are called William Symplase and Clerkplase, and all other lands and tenements, rents and services which he has in the vill of Fernlay, iuxta Otley, except Williamcroft and Percyland; to hold to them, their heirs and assigns, of the chief lords of the fee. Warranty. Sealing clause. Witnesses: William Bekwith, Thomas Bekwith,

---

[1] Seal: brown wax, broken, probably the Virgin and Child.
[2] In 1380 June 24th was a Sunday.
[3] Seal: brown wax, broken.
[4] Killinghall ?

F

John Vauasuor, Henry Schawra, Richard Williamson. At Fernley. (*Ibid.*, No. 17.)

206. Sunday after Corpus Christi [June 14, 1422]. Grant by Laurence Thomson of Fernelay to Robert, his son, his heirs and assigns, of lands [*as in* No. 202]. Sealing clause. Witnesses: Robert de Lyndlay, Thomas de Lyndley, Richard Williamson of Fernlay, William Henrison of the same, Thomas Henrison of the same. At Ferenelay. (*Ibid.*, No. 15.)

207. Sunday after the Assumption of the B.V.M., 11 Henry VI [Aug. 16, 1433]. Demise by Robert Lawrens son of Laurence Thomson of Lyndelay, to William Lawrens of Lyndelay, his brother, of a toft and a croft and 9 acres of land in Farnlay in the place called Elkstunbothom. Witnesses: Thomas Lyndelay of Lyndelay, Robert Lyndelay of Lethelay, *gentilman*, Richard Williamson of Fernelay, Thomas Angrum of Farnelay, William Wodd, rector of the church of Lethelay. At Farnlay. (*Ibid.*, No. 18.).

208. Conversion of St. Paul, 35 Henry VI [Jan. 25, 1457]. Grant by William Lawrance of Lyndeley to Roger Ees of Ottelay, and William Thakurae of Beston, of a toft and a croft and 9 acres in Farnelay in Elkstanbothom. At Farnelay. (*Ibid.*, No. 19a.)

209. June 10, 1 Richard III [1484]. Grant by John Bayldon, William Thakwray of Beston, William Thakwray of Burley, Richard Lawrence, Robert Thakwray, Thomas Thakray and John Atkynson, to Peter Medylton, knt., of a toft and croft and 9 acres of land in Elstanbothem; to hold to him, his heirs and assigns, of the chief lords of the fee. Warranty. Appointment of Constantine Curtas as their attorney to deliver seisin thereof to Peter Mydelton. Sealing clause.[1] Witnesses: Percival Lyndeley, John Arthyngton, Thomas Fraunke, John Fawkes, esqs., William Lyndeley of Letheley. At Farneley. (*Ibid.*, No. 19.)

210. June 1, 38 Henry VIII [1546]. This Byll maide the first daye of June in the 38th yere of the Reigne of our Soveraign lord Henry the VIIIth by the grace of God Kyng of Ingland, France and Ireland, defendor of the fayth and in Erthe, of the Church of Ingland and also of Irlond, the Supreme Hede; Witnesseth that where Sir Thomas Johnson knyght, lat husbond to dame Esabell Johnson, wedowe, dyd gyff lycence unto Thomas Angrome of Ferneley to edifie and make one walle upon Ferneley grene parcel of Common More of Ferneley, Conteignyng in lenghe by estimacon, to the quantite of vii rode, and in brede apon the comon to the quantite of foure fote: Know you that I, the saide dame Isabell Johnson, wedowe, halfe lord of the lordship of Ferneley aforesaid, by thes presents doith Ratifie and conferme

---

[1] Tongues for seven seals: (1) and (3) blobs of red wax; (2) letter W; the remainder missing.

to the said Thomas Angrome all suche lycences as was grauntyd unto hym by the said Sir Thomas Johnson, knyght; and ferther, I the said Isabell Johnson, wedowe, doith by thes presents gyff full auctorite and lycence to the said Thomas Angrome that yff at any tyme herafter it fortune . . . [1] Fawkes not to be Contentyd to permytt and suffer the said walle to Stande and remayn (but cast it downe) then the said Thomas Angrome shall redifie and make the walle upe ageyn and so to kepe the same in lyk manner as the said . . . . Fawks hath gyff lycence to other Tenants dwellyng and Inhabityng within the said Towne of Ferneley. In Witness wherof to this present byll I have sette my seall the day and yere above writtyn.[2] (*Ibid.*, No. 20.)

211. July 17, 31 Elizabeth [1589]. Copy of an Inquisition made at York, before Henry Thoresby, Escheator of Yorkshire, by John Myles, John Doy, Francis Arthington, Francis Temple, Walter Fraunce [?], John Skelton, Lawrence Pollard, Nicholas Morris, Walter Waddington, Edward Clerke, William Wydall, John Craven, Thomas Burges and Ingram Moyses, who say upon oath that John Garnet, on the day of his death, was seised in demesne as of fee, in 2 messuages or tenements, 10 acres and 21 acres of meadow or pasture with appurtenances within the vill and territory of Farneley, and further they say that the aforesaid lands at the time of his death were held of Reverend Father John,[3] archbishop of York, of his manor of Otley, by what service they do not know; and it is valued yearly in all profits over and above deductions at 20*s*. And John Garnet died on Nov. 1 last, and that John Garnet is his son and next heir, and was over 30 years of age at his father's death; also that at his death John Garnet held no other lands of the Queen, nor of any other person, other than that in the manner above written. Sealing clause.[4] (*Ibid.*, No. 21.)

flasby.

212. Sept. 12, 21 Henry VI [1442]. Grant by John de Rilleston, son and heir of William de Rilleston, knt., to Adam de Scardburgh and Margaret his wife, previously the wife of John de Rilleston, the grantor's son, of a messuage with 4 bovates of land and meadow in the vill of Flasby in Craven, now in the tenure of Richard Fauuell; also a messuage with 2 bovates of land and meadow in the same vill, now in the tenure of Henry Stapull; to hold to Adam and Margaret for the term of Margaret's

---

[1] Two letters, apparently *cy*; but it was a Richard Fawkes who married Margaret, the daughter of Sir Thomas Johnson and Isabella, his wife.

[2] Endorsed: This deed Nicholas Angrome gave me, Yt is a grant fro the Laydy Johnston to one Angrome towchinge the comon of Farnley.

[3] John Piers.

[4] Seal: red wax, diam. ½ in., broken; a shield of arms, a chevron between three lions rampant; "Henry Thoresby, Escaetor" written beside the tongue.

life, without impeachment of waste, of the chief lords of the fee; reversion to the grantor after Margaret's death, or to his right heirs in perpetuity. Warranty. Sealing clause.[1] Witnesses: Roger Tempest, Henry de Hertlyngton, William Eltoft, John de Catall, Henry de Preston. At Flasby. (*Ibid.*, No. 23.)

Gargrave.

213. June 20, 11 Henry VII [1496]. Grant by Richard Malgham, esq., to Oliver Witton, of a messuage, a croft and 6 bovates of land recently belonging to William Fontance, also another toft, croft and 7 bovates recently in the tenure of John Andrew, also a messuage and another toft recently held by William Huttyng, and a toft and a croft recently held by John Lister, in the vill and territory of Gargrave, co. York; also all other lands, tenements, rents and services with meadows, pastures, fishings, woods, undergrowth, wards, marriages and reliefs, also all moors, marshes and commons and other appurtenances elsewhere in the territory and fields of Gargrave; to hold to Oliver of the chief lords of the fee. Warranty. Sealing clause. Witnesses: Christopher Hamerton, vicar of the church of Gargrave, Richard Lister, chaplain, Hugh Proctour, *yoman*, William Lister, *yoman*. (*Ibid.*, No. 24.)

Garton.

214. March 2, 1335[–6]. Indenture witnessing that whereas a dispute had arisen between the inhabitants of Gerthum of the one part, and Dom. William de Hugat, rector of the church of Northburton near Beverley, of the other part, over the founding of a chantry in the chapel of Gerthum at the expense of the said rector, for the ministration of the sacraments there on three days in each week, namely Sunday, Wednesday and Friday; it was finally agreed that the rector for himself and his successors shall agree to the founding of the chantry and that he and his successors for all times shall find a suitable chaplain to celebrate at the canonical hours and mass, as well on the aforesaid days as on the other days, namely Monday, Tuesday, Thursday and Saturday in each week, and to be continually resident in the said chapel, and they shall find a clerk, bread, candles . . . .[2] a breviary, a missal, a chalice and other ornaments necessary for the celebration of masses, and these shall be maintained at the expense of the then rector; and the said chaplain shall baptize there all children born in the vill, and shall administer the other sacraments to the inhabitants in case of dire necessity . . . . And for this grant of a perpetual chantry, to be made and sustained by the said

---

[1] Seal: brown wax, diam. 1 in.; in a geometrical border, a small shield of arms; a saltire; ✠ SIGILLVM JOHANNIS DE RILISTON.

[2] The document is damaged at this point.

rector, Henry de Wyghton, burgess of Beverley, seeing the chapel desolate and deserted and the inhabitants of Gerthum lacking the consolation of the divine offices by reason of the distance of the mother church, and for the safety of his soul [*etc.*], has granted all the tenements and lands with appurtenances which he has in the vill and territory of Sighelesthorn and which formerly belonged to Dom. William de Patrington, late rector of the church of Sighelesthorn, to the rector of the church of Northburton and his successors in the same for ever, for the support of the said works; provided however that the said William [de Hugat] for himself, his church, and his successors shall procure their alienation in mortmain[1] and appropriation (*mortificacionem et apparacionem dictorum tenementorum*) by the consent of the king at his own expense before the feast of the Nativity of St. John the Baptist next ensuing and shall complete the matter as quickly as possible. It is agreed by the rector for himself and his successors that if, after Henry has given the tenements and the rector has secured their alienation and has taken peaceful possession of the same, and the books, chalice and ornaments have been provided, and a suitable house built for the chaplain to live in at the cost of the said Henry, in the territory of the chapel or elsewhere within the vill of Gerthum, it should happen by chance or misfortune that the vill of Gerthum should cease to be, or the inhabitants abandon it, that then he, and they, shall be bound to maintain a similar chantry in the church of Northburton for the souls of all the faithful during such an absence, and that if the inhabitants return the chantry shall be restored there as is agreed. The rector and his successors are to restore and repair the choir of the chapel as often as is necessary for ever; and for the better establishing of the chantry the rector promises for himself and his successors to pay 2s. of silver to the fabric of the church of St. John of Beverley each week in which by his or anyone else's fault the said chantry shall not be served as is promised [*etc.*]. Henry de Wyghton to nominate the first chaplain. The indenture to be void if the alienation in mortmain and appropriation be not obtained before the feast of the Nativity of St. John the Baptist next following. Alternate seals.[2] (*Archer-Houblon MSS.*, No. 319.)

215. Wednesday after St. Lucy the Virgin [Dec. 17], 1337, 11 Edward III. Quadripartite indenture made between William, by divine permission Archbishop of York, primate of England, and Dom. Nicholas de Hugate, provost of the church of the Blessed John of Beverley, William de Hugate, rector of the church of Northburton, and Henry de Wyghton of Beverley, merchant;

---

[1] Licence for the alienation in mortmain of 2 tofts and 4 bovates granted on Oct. 28, 1336 (*Cal. Pat. Rolls*, 1334–1338, p. 333).

[2] Seal: fragment of small red wax seal bears an interlacing geometrical pattern; device and legend not deciphered.

Recites that whereas a dispute had arisen between the inhabitants of the vill of Gerthum and the said Dom. William de Hugate of Northburton concerning the founding of a chantry in the chapel of Gerthum and the celebration of the sacraments there three times weekly, that is on Sunday, Wednesday and Friday; at last the matter was settled in this form [*recites the agreement specified in the preceding deed*] . . . . to have and to hold all the aforesaid lands and tenements to the said William de Hugate rector of Northburton and his successors in perpetuity in pure and perpetual alms for the said chantry and other the abovementioned works; and if the rector or his successors shall be deficient in the chantry and works, it shall be lawful for Henry to [enter] the said lands and tenements . . . . In witness whereof part of the indenture is to remain with the archbishop sealed . . . .[1] Witnesses: Sirs Nicholas de Hotham and Robert de [Scorburgh], knts., masters [Adam] de [Heselbeche], John de . . . ., Thomas de Cave and Dom. Richard de Melton, clerks, William del Wodhall, John de [Thorneton], John Surdevale, ... John of Beverley, Adam de Th . . . ., John le Frier. At York.[2] (*Ibid.*, No. 320.)

Glusburn.

216.   St. James the Apostle, 32 Henry VI [July 25, 1454]. Grant by James Skarburgh to John Popelay, esq., of all his lands, tenements, rents, reversions and services in the vills of Glusburne and Cononlay or elsewhere within the parish of Kildwick, co. York; to hold to John, his heirs and assigns, of the chief lords of the fee. Warranty. Sealing clause. Witnesses: Thomas Grene, John Estburne, Thomas Skott, Thomas Husteley, William Tuke. At Glusburne. (*Farnley Hall MSS.*, No. 25.)

217.   June 24, 1462. Grant by John Popelay, esq., to Thomas Hawkesworth, esq., and Elizabeth, his wife, of all his lands, rents, reversions, and services in the vills of Glusburne and Cononlay; to hold to him, his heirs and assigns, of the chief lords of the fee. Sealing clause. Witnesses: John Hawkesworth, Constantine Mohaut, esqs., John Garford, *yoman.* (*Ibid.*, No. 26.)

218.   Dec. 31, 14 Edward IV [1474]. Release by Thomas Forester of Skipton in Craven and Agnes, his wife, to Thomas Hawkesworth, esq., of all his right in all the lands, tenements, rents and services which he had of the gift and feoffment of John Smyth, otherwise John Santynglay, and which recently belonged to Richard Santynglay, in the vill and territory of Glusburn. Warranty. Sealing clause.[3] Witnesses: Percival Lynlay of Lynlay,

---

[1] Tags for three seals; seals missing.

[2] Endorsed: Wyghton. Cart' Cantar' Capelle de Gerthum.

[3] Tongues for two seals; part of a small seal of red wax remains on one.

Richard Bank of Newton in Craven, John Popelay of Hamound-thorpe, junior, esqs. (*Ibid.*, No. 28.)

219. Feb. 7, 22 Edward IV [1482–3]. Grant by John Popelay esq., John Cosse and Randolph Cosse to Thomas Hawkesworth esq., and Elizabeth, his wife, and their lawfully begotten heirs, of a messuage with appurtenances in Glusburn, which they recently had of the gift and feoffment of Thomas, as is more fully contained in their charter dated Feb. 6, 22 Edward IV; to hold to Thomas and Elizabeth and their lawfully begotten heirs of the chief lords of the fee. Appointment of Nicholas Nedderwod as their attorney to deliver seisin. Sealing clause.[1] Witnesses: William Calverlay, senior, Henry Eltosftys, Walter Boulden. At Glusburn. (*Ibid.*, No. 29.)

Gowdall.

220. Vigil of St. Michael [Sept. 28], the [first] year of the reign of Edward son of Edward the King [1307]. Grant by Lawrence de Heck son of Henry de Heck, to Stephen son of Thomas de Bernernewell [*sic*] of a toft in the vill of Goldal, lying between the toft formerly of Henry Keng and the toft formerly of Hawise Boche, the southern end of which abuts on the highway and the northern end on the meadow of Goldal; he also grants a selion of land lying in le Brotis between the land of Hugh Molling' on each side; also a selion of land lying in le Midelfeld, between the land formerly of John de Goldal and the land formerly of Robert de le Host; also a selion of land at le Stonsike between the land of Edmund, son of John and the land of William Molling'; also a rood of meadow lying in le Kar between the meadow of Hugh Molling' and the meadow formerly of . . . . son of Alan; to hold to Stephen and the heirs of his body lawfully begotten, paying yearly to the grantor and his heirs 4s. at the times appointed in the soke of Snayht, for all other services and demands, and if Stephen should die without heirs remainder to the grantor. Warranty. Sealing clause. Witnesses: Nicholas Demar, William de Wentewarht, John de Snayht, William son of Robert de Goldal, John son of Robert of the same, William Moye. At Goldal. (*Y.A.S.*, M⁰ 182, No. 22.)

221. Morrow of St. Thomas the Archbishop, 12 Edward II [Dec. 30, 1318]. Grant by Lawrence de Heck to Stephen, son of Thomas de Bernewell and his heirs, of a toft in the vill of Goldale situate between the toft formerly of Richard Boche on the west and a toft formerly of Henry Keng on the east, of which the southern end abuts on the highway and the northern end on the meadow of Goldale called le Kar; also a rood of meadow lying in le Kar of Goldale between the meadow formerly of William son of the rector (*person*') and the meadow of John Haliday, of

---

[1] Seals: tongues for three: (1) and (2) of red wax, small gems, undeciphered.

which the southern end abuts on a toft of Edmund, son of John, and the northern end on the river bank; also half an acre of arable land in le Brot' lying between the land of Hugh Molling' on both sides; also half an acre of arable land lying in another field of Goldale between the land formerly of John de Goldale on both sides; also half an acre of arable land lying between the land formerly of Richard Boche and the land of Edmund, son of John, and abutting on a place called le Stonsike; also all the common right in a bovate of land in the vill of Goldale, as well in woods as in pastures, meadows, marshes, turbaries, and in all other places within the vill or without, in any wise pertaining; also the feeding of two horses (*vesturas duorum equorum*) in the marsh of Goldale; to hold to Stephen and the heirs of his body lawfully begotten, paying yearly to the grantor and his heirs 2s. of silver at the four terms appointed in the soke of Snayth' for all other services. Warranty. Sealing clause. Witnesses: William de Wenteworht', John de Snayht', John de Courteney of Heck, William son of Robert de Goldale, John son of Robert of the same, Thomas Golding, John Keng. At Goldale. (*Ibid.*, No. 23.)

222. Grant by Robert son of Alan de Goldale to Thomas de Snaythe, clerk, his heirs and assigns, of half a bovate of meadow with appurtenances in the meadows of Goldale to which half bovate belong 6[1] roods of meadow, of which one rood lies between the meadow of William Golding towards the east and the field of the late Edmund de Goldale towards the west, and abuts on the toft of the said Edmund; and one rood lies between the meadow of Henry King on the east and the meadow of Roger Pope on the west and abuts on the toft of the late William the tailor (*cissoris*) of Snaythe; and one rood lies between the meadow of John de Goldale and the meadow of Henry King and abuts on the toft of John de Rednesse; and one rood lies between the meadow of William Golding and that of the said Robert, son of Alan, and abuts on Schiraikchened; and one rood lies between the meadow of William King and the meadow of Alexander, son of Mag. Reginald and abuts on the Ayr; and one rood lies between the meadow of Henry, son of Simon Vendiloc, and the meadow of the late Edmund de Goldale and abuts on the Ayr; and one rood lies in a place called Broggeker between the meadow of the said Edmund de Goldale and that of Henry King; to hold to Thomas, his heirs and assigns, paying yearly to the grantor and his heirs ½d. at Christmas for all secular services, demands, etc. Warranty. Sealing clause. Witnesses: Henry de Hecke, John son of Edmund de Goldale, William the merchant of Cowike, Adam of Snaythe called the tailor (*le taillour*), William de Dilham, John de Knaresburg'. (*Y.A.S.*, M[D] 153, No. 7.)

---

[1] Doubtless an error, as 7 roods are described.

223. Monday, Morrow of St. Hilary, 15 Edward III [Jan. 14, 1341–2]. Release and quitclaim by John Perqik of Snayth' to Hugh de Metham and his heirs, of all right and claim in a dole of meadow lying in the meadows of Goldale between the meadow of William Bole on the east and the meadow of John son of William on the west. Warranty. Sealing clause. Witnesses: William de Goldale, John son of Alexander of the same, Henry son of Robert le Forester of Snayth', John Bogher of the same, John Duraunt. At Snayth'. (*Y.A.S.* M^D 182, No. 24.)

224. Tuesday next after the Purification of the B.V.M. [Feb. 8], 1361[–2]. Grant by Edward son of Stephen de Snayth, to John son of Roger de Wentworth and Alice his daughter and the heirs of the body of the said Alice, of a messuage and all the lands, meadow and pasture with appurtenances in the vill and territory of Goldale which the grantor had of the gift and feoffment of Matilda, his sister; to hold to John and Alice, his daughter, and the heirs of her body, of the chief lord of the fee. Should Alice die without heirs of her body, reversion to the grantor and his heirs. Warranty. Sealing clause. Witnesses: Richard de Snayth, Henry son of Richard' of the same, Robert son of Richard de Goldale, Simon Fyssher of the same, John Spilword of the same. At Goldale. (*Ibid.*, No. 25.)

225. Monday after St. Hilarion the monk and confessor[1] [Oct. 22], 1369. Grant by William son of William Molling of Goldal to Dom. William de Garton, chaplain of the B.V.M. of Snayth, his heirs and assigns, of a strip (*selionem*) of land lying in length and breadth in the field of Goldal between the land of John son of Robert and the land of Edmund son of John, of which one end abuts on Lundikke and the other on le Bestmor, containing 3 roods of land; to hold to Dom. William, his heirs or assigns, of the chief lords of the fee. Warranty. Sealing clause.[2] Witnesses: Thomas de Goldal, Thomas son of Robert de Goldal, John Spylwode, William Malkyn, Thomas son of John. At Goldal. (*Ibid.*, No. 26.)

226. Tuesday before SS. Simon and Jude [Oct. 23], 1369. Grant by Henry son of Robert de Snayth' and William de Colby, dwelling in Couwyk, to Thomas son of Robert de Goldale, their heirs and assigns, of all the tenements, rents, lands, common pasture, grazings and meadows with appurtenances which the grantors have in the vill and territory of Goldale of the gift and feoffment of Robert son of Richard de Goldale, father of Thomas;

---

[1] An unusual feast day, not given in *Medii Aevi Kalendarium*, but noted in the Index of Fixed Feasts .... according to the Use of York (*Surtees Society*, vol. 59, xxxix).

[2] Seal: yellow wax, diam. 1$\frac{1}{10}$ ins.; device undeciphered.

to hold of the chief lord of the fee. Warranty. Sealing clause.[1] Witnesses: Simon Huwet of Goldale, John Howels of Hethensale, William de Burgoigne of Baln, Thomas Godard of Couwyk, John Long. At Goldale. (*Ibid.*, No. 27.)

227. St. Martin the Bishop, 11 Richard II [Nov. 11, 1387]. Lease by Alice de Wyntworthe of Goldale to Thomas de Redenes of the same, of an acre of land in Goldale lying in Nagkyrakys between the land of the said Thomas on the west and the land called Brigkar on the east; to hold to Thomas, his heirs and assigns, of the chief lords of the fee, paying yearly to the grantor, her heirs and assigns, ½*d.* at the Nativity of St. John the Baptist for all secular service. Warranty. Sealing clause.[2] Witnesses: John Sp[ilword], John Fox, Adam Vendilok. At Goldale. (*Ibid.*, No. 28.)

228. Nov. 28, 6 Henry IV [1404]. Indenture by which John Daunay demises to Richard Gildersome and Thomas Lowe of Goldale all the arable land and pasture which Simon de Hek lately held by the law of England[3] in the vill of Goldale; to hold from Michaelmas last for the full term of 18 years, paying yearly to John, his heirs or assigns, 8*s.* 8*d.* in equal portions at Easter and Michaelmas; and if the rent should be in arrears, in part or wholly for one month, it shall be lawful for John, his heirs or assigns, to distrain for the rent and arrears or to re-enter and occupy the lands without hindrance; and Richard and Thomas shall bear all the burdens which were owed to John during the tenure of Simon in Goldale. Warranty against all other services. Alternate seals.[4] Witnesses: Nicholas Daunay, William Broun, bailiff, Thomas de Reddenes of Goldale, John Rudde of Cowyk. At Goldale. (*Ibid.*, No. 29.)

229. Monday before the Purification of the B.V.M. [Jan. 28], 1408[-9]. Grant by William Huett of Goldale to John Aldous of Hensall and Alice his wife, of a toft built upon in Goldale, lying between the toft of Adam de Eshtoft on the south, and the toft called Beghalltoft on the north, and abutting on the king's highway on the west, and on the common field of Goldalle on the east; and of a rood of land lying between the land of John

---

[1] Seals: two, of yellowish wax, both bearing a small shield; device and legend undeciphered.

[2] Seal: fragment of white wax.

[3] Tenancy " by the law of England " was common from the time of Glanvill, and was later known as " by the curtesy of England." It signified the husband's right to hold the wife's land so soon as a child was born, which child would be its mother's heir. This right persisted even when the wife died without issue surviving and the inheritance fell to her kinsman, and endured though the husband married a second time. In contrast, according to Norman law, the husband lost this right if he married again. For a full exposition see Pollock and Maitland, *History of English Law*, ii, 414-418.

[4] Seals: two, on tongues cut from the deed; (1) red wax, a lozenge enclosed in a rectangle; (2) red wax, broken.

Fox on each side, and abutting on the said toft on the west, and on the road leading from Goldale to Polyington' [on the east]; and of an acre of land lying between the grantor's own land on the north and the land of John de Goldale on the south, and abutting on le Lundyke on the east, and on the common way leading from Goldale to Polyngton' [on the west]; to hold of the chief lord of the fee. Warranty. Sealing clause.[1] Witnesses: William Broune of Goldale, John Fox of the same, Adam Vendeloke of the same, John Cawdra of the same, Robert Mollyng of the same. At Goldale. (*Ibid.*, No. 30.)

230. March 8, 1414[–5]. Grant by John Aldous of Goldale, senior, to Richard Gildersome and Thomas Lawe of Goldale, their heirs and assigns, of one toft built upon in Goldale [*as in preceding deed*]. Warranty. Sealing clause.[2] Witnesses: William Broune, John Went of Heensell, John Henrison' of Goldale, Richard Snytall of the same, Thomas son of Robert of the same. At Goldale. (*Ibid.*, No. 31.)

231. Aug. 11, 1418, 6 Henry V. Grant[3] by Richard Gildersome and Thomas Lawe of Goldale to Nicholas Daunay, his heirs and assigns, of a toft built upon [*as in* No. 229]. Sealing clause.[4] Witnesses: William Brone of Goldale, John Henrison of the same, Robert Mollying of the same, Richard Snytall' of the same, William Fenwyk of Hek, John de Went of Hensall, John Grome of the same. At Goldale. (*Ibid.*, No. 32.)

232. Sept. 16, 8 Henry V, 1420. Indenture by which it is agreed that if William Bron', his heirs or assigns, are by force of law at any time ejected by John Daunay, son of Thomas Daunay of Escrick (*descrik*), his heirs or his wife, from those arable lands and meadows in Goldale which William had of the gift and feoffment of Robert Watton and the aforesaid John son of Thomas, and which were lately held by Richard Gildersome and Thomas Lowe of Goldale by an indenture then made, it shall be lawful for William and his heirs to enter and hold in perpetuity a messuage in Snaythe which John and others have of the gift and feoffment of William and others; and John and Robert Watton, enfeoffed of William Bron', may enter the lands and meadows aforesaid, notwithstanding the charter, and take seisin of the same, without hindrance, under the following condition, namely, if John, his

[1] Seal: yellow wax, diam. 1 in.; letter O.

[2] Seal: dark brown wax, diam. $\frac{9}{10}$ in.; device, a stag's head cabossed; ES . . U . . SME . .

[3] Quitclaim of the same by John Aldus to Nicholas Daunay, dated the following day and witnessed by William Brone of Goldale, Richard Gildersome of the same, John Henrison of the same, William Fenwyk of Hek, John Grome of Hensall. (*Ibid.*, No. 33.)

[4] Seals: two, of black wax; (1) diam. 1 in., letter B between a star and a sprig of leaves; (2) diam. 1 in., letter M.

heirs or assigns, are not able at any time to enjoy peacefully and without disturbance, according to the charter of William to John and Robert, a messuage and a toft recently belonging to Thomas Fish. Alternate seals.[1] At Snaythe. (*Y.A.S.*, M[D] 153, No. 8.)

Ⱳortb Ɠrimston, etc.

233. March 4, 12 Henry VII [1496–7]. Since Richard York, knt., and Brian Ingram, vicar of the church of Northgrymston, recently held—in conjunction with Thomas Witham, onetime chancellor of the Exchequer,[2] John Thresk of York, merchant, Guy Fairfax, recently serjeant at law, Thomas Urstwyk, recently recorder of the city of London, and William Hunterode, now deceased—the manors of Northgrymston, Nauylton,[3] Muscotes, Relyngton, Hutton and Helperthorp in the co. of York, which lately belonged to William Nauylton and which the aforesaid had of his gift, and which are more fully described in a charter made at the wish of William, now Richard and Brian, in fulfilling the wish of William, demise to Edward Bygod esq. and Katharine, his wife, widow of William Nauylton, to Richard Eure, John Bygod, and Robert Aske,[4] esqs., their heirs and assigns, all the said manors, etc., except certain lands and tenements with appurtenances in Northgrymston, formerly demised by them and their co-feoffors to Thomas Nauylton, son and heir of William, in accordance with his father's wish; to hold to Edward, Katharine, etc., their heirs and assigns, with the exception of the lands specified, for the lifetime of Katharine, for her use and sustenance, or until Katharine shall have a sufficiency and a secure state for the term of her life, from the manor of Edylthorp, which once belonged to William Nauylton, her husband; and after her death remainder to Thomas Nauylton; to hold of the chief lords of the fee. Appointment of John Ingram and Robert Foxe as attorneys to deliver seisin. Sealing clause.[5] (*Y.A.S.*, M[D] 120a, No. 19.)

Ɠuisborougb.

234. May 20, 1408. Indenture whereby John de Helmeslay, prior of Gisburne, and of the convent there, grants to Robert Conyers, knt., Richard de Norton, John Conyers of Horneby, Gilbert Eluet, John Killyngale, and Robert Dobley, their heirs,

---

[1] Seal: red wax, diam. $\frac{8}{10}$ in.; . . . H in an arabesqued border; legend undeciphered.

[2] He was Chancellor of the Exchequer temp. Henry VI and Edw. IV and died in 1480 (*Surtees Society*, vol. 59, p. 75).

[3] Nawton, N.R.

[4] Probably the Yorkshire leader of the " Pilgrimage of Grace," hanged at York, 1537.

[5] Seals: two of red wax; (1) an animal stirring a pot flanked by the letters R and Y; (2) a gem, blurred.

and the tenants of their lands and their heirs in Pynchonthorp', common pasture above a place called Bowdesdale in the vill of Hoton iuxta Gisburne in Clyuelande, within certain boundaries, which run from Ownesbergh[1] and continue by le Morebrowe towards the east as far as le Ryuestanesuawe and go down as far as Crossegate and lead on towards the west by le Senygate as far as le Staneshede, and from thence along the boundaries to le Lauerdake, and from le Lauerdake as far as le [Gern]esty, and so proceeding by le Gernesty which is divided between the said pasture of the vill of Hoton and the pasture of Pynchonthorp as far as the close of Thyng . . le towards the north, in such a way that a limit shall be made for the grazing of all their animals within the aforesaid bounds, without any hindrance there from the grantor or his successors; and should any beast belonging to Robert, Richard, etc., stray beyond the bounds they may retrieve it without hindrance or durance, and should any beast through the agency (*per*) of the forest guard (*wardum factum*)[2] cross the boundaries it shall be impounded and handed over according to the local law; provided always that if any beast shall escape, or through the agency of the forest guard cross into Bowdesdale or into the pasture called le Oxpasture of Hoton, between the Feast of the Annunciation and the Feast of the Assumption of the B.V.M., then it shall be lawful for the prior and convent or their successors yearly to impound the beasts until they can be handed over according to the local laws. Alternate seals.[3] Witnesses: John Lumley, Ralph Bulmer, knts., John Percy of Kildale, William Lambard, James de Toucotes. In the chapter house at Gisburne. (*Dorman Museum, Middlesbrough.*)

East Ibarlsey.

235. Sunday before St. Thomas the Apostle [Dec. 18], 1345. Quitclaim by Peter, son of David de Tresk, to Marmaduke Darelle of all right in an annual rent of 5 marks of silver, granted to him by Marmaduke for the term of his life, from all the lands and tenements of Marmaduke within the vill and territory of Est Herlsay. Warranty. Sealing clause.[4] Witnesses: Thomas de Salcok of Herlsay, John de Multon' and Roger de Cousby. At Herlsay. (*Y.A.S.*, M[D] 182, No. 34a.)

[1] Roseberry Topping.

[2] *Wardum factum* is an unusual phrase, and the Latin is not very explicit: *per* should mean through, or by the agency of, but in this case might mean something like despite, or through the negligence of.

[3] Seal: the seal of the Priory, and (reverse) probably that of John de Helmeslay.

[4] Seal: fragment of light brown wax.

Ibarswell.

236. Monday before St. Gregory the Pope [March 8],
1288[-9]. Indenture by which Gerard, son of Robert Saluayn,
grants to Sybil, widow of Robert Saluayn, his mother, his capital
messuage in Herswelle, with a dovecot and all the dwellings and
gardens belonging thereto, saving to Gerard and his heirs the
three houses and lands which Sybil holds as dower; also grants
26 and 11 acres of arable land in Herswell with appurtenances,
also folds for all manner of cattle, such as were accustomed to
pasture there in the time of Robert his father, except for the
animals belonging to the grantor; also grants 62 acres of pasture
and a rood and a half in Harswell, namely in Swethilles 2 acres,
in Hotham 5 acres and a rood, in Fyueandtwentakers 10 and 18
acres, between the Fyrehakes and Derlunde 15 acres and half an
acre, [in] Hobonenderlundelere 6 acres, in le Smythens 6 acres
and a half, in the meadows towards Holmdike 9 acres and a half;
also grants 2 mills, namely, a water mill in Herswell, and a windmill in Rugthorp with appurtenances; also grants 73s. 7½d. annual
rents from his men in Rugthorp and Herswell, namely, from
Richard de Barnbrig 24s. for a toft and 2 bovates of land which
he holds in Rugthorp; from Henry le Wra 24s. for a messuage
and 2 bovates which he holds in the same vill; from Richard
Gerardman 24s. for a messuage and 2 bovates which he holds in
the same vill; from Edelina Attegate 19½d. for a toft in Herswell,
to be received in equal portions at Whitsuntide and Martinmas;
to hold to Sybil for the term of her life, freely, [etc.], paying yearly
to the grantor a clove gillyflower at the Nativity for all services.
For this grant Sybil quitclaims to Gerard all her right in the manor
of Northduffeld with appurtenances, which Gerard had of her
gift; and she is to maintain all dwellings, mills, walls and hedges
in her custody in as good repair as when she received them; and
she shall have from Gerard or his foresters, from the woods of
Herswell, a supply of timber for the maintenance of the carts,
ploughs and harrows on the manor, and if any house, mill, wall
or hedge shall deteriorate through her defection, Gerard or his
heirs to have power to repair the same out of Svbil's rents from
Rugthorp; Sybil to find pasture, custody for the animals, agist-
ment dues, food and suitable folds, from the Invention of the
Cross [May 3] until Martinmas. Remainder to Gerard, his heirs
and assigns, after Sybil's death. Sybil shall have possession of the
messuage, dovecot and gardens on the day of the making of this
charter, the lands at the next fallow (*warect'*), and the pastures,
mills, rents at Whitsuntide 1290. Should the rents be in arrears,
power to Sybil to enter and distrain until satisfaction be obtained,
and if sufficient rent is not forthcoming then Gerard binds
himself to distrain on other lands in Rugthorp until she is fully
paid. Alternate seals. At Herswell. Witnesses: Sir Thomas de

Normanvil, Sir Peter Bekarde, Sir William Const[able], knts., John de Hothum, William Sturmy, Thomas de Houeton. (*Slingsby MSS.*, No. 1.)

237. Sunday after Martinmas [Nov. 13], 1361. Indenture by which Gerard Saluayn, knt., leases to John de Wa . . .,[1] rector of the church of Herswelle, and Dom. Robert de Dalton, chaplain, a piece of land called le Thewe[nty]acre, another piece called le Hassokes and a third piece containing 3 acres which lies below the garden of William . . . . in the fields and territory of Herswelle; also grants a piece of pasture called le Milnecroft in the same vill; to hold to John and Robert, their heirs and assigns, from the Purification of the B.V.M., 36 Edward III [Feb. 2, 1361-2], to Michaelmas next following, paying yearly to the lessor or his heirs a rose at the season of roses if demanded for all services and demands. Warranty. Alternate seals.[2] At Herswell. (*Ibid.*, No. 2.)

238. Wednesday after St. Luke the Evangelist, 1 Richard II [Oct. 21, 1377]. Appointment by Gerard Saluayn of Hersewell, of John de Saltmerssh, his brother, as his attorney, to distrain upon, dispossess and re-enter into all his lands, tenements and rents everywhere. At York. (*Ibid.*, No. 3.)

239. Nov. 12, 13 Henry VI [1434]. Indenture[3] by which Roger Saluayn, esq., quitclaims to Mag. John Carleton, clerk, junior, Robert Rudestone, Thomas Ward, William Reuetus of York, chaplain, their heirs and assigns in perpetuity, all right which he has in the manors of Hersewell, Holme in Spaldyngmore and Thorp in Strata,[4] and in all the lands and tenements with appurtenances in Otteryngham in Holdernesse; also in an annual rent of 20*li.* from the manors, lands and tenements which Alice Saluayn had of his gift for the term of her life, in Northduffeld, but not in that tenement with appurtenances which Thomas Saluayn holds there; also in all the other lands, tenements, rents, services, and in all reversions after the lives of the holders or the conclusion of their years of tenancy (*annorum feodis*), also all advowsons, liberties and other rights wheresoever existing in co. York, all of which the said John, Robert, Thomas and William had of his gift. Warranty. Sealing clause.[5] Witnesses: Robert Ughtred, knt., Robert Constable, Robert Elys, esqs., William Hundgate, Robert Stodehowe. (*Ibid.*, No. 4.)

[1] John de Wartre.

[2] Tongues for two seals; a small portion of brown wax remains on the second; S ✠ DA . . . AR.

[3] See *Yorks. Deeds*, vol. I, p. 83, for the settlement on Roger Salvayn and Margaret Bolton dated Nov. 15, 1434.

[4] Thorpe-le-Street.

[5] Seal of red wax, diam. ⅝ in.; surrounded by sprigs of leaves, an armorial shield; on a chief, two mullets.

240. July 24, 28 Henry VI [1450]. Demise by Christopher Boynton, Robert Danby and John Thwyng to Henry Gascoigne, esq., and Margaret, his wife, of full right and possession in the manor of Herswell with appurtenances, with all lands and tenants, and services in Herswell, Holme in Spaldyngmore and Thorp in Strato, which they had of the demise of John Bolton, late citizen and alderman of York, for the term of Margaret's life; provided that if Henry Gascoigne should make any feoffment or alienation of the said manor or lands, it be lawful for Christopher, Robert, and John to re-enter and take possession, this charter notwithstanding. Sealing clause.[1] Witnesses: John Portyngton, justice of the king's bench, William Gascoigne, Robert Ughtred, knts., John Conestable, William Seintquyntyn, John Hothom, William Routh, esqs. At Gunby. (*Ibid.*, No. 5.)

241. Sept. 1, 29 Henry VI [1450]. Confirmation by John Saluayn of Northduffeld, knt., to Margaret, now the wife of Henry Gascoigne, by name Margaret Bolton, daughter of John Bolton, alderman and citizen of York, of the manors of Herswell, Holme in Spaldyngmore and Thorp in Strata, late in the seisin and possession of Roger Saluayn, deceased, and Margaret and their lawful heirs; by virtue of a charter of feoffment to John Carleton, clerk, junior, Robert Ruddestane, Thomas Warde, William Reuatus of York, chaplain, but now in the possession of Henry and Margaret, by right of the same Margaret; John confirms to Henry and Margaret, their heirs and assigns, for the term of Margaret's life, possession of the said lands. Warranty. Sealing clause.[2] Witnesses: John Portyngton, justice of the king's bench, James Pikering, John Melton, junior, knts., John Constable, John Hothom, William Routh, esqs. At Gunby.[3] (*Ibid.*, No. 6.)

Ibeadingley.

242. Memorandum of the Lands and Tenements which the abbot and convent of Kirkestalle hold in Heddinglay of [the gift of ?] William Paytefyn.[4] All the site of Kirkestalle; namely, le close; Bargram grove, the mill; Mikelleyam; Wesrode, Eskelrode; Lynley. Item: the abbot holds in Westheddinglay, 2 carucates of land with the Northwode; a toft and a croft with the meadow in Burlay which Mase holds, and an assart of 9 acres; an assart with wood and meadow which Robert Harewod holds; a toft which Matilda Long holds and 20 acres of land. Item: a toft and a croft which Robert Maunsel holds, and 6 acres of land, and

---

[1] Fragments of three seals of red wax.

[2] Fragment of red wax; armorial shield, on a chief, two mullets.

[3] Endorsed in a later hand: A lease for life to Gascoigne of the mannor of Harsewell.

[4] The charters granting the lands enumerated in this memorandum are to be found in the *Coucher Book of Kirkstall Abbey*, p. 58 *et seq.*

next to the same toft, 2 acres of land and a half which the abbot and monks have of the gift of Roger, son of Robert; and a toft and a croft which Ralph le Eril holds; all the land which Gilbert Donius holds; all the land called Langilwelleker and 5 acres of land adjoining; the assart of Roger Ruffy; 4 acres of land and a half which lie next to the croft of Roger the chaplain towards the north of Linley; one bovate of land with a toft and a croft which Robert Cary holds; 10 acres of land which lie next to the cultivated piece of ground of 4 acres. Item: 24 acres of land in Burlay, and in addition that which Thomas Paytefyn gave to the abbot and monks next to the aforesaid [?] toft with woodland adjoining; also le Est-Rode; 24 acres of land in Burlay; an annual rent of 5s. from land in Saxetun. Item: 2 carucates of land in West Heddinglay and ½ a carucate of land in Est Heddinglay which is called Wymarkesflat. Item: the performance of forinsec service. (*Bramley MSS.*, No. 20.)

243.   Epiphany, 1311 [Jan. 6, 1311–2]. Indenture whereby Thomas, son and heir of William Pictauensis of Heddingley, quit-claims to the abbot and monks of St. Mary of Kyrkestall an annual rent of 2 marks which they used to pay to him at the two terms, namely Whitsuntide and Martinmas in equal portions, for certain lands and tenements which they held of him and his ancestors, for the 25 years next following this indenture, in return for a sum of money. Warranty. Alternate seals. At Kyrkestall. (*Ibid.*, No. 21.)

ibeck.

244.   Oct. 13, 1341, 15 Edward III.   Grant by Matilda, widow of Richard Frere of Balneheck,[1] to John de Neuton' of Snayth and William son of the same John, of a toft with croft and half a bovate of land and meadow with appurtenances in Balneheck; to hold to John and William, their heirs and assigns, of the chief lords of the fee. Warranty. Sealing clause.[2] Witnesses: John son of Thomas the clerk of Snayth, John Elys, junior, John le Warner of Snayth, John son of William de Snayth, William Dennysone of Heck, Robert son of Robert de Heck, Simon Dyan, of Heck. At Balneheck. (*Y.A.S.*, M[D] 182, No. 35.)

245.   Wednesday after St. Wilfrid the Bishop [Feb. 16], 1362[–3].   Grant by Joan, widow of John de Neuton to John Chylde of Balneheck and Beatrice, his wife, and Thomas, son of Rayner Dilcock and Alice his wife, and the heirs of Thomas and Alice, of a messuage and half a bovate of land and meadow with appurtenances in the vill and territory of Balneheck, which were

[1] This is not a separate hamlet but the part of Heck nearest to Balne (*Y.A.J.*, **x**, 352).

[2] Seal: reddish brown wax, oval, ⅘ × 1¼ ins.; 6-pointed star; S. RICARDI F' AD.

G

formerly held by Richard Frere of Balneheck; to hold of the chief lord of the fee, paying yearly to the grantor and her heirs 6s. 8d. of silver at the four terms of the year as established in the soke of Snayth' in equal portions. Warranty. Sealing clause.[1] Witnesses: William son of Lawrence de Balneheck, William son of Robert of the same, Robert Little (*parvo*), John son of Thomas, Henry Fox of the same. At Balneheck. (*Ibid.*, No. 36.)

246. Friday before the Conversion of St. Paul, ... Richard II. Grant by Thomas son of John Elys of Hek to the lords Alexander, archbishop of York,[2] Ralph, Baron de Graystock, and Simon de Elvington, their heirs and assigns, of all his manor of Lytelhek with all appurtenances, rents, services, also all the lands and tenements, woods, meadows, rents and services within the soke of Snayth or the parish of the same; to hold of the chief lords of the fee. Warranty. Sealing clause.[3] Witnesses: Hugh de Hasyleges, Brian de . . . ., Thomas de . . . ., John de Marrays, Thomas Daunay, John Maples, ... John Frere, John . . . . At Littlehek. (*Ibid.*, No. 39.)

247. Sunday before All Saints [Oct. 30], 1390. Grant by John de Balne living in Knottyngle to John Aldous of Heck, Ellen his wife and the heirs and assigns of the said John, of a messuage in Little Heck lying between a messuage formerly belonging to Hugh Pynder and Henry son of Alice on the west, and which now belongs to Thomas Spilwode, and the common lane (*venella*) on the east, and abuts on the highway on the south and on the common pasture on the north; he further grants all the lands which had descended to the grantor by inheritance in the fields of Heck; to hold of the chief lords of the fee. Warranty. Sealing clause. Witnesses: Adam de Wynteworth, William de Heck, John Fenewyk, John Adam, Simon de Heck. At Heck.[4] (*Ibid.*, No. 38.)

248. Oct. 4, 1392. Grant by John Aldous, living in Hethensale, and Ellen, his [wife], to Thomas Thompson of Horneby, living in Balne, and Alice, his wife, and his heirs and assigns, of a tenement in North Heck, of which one part once belonged to John Snowe of Goldale and the other part to John Pynder of Polyngton', and which lies between the tenement of Adam de Wenteworthe on the west and the tenement which the grantor holds of Adam for the term of his life [grantor's] on the east, and abuts on the highway on the south, and on a meadow called le Sprynges on the north; he also grants a croft lying in Heck and 8 acres separated and lying in the three fields of Heck, which toft

---

[1] Seal: brown wax, diam. 1½ ins.; Virgin and Child.

[2] Alexander Neville was archbishop from 1374–1388.

[3] Seal: red wax, oval, 2 × 1½ ins.; Virgin and Child; AVE MARIA GRACIA.

[4] Endorsed: Carta J. de Balne, Johanni Aldous.

[*underlined and* croft *written over*] is called le Morecroft, lying between the common pasture on the east side and a certain close of Thomas de Metham, knt., on the other side, abutting on the broad way to the south and on the croft of Simon de Heck on the north; to hold in perpetuity to Thomas and Alice and the heirs and assigns of Thomas, of the chief lord of the fee. Warranty. Sealing clause.[1] Witnesses: Adam de Wentewrothe, William de Heck, John Adam, John attEk [*sic*], William de Fenwyk of Heck. At Heck. (*Y.A.S.*, M^D 153, No. 9.)

249. May 16, 20 Richard II [1397]. Grant by John Daunay to Thomas Rayner and Alice, his wife, of a toft in Hek lying between a messuage of Thomas on the east, and the common lane on the west and abutting on the highway of the vill and upon Lucok croft of William de Hek; also grants the wood called Wellsfall and all the arable land lying in Colmancroft, Midilfeld, and Estfeld, and les Buttes of the vill of Hek, all pertaining to the said toft, also one Intakgate pertaining to the toft; to hold to Thomas, Alice, and the heirs and assigns of Thomas, of the chief lords of the fee. Warranty. Sealing clause.[2] Witnesses: William de Fenwyk, William de Hek, Henry Coke, John Lowe. At Balnehek. (*Y.A.S.*, M^D 182, No. 40.)

250. March 14, 1 Henry V [1413-4]. Grant and quitclaim by Joan, widow of Henry Lowe of Hek and kinswoman and heir of Henry, son of Simon Prest of Balne Hek, in her pure widowhood, to Robert Watton, esq., Nicholas Norfolk of Naburne, William Rosselyn' of Cottenes and William Darthyngton, chaplain, their heirs and assigns, of an annual rent of 8s. 4d. which Laurence de Hek lately by his charter granted to the said Henry son of Simon, and which rent the same Laurence was accustomed to take from the lands and tenements and appurtenances which John the miller holds of him in the vill and territory of Balnehek; to hold the rent with all manner of arrears pertaining to the said rent within the vill of Baln'hek and without. Warranty. Sealing clause.[3] Witnesses: John Daunay, Nicholas Daunay, William Fenwyk, William Hek, John Robyn, John Adam, William More. At Hek. (*Ibid.*, No. 41.)

251. March 20, 2 Richard III [1484-5]. Grant by John Adam of Great Hek, *yeoman*, within the soke of Snaith, to John Daweney of Coweike, esq., and Guy his son, of all his lands, tenements, rents, services, meadows, woods, pastures, and grazings, which he has or might have within the said soke or elsewhere

---

[1] Seals: two of white wax with impression in red wax; (1) diam. $\frac{7}{10}$ in., a stag to the dexter, legend undeciphered; (2) broken, apparently an armorial shield.

[2] Seal: small, brown wax, rather blurred, probably the Virgin and Child.

[3] Seal: fragment of red wax, round, not deciphered.

within co. York; also grants all his goods, movable or fixed, living or dead, of whatsoever species or kind, wherever they may be; to hold the said lands, goods, and appurtenances of the chief lords of the fee. Warranty. Sealing clause.[1] Witnesses: John Lawe of Hek, senior, John Atkynson of the same, Richard Atkynson of the same. At Hek. (*Ibid.*, No. 42.)

Ibedon.

252. Saturday after St. Andrew the Apostle [Dec. 4], 1322. Quitclaim by Simon de Wynested of Hedon to Dom. Hugh, the priest of the chapel of Nuttill, of all right and claim in that croft with appurtenances which lies outside the ditch of the vill of Hedon on the north side of the road leading towards the chapel of blessed Mary Magdalen; in length it extends east and west from the said ditch to the croft of Dom. Hugh, and in width north and south between the croft of John de Preston and the highway. Sealing clause. Witnesses: John de Nuttill, ... William du Lund, Peter Skilling', John Gilt, Richard le Taverner, Peter de Kellesay, Peter Reyn'. At . . . . (*Archer-Houblon MSS.*, No. 326.)

Ibensall.

253. Vigil of St. Margaret the Virgin [July 19], 1365. Indenture witnessing grant by John Huglot of Hethensale to William of Lancaster living in Hethensale and Agnes, his wife, of a toft with appurtenances in Hethensale, lying between the toft of Robert Lady on the east, and a certain piece of ground (*placea*) called Bridtoft on the west, and abutting on the common way of the said vill on the south, and on the north field towards the north; to hold to William and Agnes, their heirs and assigns, of the chief lord of the fee, rendering yearly to the grantor or his heirs 6*d.* of silver in two equal portions at Whitsuntide and Martinmas. Warranty. Alternate seals.[2] Witnesses: John de Schirwod, Henry de Schirwod, Adam Raynald of Hethensale, Thomas de Goldale, Robert son of Richard of the same. At Hethensale. (*Y.A.S.*, M[D] 182, No. 42a.)

254. Saturday in the Octave of Easter (*Clausam Pasche*), 3 Richard II [April 13, 1380]. Bond by Adam de Seuster of Hethensale to John Fendard, in the sum of 100*s.* to be paid to John or his attorney at Hethensale on the Feast of St. Michaelmas next following. Sealing clause.[3] At Hethensale.

Dorso: The condition of this obligation: John Fendard and his heirs to enjoy peaceful possession of a messuage with appurten-

---

[1] Seal: small blob of reddish brown wax on tongue cut from bottom of deed; device not deciphered, probably a letter.

[2] Seal: brown wax, $\frac{7}{10} \times 1\frac{1}{10}$ ins.; undeciphered.

[3] Seal: brown wax, $1 \times \frac{3}{4}$ in.; undeciphered; ✠ S. IOHIS GRO . .

ances in Hethensale, which messuage the said John had of the gift and feoffment of Joan, widow of John Seuster, without impediment of the said Adam, his heirs or anyone acting on his behalf. (*Ibid.*, No. 48b.)

255. Oct. 2, 6 Henry V [1418]. Grant by Aveline de Layburn' of Snaythe to Nicholas Norffolk of Naburn', William Rosselyn of Cottenays and John Daunay of Hek, senior, of all her lands, tenements, rents, services, reversions, with appurtenances in the vills of Hensalle and Whitlay, which recently belonged to Richard de Snaythe; to hold to Nicholas, William, John and the heirs of John, of the chief lord of the fee. Warranty. Appoints Robert Lady of Hensalle and Richard Flot of the same to deliver seisin according to the present charter. Sealing clause.[1] Witnesses: Richard Burgoyne, Thomas Dylcok, senior, Nicholas Daunay, Richard Dylcok, son of the aforesaid Thomas, John de Wente, John Grome, Richard Mekesburghe, Richard Heworthe. At Snaythe. (*Y.A.S.*, M^D 153, No. 10.)

Ibessle.

256. II Non. April [April 4], 1220. Ratification by the Chapter of St. John of Beverley of an exchange made between the prior and convent of Watthon and Richard Caretarius of Beverley, in connection with the lands which Richard holds of them [the Chapter] in the vill and territory of Hesel, of the gift of Robert de Hesel, that is, 2 bovates, one of which is held by Thomas, son of Osbert, with a toft appertaining, the other is held by the widow, Maysant; also 7 acres of land towards the marsh, and one piece of cultivated land called Sandayle; and 7 acres of meadow, of which 5 acres lie between the meadow of Robert, son of Hubert, and that of Ralph, son of Siward, and 2 acres lie in Sculeholm adjoining the meadow of Alan, son of Ernest, towards the south; also good pasture for 300 sheep and 6 cows, with a way out for them every two years; also of the gift of the same Robert, a bovate in the territory of Hesel, which Geoffrey Lang holds, with a toft and a croft adjacent with all appurtenances; also that land and territory of Hesel which is called Tockecroft with all easements appertaining; and in addition, pasture for 100 sheep in the pasture of Hesel, with their issue; also of the gift of Alan son of Ernest of Hesel, 6 acres of land in the territory of Hesel, namely one acre and a rood lying in the southern part of the same vill between the land of Henry de Traneby, and the land of Geoffrey Lang, and one acre in the east part of the cultivated land belonging to Alan, above the Humber and next to the land of Henry, and one acre at Wrah on both sides of the land of Alan, the monk, and one acre above Nordlangs, lying between the land of William

---

[1] Seal: small, red wax, undeciphered.

Bonde and the land of Geoffrey Lang; and 3 roods (*percatis*) towards the pathway of Traneby, and one acre on the east part of the way to Anloftby next to the land of Mauger de Langetoft towards the south; also one acre of meadow adjoining the meadow of William Palmerus towards the north, and an acre and a half towards the west part of the vill of Hesel, lying between the land which Richard Caretarius holds of Robert, son of Osbert, and his demesne land; moreover, of the gift of the same Alan, 3½ acres of meadow in the territory of Hesel, lying between Sculeholm and the meadow of the Brethren of the Temple, dwelling in Feriby, and half an acre of meadow in Sculeholm, lying on the west of the meadow which Robert de Hesel gave to the altar of Blessed John of Beverley, and an acre and a rood of arable land on the west of the vill of Hesel, adjoining the land which Richard Caretarius holds of St. John of Beverley, of the gift of the same Alan towards the south; also of the gift of Alan son of Alan the monk of Hesel, 9 acres of land in one piece of cultivated land (*cultura*) in the territory of Hesel, lying to the south of the land of Geoffrey, son of Saxelin, and extending from the highway which leads from Hesel as far as the boundary of Traneby, and 3 acres of meadow called Hubert's meadow in the vill of Hesel; also of the gift of Robert son of Hubert the deacon, 3 acres of land in the fields of Hesel, that is, one acre to the east of the vill adjoining the land of Alan the monk, and one to the west adjoining the land of Alan, son of Ernest, and one in the fields of Traneby, adjoining the lands of the church; also of the gift of Alan, son of Ernest, 7 acres of arable land and one rood in the territory of Hesel, namely 2¼ acres called le Gayre towards Feriby and 4 acres which lie between the land of Hesel church and the land of Gilbert de Willardeby, towards Traneby, and 3 roods at Sandayle which lie between the land of Robert de Hesel and the land of Geoffrey, son of Saxelin, and 3 acres of meadow and one rood lying in Nordheng between the meadow of Dom. Robert de Hesel and the meadow of the said Alan towards the south, which is of the same Dayla [?]. The prior and convent of Watton to hold the above lands, of the chapter of St. John of Beverley, in pure and perpetual alms, paying yearly 6s. 8d. at the Nativity of St. John the Baptist for all services and secular demands. Witnesses: Mags. Roger de Rich', Ralph de dei Bone, Richard de Vescy, Richard Hornblower (*cornubiensi*), canons of Beverley, Dom. Nicholas de Stuteville, Walter de Soureby, Peter de Kaua, Mauger de Langetoft, Alan the monk of Hesel, Walter de Mathom, William de Bilter, William the clerk of Semar, John, son of Siward, Walter, his brother. (*Y.A.S.*, Mᴰ 120a, No. 3.)

257. April 8, 46 Edward III [1372]. Grant by Richard of Chesterfield, canon of the church of St. John of Beverley, and Adam Coppandale of Beverley, son of William Coppandale, senior,

to Sir John de Hotham, knt., of an annual rent of 20 marks from all their lands and tenements in Hesill, which they have of the gift and feoffment of Geoffrey de Hanby and which formerly belonged to Sir John de Hothom, ancestor of the present Sir John; the rent to be paid yearly in equal portions at Whitsuntide and Martinmas, and should it be in arrears Sir John to have power to distrain. Sealing clause.[1] Witnesses: Thomas de Sutton, Simon de Heselarton, John Constabile, knts., Patrick de Langdale, Peter de Santon of Caue. At Hesill. (*Archer-Houblon MSS.*, No. 328.)

Ibetton.

258. St. Barnabas the Apostle [June 11], 1312. Release and quitclaim by John son of Thomas de Berewyck, of all right and claim in an annual rent of 1*d*. from A[gnes] who was the wife of William de Bru . . . . for a toft and croft in the vill of Heton, which the said Agnes holds, to the same Agnes. Sealing clause. Witnesses: William Darel, John Mansel, Robert de Foxoles, Richard Bigot. At Heton. (*Y.A.S.*, M⁰ 182, No. 43.)

Ibewby.

259. Lease by Adam Faukes of Helthuayt[2] to William de Wucherton,[3] his nephew, of a toft with a croft at the top of the vill of Hueby in Wycherton, with appurtenances within and without the vill; to hold to him his heirs and assigns, freely, quietly and peacefully in woods, plains, grazings, and pastures, with all easements, paying yearly to Adam and his heirs a rose at the Nativity of St. John the Baptist. Warranty. Sealing clause.[4] Witnesses: Alan de Stokeld, William de Casteley, Robert Fraunke, Henry de . . . . of Wycherton, John de Barkeston of the same, William Stute of Dygton. (*Farnley Hall MSS.*, No. 42.)

Ibougbton.

260. Sunday after St. Matthew, 19 Richard II [Sept. 25, 1395]. Grant by Ellen de Langedall' of Etton to John Langedall' and Richard de Langedall', her sons, of an annual rent of 100*s*. after her death for the term of their lives or for the lifetime of the survivor, from the lands, tenements, rents and possessions which she has in the vills and territories of Hoveton, W atre,[5]

---

[1] Seals: two, of black wax; (1) diam. ¾ in., a lion passant guardant to the sinister; ✠ SIG . . . . A . . . TIRE . . . RI; (2) diam. 1 in.; a mark like the letter A surmounted by a cross; ✠ SIGI . . . . . . ALTRE.

[2] Possibly Wallerthwaite, near Ripon.

[3] Weeton in the parish of Harewood.

[4] Seal: green wax, vesica shaped; a fleur-de-lis; S'M DE E . . T DE WESC . . . .

[5] Warter.

Wyghton, Ellerker, Etton, Beverley, Sywardby,[1] Merton, and Hilderthorpe, at the two terms, namely, Whitsuntide and Martinmas, in equal portions; should the rent be in arrears in whole or in part for longer than one month, power to enter and distrain; and if Richard should be promoted to any ecclesiastical benefice to the value of 40 marks, the said rent to go to John for life, and if he should predecease Richard, remainder to the latter for his life, notwithstanding the ecclesiastical benefice. Warranty. Sealing clause. Witnesses: Robert Conestabill', lord of Flayndburgh, John de Sancto Quintino, knts., Edmund de Hothume, William Jakelyn, William Scot, Richard Lelome, Thomas Cumaye [?], Robert de Caue, Patrick Cook. At Etton. (*Y.A.S.*, M^D 120a, No. 15.)

Ibowden.

261. St. Matthew the Apostle, 5 Henry VI [Sept. 21, 1426]. Acquittance by Richard Esshelay, keeper of the park of Howden (*parcarius parci de Howden*), who says that he has received of Nicholas Dawnay and Alice Pultar, executors of William Pultar, all the goods called heirlooms (*ayerloms*) belonging to [*blank*] his wife as kinswoman and heir of the said William Pultar. Sealed in the presence of Richard Dilcok of Snayth. At Howden. (*Y.A.S.*, M^D 182, No. 44.)

Ibovland=Swaine.

262. Whitsunday [June 5], 1362. Grant by William Arnald of Holand Swayn, to John Swynden of the same, of a messuage in Westthorpp', with a bovate of land and meadow within the fields and territories of the same, in the bounds of Holand Swayn, of which one parcel of land and meadow is called Brelas and lies between the grantor's land on one side and the common of Westthorpp' on the other, and adjoins the common way towards the west, and is above Byredoleynges towards the east; and the other parcel is called Wodwall ' hill ' and lies between the grantor's land on the north and the land of the prior and convent of Hampoll' on the south, and adjoins the land of William Clarell called Inchburnesyke towards the east, and the grantor's land towards the west, called Hannerodesyke; also an acre of land and a rood lying separately above Sowrelandes, and an acre and 2 roods above Wellclyffes, and a rood lying above Longfurlonges, and 4 *rode byttes* lying above Wellclyffebuttes, and an acre in the fields of Westthorpp' called Trysterlandes above Brekes towards the west, and above Wellclyffe towards the east; to hold to John and his heirs lawfully begotten, paying yearly to the grantor and his heirs 2*s*. at Whitsuntide and Martinmas in equal portions; and for blanch farm 1*d*. and 3 eggs for all secular services. Rever-

---

[1] Sewerby.

sion to the grantor in default of lawful issue. Sealing clause.[1] Witnesses: John Catelyn, William Horne, Richard Bylclffe of Holand Swayn. At Westethorpp'. (*Farnley Hall MSS.*, No. 30.)

263. Sunday, St. Matthew [Sept. 21], 1393. Grant by Robert son of Thomas de Holandswayn, in the parish of Silkeston, to Richard de Turtun of the same, his heirs and assigns, of all the lands, tenements and appurtenances which he had of the gift and grant of Roger, the clerk of Silkeston, in the vill and fields of Holandswayn; to hold to Richard, his heirs and assigns, of the chief lords of the fee. Warranty. Sealing clause.[2] Witnesses: Robert de Scwynden of Holand, William Scott of Oxspring, William Masun of Holand, John del Grene of Thurgerland. At Holandscwayn. (*Ibid.*, No. 31.)

264. Jan. 4, 1485[6]. Indenture by which Robert Addy of Elmehirst grants to Thomas Addy, his brother, an annual rent of 6s. 8d. from certain lands and closes in Holand Swayne, called Smethyrodes, to be received at Whitsuntide and Martinmas in equal portions; power to Thomas to enter and distrain if rent be in arrears, until satisfaction is obtained. Warranty. Sealing clause. Witnesses: Robert Barnby, esq., Thomas Fletchar of Calthorn, Richard Elys of Elmehirst. (*Ibid.*, No. 32.)

Ibunmanby.

265. Friday after the Epiphany, 1372, 46 Edward III [Jan. 9, 1372-3]. Grant by Gerard de Grymeston, knt., to Stephen Yueson of Hendemanby, clerk, and Christiana, his wife, in return for Stephen's frequent good services to him, of a messuage with a courtyard (*curtilagio*) adjoining, a rood of arable land, and a certain butt of meadow called *le littel pighel*, with appurtenances and easements in the vill, fields and meadows of Hundemanby, that is, the messuage and courtyard which John Hert once held of the grantor, and which are enclosed by stone walls, and lie in length from the highway del Southgate as far as the grantor's capital messuage towards the east, and in breadth between the messuage which John del Aumary held of him on one side towards the north, and a messuage which John Yueson held of him on the other, towards the south; the rood of land lies at Northdale near the land of the abbot of Barthenay,[3] and the butt of meadow lies in the meadows of Hundemanby near the lane called Cougate which leads as far as Pekebrig, between the said lane on the north and a croft belonging to Stephen, called Tedenhill croft, on the south and between Tednal croft on the west and a croft of John

[1] Seal; black wax; diam. $\frac{4}{10}$ in.; a hare to the sinister and sprays of eaves.

[2] Seal: brown wax, diam. $\frac{6}{16}$ in.; shield of arms, a lion [?] rampant to the dexter; legend undeciphered.

[3] Bardney, Lincs.

del Aumarye, called Gregmancroft, on the east; to hold to Stephen, Christiana and the lawfully begotten heirs of Stephen, freely and quietly, paying yearly to the grantor and his heirs 2s. of silver in equal portions at Whitsuntide and Martinmas; should Stephen die without lawful heirs remainder to William son of John Yueson of Hundemanby, and in further default of issue remainder to (1) John, son of John Yueson, (2) Margaret, sister of Stephen, (3) the lawful male heirs of Christiana, sister of the aforesaid William, (4) William de Semer, *sadeler*, kinsman of Stephen, (5) Margaret, daughter of John Paulyn of Hundemanby, (6) John Paulyn, brother of Margaret, (7) the grantor and his heirs in perpetuity. Warranty. Sealing clause.[1] Witnesses: William Horegh', Thomas Coke, John de Corbrig, William de Corbrig, chaplain, John de Aumarye, Stephen Lightfote, John Bakster, Richard de Raygate, chaplain, Stephen del Hill', John de Cayngham, John Dawnay, Roger Lufgod. At Hundemanby. (*Y.A.S.*, M^D 116, No. 1.)

266. Wednesday before St. Margaret, 50 Edward III [July 16, 1376]. Grant by William de Kerdston' knt. to Nichola, widow of Richard Harpham, Dom. Richard de Fraythorp', vicar of the church of Hunmanby and Dom. William Orie, chaplain, of 2 messuages, 4½ tofts, 15½ bovates of land, and a fourth part of a bovate with appurtenances in Hunmanby and Folkethorp'[2]; to hold to them and their heirs of the chief lords of the fee. Warranty. Sealing clause.[3] Witnesses: Sir Robert de Boynton, Sir William de Argum, knts., Robert de Bossale, Peter de Bukton, John de Lascy and Dom. Laurence Oundell, vicar of Neuton. At Hunmanby. (*Ibid.*, No. 2.)

267. Aug. 16, 3 Richard II [1379]. Grant by Richard de Fraythorp', vicar of the church of Hunmanby, and William Horry, chaplain, to Dom. John de Akom, rector of the church of Almonbiry, and John Paulyn of Hunmanby of [*as in previous deed*]; to hold to them and their lawful heirs of the chief lords of the fee. Warranty. Sealing clause.[4] Witnesses: William de Acon, William de Ergham', knts., John de Aske, Peter de Bukton, Robert de Thorp', Hugh de Erderyn, John de Thornehom', Roger Swan. At Hunmanby. (*Ibid.*, No. 3.)

268. June 5, 29 Henry VI [1451]. Indenture by which William, Lord Fitzhugh, grants to John Wencelagh', John Mar-

---

[1] Seal: dark brown wax, diam. 1 in.; a shield couchée, on a fess three mullets pierced; crest, a helm and mantling ermine, from which issues a dragon's head. ✠ . . . . GERARDI DE GRI . . TON.

[2] Folkethorp', *sic;* but presumably Folkton is intended.

[3] Seal: red wax, diam. 1⅟₁₆ ins.; in a cusped border a shield of arms pendant from two sprays of flowers; on a hatched field a saltire engrailed; ✠ SIG . . . WI . . . . RDSTONE.

[4] Seals: two, of dark brown wax; (1) shield of arms, a dragon rampant; leg. undeciphered; (2) blob of wax, blurred.

shall, chaplain, and Thomas Siggeswyk, their heirs and assigns, all lands, tenements, rents, reversions and services with all appurtenances which he has in Hundmandby; power of attorney to William Doront, John Darbour and Robert Miton' to deliver seisin. Sealing clause.[1] Witnesses: Ralph, Lord de Graystok, Robert Ughtred, John Melton, knts., William Twyer, Thomas Grymston, Robert Hartefeld, Robert Twyer, esqs. (*Ibid.*, No. 4.)

269. June 10, 29 Henry VI [1451]. Indenture by which John Wencelagh, John Marshall, chaplain, and Thomas Siggeswyk demise to William, Lord Fitzhugh all the lands etc., which they had of his gift in Hundmandby; power of attorney to William Durant and Robert Miton to deliver seisin. Sealing clause.[2] Witnesses: Ralph, Lord de Graystok, Robert Ughtred, John Melton, knts., William Twyer, Thomas Grymston, Robert Hartefeld, Robert Twyer, esqs. (*Ibid.*, No. 5.)

270. Aug. 20, 29 Henry VI [1451]. Indenture between William, Lord Fitzhugh, of the one part and John Portington, junior, Thomas Ripplyngham, Thomas Huknall, chaplain, John Gower and William Mapilton of the other, witnessing that William, Lord Fitzhugh grants to John, Thomas [*etc.*], all the messuages, lands, tenements, rents, reversions and services with appurtenances in Hunmanby, co. York; to hold to them and their heirs and assigns in exchange for all those lands, messuages [*etc.*], which recently belonged to John Ellerker and Isabel his wife or her sister in Brandesburton and Bristhill', co. York, except 2 messuages and 4 bovates of land in Brandesburton recently given to Lord Fitzhugh, his heirs and assigns, by John, Thomas, etc.; under the following condition, that if it happen that the aforesaid lands, except those specified, should in any way, by reason of law or title by any person or persons, be removed from the possession of Lord Fitzhugh, his heirs or assigns, without fraud or collusion (*covina*) on his part, before the date of the present charter, then it shall be lawful for him or his heirs to re-enter and occupy all those lands in Hunmanby, or any portion of them which might be taken from him, notwithstanding the present charter. John, Thomas, etc., grant the lands in exchange, in Brandesburton and Bristhill', under a similar condition. Alternate seals.[3] Witnesses: Robert Ughtred, Ralph Bigod, John Melton of Swyne, knts., Robert Constable of Flaynburgh', John Constable of Halsham, William Seyntquyntyn, Thomas Grymston, esqs. (*Ibid.*, No. 6.)

Jlkley.

271. Grant[4] by Henry de Percy, lord of Wodehouse to his lord Peter de Middelton and his heirs, of the suit of all his tenants

---

[1] Seal: as to No. 86.
[2] Seals: three, blobs of red wax, undeciphered.
[3] Seal: red wax, gem, possibly a dragon.
[4] In French.

of Wodehouse of the mill, that they shall grind every 20th vessel both of the corn which they buy for their sustenance, as well as that which they grow on their land, either at Sir Peter's mill in Ilkelay or at his other mill which he has built (*plaunte*) on the Qwerfe in the parish of Ilkelay; and for the said right Sir Peter or his heirs shall pay to the grantor and his heirs 6s. 8d. yearly in equal portions at Whitsuntide and Martinmas; also grants that if the tenants should not grind the said portion at his mill, then the corn which they grind elsewhere (*ailioront*) shall be forfeit to Sir Peter in default of their suit at his mill. Sealing clause. Witnesses: Peter son of Richard de Middelton, Sir John Querderay [?], chapelayn, Robert son of Simon the smith (*le feu'*) of Ilkelay, Thomas Scalwra of Metlay, John the clerk. (*Y.A.S.*, M^D 59/12, No. 1.)

272. Grant by Adam son of Thomas de Ingemanthorp to William de Heby for his services, of all that moiety of all his lands, with appurtenances in Stubhuse[1] which he had granted (*incartaui*) by a writ of the king before his justices at York, namely 20 acres of land and appurtenances of the 40 acres in the territory of Jordan de Benetham, and 3½ acres of the 7 acres in the lands of Serlo de Ilkley, and one acre of the 2 acres of Matilda Hurel and half an acre of the lands of Peter de Ilkeley; to hold to William, his heirs or whatever assigns he wishes, of the grantor and his heirs, paying yearly a pair of white gloves or ½d. at Easter for all services saving forinsec service, if any such service is due from the said land. Warranty. Sealing clause.[2] Witnesses: Sir Patrick son of Thomas, Sir John son of Thomas, Sir Patrick de Westwyc, knts., Henry de Walingford, clerk, William de Herthlington, Nigel de Rigton, William de Lumley. (*Ibid.*, No. 2.)

273. Morrow of St. Luke, 33 Edward III [Oct. 19, 1305]. Acknowledgement by Robert de Cotingham, clerk, of the sum of 10 marks sterling from Sir Adam de Middleton in part payment of 50 marks for the rent (*firma*) of the church of Ilkelay. Sealing clause. At London. (*Ibid.*, No. 3.)

274. Sunday after St. Nicholas [Dec. 7], 1320. Indenture by which Peter de Middilton, knt., demises to John Brantyngh' of Kenton [?] all the messuage and land with the meadows adjacent and all the pastures in Eklesgarth, also reasonable estovers of *housebote* and *aythebote* and other appurtenances in Westelay in the parish of Hilkelaird, which tenement Peter, son of Richard de Middelton, once held of the grantor, with the exception of a piece of land which is called Holrydding and the furthest 3 roods of meadow in Holrydding towards the east; to hold to John for the term of his life of the grantor and his heirs, paying yearly

---

[1] Stubham in the parish of Ilkley.

[2] Seal: green wax, vesica shaped, 1½ × 1 in.; an ornate type of fleur-de-lis. ✠ S.ADE .... THOME DE INGMANTHORP.

36*s*. 8*d*. in equal portions at Whitsuntide and Martinmas. Warranty. Sealing clause.[1] Witnesses: Peter del Stode, Robert son of Simon del Hilkelay, John Crokebayn, Thomas de Scallwro', Richard de Wythelay. At Hilkelay. (*Ibid*., No. 4.)

275. Sunday, St. Mary Magdalene, 15 Edward III [July 22, 1341]. Grant by Thomas Skallewra of Middilton to John his son, of a messuage and 18 acres of land with appurtenances in Ilklay, of which Alice daughter of Richard Boulton enfeoffed him; to hold to John and the heirs of his body of the chief lord of the fee; should John die without heirs, remainder to William, the grantor's younger son, to hold to him and the heirs of his body, and should he die without heirs reversion to the grantor. Warranty. Sealing clause. At Ilkelay. Witnesses: Peter de Sted', Simon del Chirche, William de Wetherby, chaplain, Robert son of Simon, John le Mohaut. (*Ibid*., No. 5.)

276. Purification of the B.V.M., 4 Edward IV [Feb. 2, 1464–5]. Quitclaim by William Skalwra of Whetelay to Robert Thakwra, William Thakwra and John Herfeld, their heirs and assigns, of a messuage and 18 acres in Ilkelay which they had of his gift. Sealing clause. At Whetelay. (*Ibid*., No. 6.)

277. Sept. 28, 1482. Grant by Robert Thakwra, William Thakwra and John Herfeld to Thomas Middilton of Kyrkbyoverblawys and Nicholas Middilton of Northdyghton, of a messuage and 18 acres in Ilkelay. Sealing clause. Witnesses: William Gascoigne, Peter Middilton, Robert Plompton, knts., Thomas Ros, John Vavasur, esqs. At Ilkelay. (*Ibid*., No. 7.)

278. April 20, 5 Edward IV [1465]. Quitclaim by Margaret Plessyngton at the special request of John Fraunces and Isabel his wife, to William Vauasur, rector of the church of Bronsall, and Robert Roos esq., of all right in the manor of Ilkley, with all appurtenances, tenements, rents, reversions, which recently belonged to . . . .[2] Plessyngton, her kinsman; to hold to William and Robert, their heirs and assigns, of the chief lords of the fee. Warranty. Sealing clause. Witnesses: William Gascoigne, Henry Vauasur, knts., John Thwat, William Carverlay, esqs. (*Ibid*., No. 8.)

Ikilburn.

279. [Nov. 28, 1538.] Thys Indenture made the xxviij day of November in the xxxth yeir of the reign of our sovaraign lord Kyng Henry the viijth by the grace of God Kyng of England and of France, defender of the Fayth, lord of Yrland and in Erth the Supreme hede of the Church of England, betwen Wylliam, pryor of the monastre of our Blessed Lady of Newburgh[3] in the

---

[1] Seal: brown wax, diam. $\frac{7}{10}$ in.; device of leaves; leg. undeciphered.

[2] Hole in deed.

[3] This Priory was not surrendered until 1539.

countye of Yorke and the convent of the same, of the one partye, and Bryan Egglyfyld of Hood in the seyd Countye, gentylman, of the other partye; Wytnesseth that the seyd Pryor and Convent of their holl and free assente and consent hayth demysed, graunted and to ferm letten, and by these presents demyseth, graunteth and to ferm letteth to the seyd Bryan, their Tythe Corne and hay of the lordshyp of Kylburn in the Countye of York beforeseyd, except certayn tythe hay belonging to the parysshe preyst, and a frunte[1] wyth a croft, sett, lying and beyng in the Southend of the Towne of Kylburn beforeseyd, wyth all the appurtenances and their Shepe rayke.[2] To have and to hold the seyd tythes and frunte wyth the croft wyth all and singuler their appurtenance to the seyd Bryan and his assygnes from the fest of Seynt Andrewe the appostell [Nov. 30] now next comyng after the day herof unto the full ende and term of lxx yeir then next folowyng and fully to be complett and endytt, yeldyng and payyng therfor yerely to the seyd Pryor and Convent and to their successors, iij*li.* iij*s.* iiij*d.* of lawful Englysh money at twe tymes in the yeir, that is to sey at the fest of Seynt Peter called *ad vincula* and the purify-caton of our Lady by even porciones, or wythin xxth days next after eitheir of the seyde fests. For the whych lease covenaunteth and graunteth to be performed and fulfylled appon the partye of the seyd Pryor and Convent, the seyd Bryan covenaunteth and graunteth to be content to pay or cause to be payd to the seyd Pryor and Convent, viij*li.* of lawfull Englysshe money at the day of enseallyng of thes Indentures. In wytnesse wherof to the one parte of thys Indentur remaynyng with the seyd Bryan the seyd Pryor and Convent hayth putt their Common or Conventuall Seall[3] to the other parte of the same remaynyng wyth the seyd Pryor and Convent the seyd Bryan hayth putt his seal. Geven at the seyd monastre of Newburgh in the Chapytre house the day and yeir aboveseyd. (*Farnley Hall MSS.*, No. **33**.)

Ikilbam.

280. Grant by Alan ad Hogam to Juliana, daughter of Elias, son of Richard, of a butt of land above le Suthwandaylbuttes in the south field of Kyllum, extending from the path which leads to Louthorp as far as the water course, and lying between the land of Sir Robert Conestabularius on one side, and the land once belonging to Geoffrey Jolle on the other; to hold to Juliana and her heirs, of the chief lords of the fee. Warranty. Sealing clause. Witnesses: William de Middleton, John Beaudr', Henry Damyot,

---

[1] An obscure word possibly derived from *front* or *frunstead*, the site on which a house stands or has formerly stood (*Glossary of the Cleveland Dialect*).

[2] Raik, a range or walk for cattle, sheep, etc. (*Eng. Dialect Dict.*).

[3] Seal: Chapter seal of Newburgh Priory; reverse, Secretum of the Chapter (*Archæologia*, lxxviii, 27).

Geoffrey Randolph, William *le tanner*, Alan Colus, John the clerk. (*Y.A.S.*, M^D 120, No. 9.)

281. April 20, 15 Edward IV [1475]. Quitclaim by William Buron of Killom, co. York, chaplain, his heirs and executors, to William Attehowe of the same and Agnes, his wife, of all actions and damages (*vasta*) which he might bring against the latter. Sealing clause. At Killom. (*Ibid.*, No. 18.)

282. Kyllom.[1] The Answer of Rychard Webster vicar of the parish church of Kyllom and of Thomas Stropton, William Fenton, Barthelmow Hathwey, Robert Johnson, churchwardens, and of Rauph Paston and Edward Johnson, parishioners of the said church, to the articles sent by Robert, lord archbishop of York and the king's commissioners deputed for surveying colleges, hospitals, chantries, etc.

First we certify that there is no college, hospital, fraternities, guilds nor stipendiary priests being perpetuities within our said parish or church.

Item: We certify that there is a chantry within our town and parish founded to the intent that the incumbent thereof should pray for the founders and patrons of the same, and that the said chantry is served by Richard Wryght, clerk, now the incumbent of the same or by his deputy, according as it has been served *tyme wythout mynd*, for the said incumbent could never get into his hands the foundation of the chantry or composition of the chantry or any other writing thereunto appertaining, nor could five other incumbents of the said chantry. The founder and patron of the chantry was George Darsy, knt.;

Item: We certify that the lands, tenements, possessions and revenues of the chantry are such as appear in a rental exhibited to you;

Item: We certify that the plate, jewels, ornaments and other goods belonging to the chantry are also truly and severally [set forth] in our inventory indented, as well as the true weight, price and value thereof;

Item: We certify that there is no other thing in any other of the articles contained within our town or parish.

In witness of all and singular the premises hereunto we have put our seals[2] and subscribed our names.

Richard Webster, vicar.[3]   (*Archer-Houblon MSS.*, No. 337.)

[1] The document is in English.

[2] There have been seven seals of red wax affixed to tongues cut from the bottom of the document.

[3] There is no date given, but it is endorsed in an early hand 37 H. 8. [April 1545–April 1546]; Archbishop Robert [Holgate] was translated from Llandaff to York on Jan. 16, 1545.

𝕂ilnsea.

283. Thursday before the Annunciation of the B.V.M., 15 Edward III [March 22, 1340–41]. Copy[1] of an indenture made at Beverley between the Prior of Warter and his fellows (*socios suos*), the sellers and assessors of the tithe of corn, wool, and lambs (*venditores et assessores none garbarum, vellerum et agnorum*) lately granted to the king in the East Riding of the county of York, of the one part, and John Gaway, John son of Alan, Peter son of Constantine, Alan le Stoerur, Stephen West, Robert West, cook, Nicholas Grayne, Stephen son of Simon Grayne, Stephen Crapes, Peter son of Alan, John son of Simon, and Simon Doust, parishioners of the church of Kilnsey, jurymen, of the other part. The jurors say on their oath that the tax on the church of Kilnsey is 17*li*. 6*s*. 8*d*., also that the tithe (*nona*) of corn, wool and lambs from the laity of the same parish is worth that year 9*li*. 16*s*. 3*d*., also that the abbot of Thorneton holds temporalities in the same parish of which the tithe is worth that year 26*s*. 10*d*., and that the tithe of the priory of Birstall in the same parish is worth that year 14*s*. 10*d*., they also say that the tithe of hay (*decima feni*), mortuary fees, oblations, the lesser tithes and other income which come under the taxation of the church (*que cadunt in taxa ecclesie*) and not under the aforesaid tithe (*nona*) are worth 6*s*. Sum of tithes from the laity 9*li*. 6*s*. 3*d*.; and from religious 41*s*. 8*d*. Alternate seals. (*Ibid.*, No. 338.)

𝕂irkby 𝕄isperton.

284. Saturday after St. Leonard [Nov. 8], 1393. Grant by Thomas Barri of Pikeryng to John de Haymunderby, rector of the church of Kyrkbymysperton, and Robert de Pikeryng, rector of a moiety of the church of Heyholand, their heirs and assigns, of a messuage and 3 bovates of land and meadow in the vill and territory of Kyrkbymysperton, which messuage lies between the messuage of the prior and convent of Malton on one side and the messuage of William de Bretherton on the other; and 2 bovates of land and meadow lie between the land of the abbot and convent of Blessed Mary of York on one side and that of the cantarist Walter de Bergh' on the other, and the third lies between the land of the said abbot and convent and the land of the prior and convent of Malton; also grants an annual rent of 2*d*. from a bovate of land which William Clerk holds, and an annual rent of 1*d*. from a piece of land held by John of York; to hold of the chief lords of the fee. Warranty. Sealing clause. Witnesses: Thomas Prestcosyn, Stephen Smeyht, William Kepwyk, John Chalouner, John Forster. At Kyrkbymysperton. (*Y.A.S.*, M^D 120a, No. 11.)

---

[1] In a much later hand, probably sixteenth century.

285. Nov. 11, 1439. Grant by Richard Barry of Danby, kinsman and heir of Alice Barry, to William Boynton of Estheslordton of the lands [*as in the preceding deed*]. Warranty. Sealing clause. Witnesses: John Schyrbirn, Robert Walton, John Lamnott. At Estheslardton. (*Ibid.*, No. 12.)

Ikirkby Wiske.

286. May 6, 4 Henry VI [1426]. Appointment by John Grene of Neuby on Swale, esq., of Dom. Nicholas Grene, rector, of a moiety of the church of Southotryngton and Thomas Paliser as attorneys to deliver to Richard Grene, his brother, full and peaceful seisin of a messuage with . . . .[1] of land and meadow with appurtenances in the vill and territory of Kyrkby super Wysk. Sealing clause. At Neuby. (*Y.A.S.*, M° 182, No. 45.)

Iknaresborough.

[2]To the King oure Soueraigne lorde and to his noble and discrete counsaill of his Duchie of Lancastre.

287. Besecheth humbly John Slyngesby Squier that where oon William Slyngesby his grauntfadr whos heire the same John is, was seased and possessed of the office of Master Forester of youre Forest of Knareburgh in the Shire of Yorke, nowe parcell of youre seid Duchie, with men under him, to him and his heires in fee simple, and that the same William and all his auncestres whos heire he was of tyme that no mynde is, have been seased of the seide Office, Of the which Office and also of vj*d*. duly to be taken of the free and bond tenaunts and inhabitaunts within the seide Forest in the name of puture[3] as parcell of the seide office, the seide William the Grauntfader died seased, after whos deth the said Office and vj*d*. by the day in the name of puture descended to William son of the said William and fader to youre saide Besecher as Son and heire, by Vertewe whereof the seide William, fader to youre said Besecher was seased until he was interrupted by Sir William Plumpton knyght, Styward of the said Lordshipp of Knaresburgh, and over this where the seide William the Grauntfader and his auncestres whoos heire he was were seased of commone of pasture to all manre thair bestes within the said forest as well in the severall pastures of the lord there as in the commone pastures within the same Forest, and of housbote and firebote sufficient to be taken within the demayne wodes of Knaresburgh out of the park there, as of fee and right of tyme that noo mynde is the contrarye, and of the same the said William the Grauntfader died seased, after whoos deth the said William fader to

---

[1] Hole in document.   [2] In a late fifteenth-century hand.

[3] Putura, the custom of taking men's, horses' and dogs' meat of the tenants—gratis, within the bounds of a forest, claimed by the keepers of the forests.

H

youre said Besecher was possessed of the same as Son and heire
to the seide William the Grauntfader, unto the tyme he was also
wrongfully interrupted and letted by the seide Sir William
Plumpton then Stiward of the saide lordshipp, after which inter-
rupcion the said William fader to youre said Besecher died, after
whoos deth the Right of the saide Office, commone of pasture
and estovers with the appertenaunce descended to youre saide
Besecher, as son and heire of the said William his fader. Wherefore he humbly bescheth youre noble grace that he may bee
restored to his said Office with the saide vj*d*. by the day, and
also to the said commone of pasture and Estovers according to
his Right and title. And he shall pray to God for you. (*Slingsby
MSS.*, No. 7.)

Langton.

288. SS. Peter and Paul [June 29], 1362. Grant by William
Madame, chaplain of the parish of Grymeston iuxta Setryngton,
and Thomas de Rylington dwelling in Langton', to William, son
and heir of William de Langton' and Matilda, his wife, of all the
lands and tenements with meadows and pastures with appurtenances, that is, the lands and tenements which the grantors had of
the gift and feoffment of the said William in the vill and territory
of Langton' iuxta Bridsale; to hold to them, their heirs and
assigns, of the chief lords of the fee. Warranty. Sealing clause.[1]
Witnesses: John de Middelton [of] Thorgrymthorp', Stephen
Wasseline of Kenerthorp',[2] John de Foxholes, Thomas Wascelyne,
Richard de Santon', William del Selar of Kenerthorp, Robert
Bonefayth. At Langton'. (*Y.A.S.*, M^D 120a, No. 7.)

Great Langton (R.R.).

289. Sunday the morrow of SS. Simon and Jude [Oct. 29],
1329. Indenture whereby Nicholas de Stapilton grants and
demises to Mag. William de Langton a toft and a croft which
Roger de Aynderby once held in Great Langton; to hold with
all appurtenances to William for the term of his life, paying
yearly to the grantor and his heirs 3*s.* of silver at Martinmas
and Whitsuntide in equal portions for all services and secular
demands. Reversion to the grantor and his heirs after the death
of William. Alternate seals.[3] Witnesses: Thomas de Fencot',
bailiff of Richmond, William de Scrueton, Henry de Kyrkeby,
William de Hunton in Langton, Geoffrey de Gormyr of the same.
At Kyrkeby. (*Y.A.S.*, M^D 40.)

---

[1] Seals: two, of light brown wax; (1) broken, blurred; (2) diam. ½ in.,
possibly a stag's head; legend undeciphered.

[2] Kennythorpe, par. Langton.

[3] Seal : oval, white wax; a man's head to the sinister, blurred.

Lindley (Otley).

290. June 3, 18 Edward IV [1478]. Lawrence, archbishop of York, to all his stewards, bailiffs, reeves and other ministers of his lordship of Otley, salutation. Since Percival Lyndeley of Lyndeley has this day, at our manor of Sorowby, done homage for the lands and tenements in Lyndeley, which he holds of us by military service pertaining to the lordship of Otley, we wish and ordain that no distraint or other proceeding be taken against him on this ground, and that these letters shall serve as an acquittance. Given under our seal at Scrowby. (*Farnley Hall MSS.*, No. 37.)

Liverton.

291. Monday before St. Wilfrid the Confessor, 49 Edward III [Feb. 5, 1374–5]. Grant by William Colle of Livyrton', chaplain, to William Colle and John Colle, his kinsmen, of a bovate of land and three parts of a bovate lying in the field of Lyvirton' between the land of the lord (*domini*) of Lyvirtonn on each side, with all appurtenances in fee for ever by the services due and accustomed. Warranty to William and John Colle, his nephews. Sealing clause. Witnesses: Richard de Ellyrby, Walter de Boyngtoun, John de Whetlay, John Bertram, John Gregsoun. At Lyvirton'. (*Y.A.S.*, Mᵇ 182, No. 46.)

292. June 18, 10 Edward IV [1470]. Grant by Henry Toey, otherwise Henry Bifeld of Beverley, *steuenyour*,[1] and Joan, his wife, to William Colle of Esyngton, son of John Colle of the same, of a toft and a croft in the vill of Lyverton in Whitebestrand, which lies in length between the messuage of the prioress and convent of the nunnery of Handalle on the south and a messuage of the chief lord of the same vill on the north; also grants a bovate of land and 3 acres of meadow with appurtenances in the vill and territory of Lyverton which the grantors have there at the date of these presents, without reservation (*retinemento*); to hold to William, his heirs and assigns, of the chief lords of the fee. Warranty. Sealing clause.[2] Witnesses: Alan Lame of Lyverton, Robert Gelle, William Toyes. At Lyverton.

On a strip of parchment attached to the deed: The above Joan swears before God that she will not claim any title to the aforesaid toft, croft or lands as contained in the present charter, neither during the life of the said Henry nor after his death should he die before her; and this under oath before the following respected persons, namely William Warwike of Beverley, merchant, Thomas Taverner,

---

[1] This may possibly be the occupation referred to as ' le pressing ' or ' le stenyng ' (read steuyng) of wools (*Cal. Pat. Rolls*, 1476–1485, p. 300). Alternatively it may be a corruption of steynor, a glazier.

[2] Seals: two of red wax; (1) a merchant's mark; (2) a bird.

clerk of the parish church called *holmekyrke*, Robert Johnson of the same, *litster*. (*Ibid.*, No. 46a.)

Loftsome.

293. Aug. 6, 27 Henry VI [1449]. Indenture by which Constantine Maude and Richard Marshall demise to John Hawkesworth esq., and Joan, his wife, their manor of Lofteshome in Spaldyngmore, with all appurtenances, which they had of the gift of the said John; to hold to John and Joan and the heirs of John, of the chief lords of the fee. Appointment of William Marshall, Robert Bilburgh, separately or together, to deliver seisin according to this indenture. Alternate seals.[1] Witnesses: Ralph Graystock, William Gascoigne, William Rither, knts., Ralph Babthorp, John Vauasour, esqs. At Lofteshome. (*Farnley Hall MSS.*, No. 47.)

Londesborough.

294. Thursday before St. Augustine the Bishop [Aug. 28], 1370. Grant by Adam Coke of Heryngham, son of Richard Coke of Waltham to Sir Edward de St. John of Lounesburgh, knt., son of Sir Edward de St. John, knt., of his manors of Lounesburgh and Wyuerthorp with all the lands, tenements, woods, waters, meadows, grazings, pastures, agistements, rents, mills, profits of courts, services and tenants with all commodities etc., pertaining to the said manors, also the advowson of the church of Lounesburgh when it should occur, which he had of the gift and feoffment of the said Sir Edward, son of Sir Edward; to hold to the grantee, his heirs and assigns, of the chief lords of the fee. Warranty. Sealing clause.[2] Witnesses: Sir Roger Lascels, Sir Gerard de Grymeston, knts., Edward Fancourt, Richard le Veyle of Brunby, John Toche of Midelton, John Roland of Gothmandham, Hugh Coluyle of the same. At Lounesburgh. (*Y.A.S.*, M[D] 239, No. 11.)

295. All Saints, 12 Edward IV [1 Nov. 1472]. Delivery[3] by Richard Chokke, knt., a king's justice of the Common Bench, and William Rilston to Margaret dame Clyfford,[4] daughter and heir of Henry Brounflete, knt., late lord Vessy, and now wife of Lancelot Threlkeld, knt., of all the lands, tenements, rents, reversions, services, meadows, feedings, woods and pastures with appurtenances in Lounesburgh', Esthorp', Towthorp', Kyblyngcot, Wyghton', Shupton', Brompton', Heslarton' and Saulden', co. York, which they had of the gift of the said Henry Brounflete to his use; to hold to her, her heirs and assigns, of the chief lords

---

[1] Seals: two of red wax; (1) undeciphered; (2) small gem, and eagle with wings displayed.

[2] Seal: red wax; gem, a bird.

[3] Also *Y.A.S.*, M[d] 239, No. 10.

[4] For the Clifford family see *Y.A.J.*, xviii, pp. 355 *et seq.*

of those fees. Also appointment of Robert Rilston and Thomas Dene as attorneys to deliver seisin. Witnesses: Richard Tunstall, William Stapulton', knts., Thomas Tunstall, esq., Robert Sheffeld, esq., William Eland, esq., Edward Saltmerssh, esq., Edmund Skeerne. At Wyghton.[1] (*Duke of Devonshire, Bolton Abbey Estate MSS.*)

296. Feb. 4, 6 Henry VII [1490–1]. Indenture between Dame Margaret de Clyfforde, daughter and heir of Henry Bromflet, knt., late lord of Vescy, of the one part and Richard Clyfforde, her son, of the other part, witnessing that the said Richard had demised and let to the said Margaret his manors of Lonesburgh, Brompton, and Highall in Wighton, co. York, and a moiety of the manors of Sutton and Willom[2] in the same county; also a third part of the manor of Aton and of the manor of Castle (*Castri*) and the lordship of Malton in Rydayll in the said county; also a third part of the manor of Newmalton, a third part of the manor of Barlbe and all other lands, tenements, rents, reversions and services with appurtenances in Lonesburgh, Brompton, Wighton, Sutton, Willom, Malton, Hayton, Bromflet, Saldon, Snayton, Newmalton, Barlbe, Wikham, Ruston, Preston, Marton, Kyplyngcott and Rillyngton in the said co. York, which Richard holds for the term of his life by the demise and grant of the said Dame Margaret; to hold and occupy the said manors, moiety and third parts of all the premises with appurtenances to the said Dame Margaret and her assigns from Whitsuntide last for the term of 60 years following, paying yearly to Richard a rose at the Nativity of St. John the Baptist if demanded, and to the chief lords of the fee the due and accustomed services. If Dame Margaret should die within the said term, power to Richard to re-enter the lands and to hold them as in their original state. Sealing clause. Witnesses: Brian Stapilton, Robert Aske, John Ros, Richard Rukysby. (*Y.A.S.*, M^D 239, No. 12.)

Xowtborpe.

297. Indenture witnessing that whereas by a fine[3] made in the court of the then king (*in curia domini regis qui nunc est*) Simon de Heselarton, knt., granted a moiety of the manor of Louthorpe, 2 messuages, 3 bovates of land in Harpham near Louthorpe, and the fourth part of 400 acres of moor in Katilholme in Louthorpe, after the death of Eufemia, late wife of Sir Walter de Heselarton, knt., and after the death of the said Simon

---

[1] Two seals, red wax: (1) broken; (2) a bird; a motto not deciphered.

[2] Welham.

[3] For this fine dated Dec. 5, 1371, see *Cal. Pat. Rolls*, 1370–1374, p. 161, also p. 259 for the confirmation of the licence to alienate the same in mortmain, Feb. 28, 1373, due to its failure to become effective owing to the death of John de Ingleby in 1372.

de Heselarton, to John de Ingelby, then rector of the church of Louthorpe and his successors for ever; now **Robert de Buckton** grants for himself, his fellows (*sociis*) and his successors that Simon de Heselarton shall have a moiety of the said manor and aforesaid lands for the term of his life, with reversion to Robert de Buckton for ever as contained in the said fine by licence of our lord the king. Sealing clause: Robert de Buckton seals with his common seal; Simon de Heselarton with his seal of arms.[1] (*Archer-Houblon MSS.*, No. 340.)

Lund.

298. May 21, 15 Henry VII [1500]. Copy of a grant by Edmund Twhaytts to Ralph Bygott, William Bulmer, knts., Robert Constable, sergeant-at-law, Ralph Salven, esq., Edmund Salven, John St. Quintin (*Sanctoquintyne*), esq., William Bapthroppe, John Arthyngton, John Vavysor of Newton iuxta Rypplay, William Danyell, Edmund Twhaytts, the grantor's son, John Langdayll and Richard Yedone, of 2 bovates of land with appurtenances in the fields of Lunde near Watton, co. York, which lie between 2 bovates of land of the said Edmund called les Braide oxganges on the east and a bovate of land of the same Edmund called le Narrow oxgang on the west; also of a messuage in Lund near le Marr which the grantor holds of the gift and feoffment of Isabel Farrour, also a close in the same vill called Mossecrofte and an orchard opposite the house of the said Edmund in Lunde; he also grants 2 messuages, a toft and 2 crofts, 3½ bovates of land with appurtenances in the vill and territory of Burdsall which lately belonged to Robert Kyldayl, also a messuage, a toft, 2 crofts and 5 bovates of land in Fulsutton, and a cottage and 4½ acres of arable land in Myddylton near Lound, also half a cottage and a garden in Myddylton, and 7 acres and 3 roods of arable land in the same vill with appurtenances; to hold all the lands and premises in Lund, Byrdsall, Foulsutton and Myddylton, of the chief lords of the fee. Warranty. He appoints as his attorneys John Noble, chaplain, and Thomas Goill[er] to deliver seisin. Sealing clause. (*Ibid.*, No. 157.)

299. May 24, 15 Henry VII [1500].[2] Copy of grant of lands in trust for the foundation of a chantry at Lund. Recites that Edmund Twhaytts, by his deed bearing date May 21, 15 Henry VII, enfeoffed Sir Rauff Bygott, knt., Sir William Bulmer and others, of a messuage, a close, an orchard, and 2 oxgangs of land with appurtenances in Lunde near Watton, and of all the lands

---

[1] Endorsed: i feme qui iadys la feme mons[ieur] Wauter Haselarton chi[valer]. This is in a contemporary hand. The document is on paper, and there is no sign of tongue or seal. It may be either a draft or copy; the hand is probably fifteenth century.

[2] In English.

and tenements with appurtenances which he held in Byrdsall, Fulsutton and Myddleton near Lund; to hold to them, their heirs and assigns, as in the said deed more plainly appears, to the use of the grantor;

Now Edmund wills that the feoffees, their heirs and assigns, of the said lands shall suffer [John] Noble, the grantor's priest, and every other priest after him who shall be named and assigned, to sing divine service and other obsequies and prayers in the chapel of our Lady newly builded by the said Edmund on the north side of the church of All Hallows in Lund, for his soul and the souls of such others as he shall appoint and all christian souls, according to such ordinances and compositions as shall be made by him, the profits and revenues from the said messuages, lands [*etc.*] to be taken for the support of the same; and the feoffees to enfeoff other persons of the said lands according as shall be specified in the composition, for the continual support of the priests. Sealing clause. (*Ibid.*, No. 157a.)

Malton.

300. St. Mary Magdalene, 14 Edward IV [July 22, 1474]. Indenture by which John Malton, gent. of co. York grants in fee farm to Roger Malton, vicar of Yhedyngham, an abandoned (*vastum*) toft with appurtenances in New Malton, lying in Yorkesgate on a certain corner between the tenement of the prior and convent of the monastery of Old Malton, and a tenement of the lords of New Malton; to hold from Martinmas next for the term of 41 years following, paying yearly to the chief lords' of the fee 2*d.* at Michaelmas. The lessee may erect thereon a house at his own expense and repair it as seems best to him, and at the end of the term he shall leave the house in reasonable repair. Alternate seals. Witnesses: Richard Danby, William Danby, Richard Brydekirk. (*Y.A.S.*, M^D 120a, No. 17.)

Market Weighton.

301. Jan. 8, 7 Elizabeth [1564–5]. Letters patent of Elizabeth. In respect of the sum of 14*li.* 6*s.* 7½*d.* paid to the hanaper, she grants and licences her kinsman Henry, earl of Cumberland the right to grant, sell, alienate by a fine in court before the justices of the Bench or otherwise according to the wish of the said earl, to William Franklande and Richard Gurney, all his manor of Wyghton with appurtenances and 3 messuages, 20 tofts, a water mill and a wind mill, 6 dovecots, 30 gardens, 40 acres of land, 40 acres of meadow, 300 acres of pasture, 20 acres of wood, 40 acres of heath (*jampnorum*) and broom and 60*s.* rent with appurtenances in Wyghton and Shipton in co. York, which he holds of her in chief; to hold the manor, lands and rent to William and Richard to the use and profit of them, their heirs and assigns

in perpetuity, of Elizabeth and her successors by the due and accustomed services as previously held; and neither the earl and his heirs nor the said William and Richard and their heirs and assigns be vexed, molested, disturbed, etc., by Elizabeth, her justices, escheators, sheriffs, bailiffs or by similar ministers of her successors. Sealing clause. At Westminster.[1]   Fy. Cordell.

Sol. xiiij*li*. vi*s*. vii*d*. ob, pro fine.
Sol. xx*s*. iiij*d*. pro. Sigill.   T. Scotton.
Sol. iiij*s*. ij*d*. pro. irr. ex.   (*Y.A.S.*, M^D 239, No. 13.)

ᚹarton.

302. Grant and confirmation by Peter de Faukenberg to Richard de Risa and his heirs, for his homage and service, of a bovate of land in the territory of Estmerton,[2] namely, that bovate which Drev held with all the appurtenances, easements and liberties which belong to the same, within the vill and without; to hold of the grantor and his heirs, freely, quietly, honourably and in peace by performing the forinsec service which pertains to a bovate where 48 carucates make a knight's fee, for all services and exactions. Warranty. Witnesses: Sayer de Sutton, William Foliot, Andrew de Faukenberg, Philip de Faukenberg, William de Withornewic, steward. (*Archer-Houblon MSS.*, No. 347.)

303. Demise by Peter de Bokkesword to Agnes daughter of Matilda de Marton, for the term of her life, of a messuage and 2 acres of land with appurtenances in the vill and territory of Marton which William de Marton formerly held, of which one acre lies in the south field between the land of the prioress of Swine, and the land of Richard son of Ralph de Mertoun, and one in the north field between the land of Agnes atte Wodhouse and that of the said Richard; to hold the messuage and 2 acres of land to Agnes for the term of her life, paying to the grantor and his heirs a rose at the feast of the Nativity of St. John the Baptist, and performing the services due and accustomed to the chief lords of the fee. Warranty. Witnesses: William Hawtayn, William de Estorp, Richard son of Ralph de Mertoun, John Fournes. (*Ibid.*, No. 348.)

304. Grant by Robert Hauteyn of Wythornewyk[3] to Peter de Bokesworthe of a toft with the buildings on it and 2 acres of arable land in the vill and territory of Marton, namely, that toft and 2 acres of arable land which William de Marton once held in

---

[1] Endorsed: A lycens of alienacion graunted unto the Erle of Cumbrd to alien unto Wyllyam Frankland. Fylbe.

[2] The Marton in Holderness, not the vill of East Marton in the West Riding.

[3] Withernwick.

the vill, of which one acre lies in the south field between the land
of the prioress of Swine and that of Ralph de Marterton, and one
in the north field between the land of Dame Wymark formerly
widow (*quondam relict'*) of Sir Robert de Gousil, and that of the
said Ralph de Marterton; to hold to Peter, his heirs and assigns,
of the grantor and his heirs and assigns, freely and in peace with
all liberties and easements within the vill and without, for ever,
paying yearly on the altar of St. Peter in the parish church of
Swine one pound of wax on the feast of the Apostles Peter and
Paul, for all secular services, customs, exactions, suits of court
and demands. Warranty. Sealing clause.[1] Witnesses: Sir Walter
de Faucumberg, Sir William de Faucumberg, knts., William de
Wytik, Roger de Aol, Hugh ad Aulam of Wythornewyk, John son
of Walter of the same, Thomas Darreine of Haytfeld, Walter
Nerthiby of Ryse. (*Ibid.*, No. 349.)

305. April 14, 1322, 15 Edward II. Grant and confirmation
by Richard son of Ralph de Merton to Stephen Storme of Merton,
Matilda, his wife and Simon, their son, and to the survivor, of
4 acres of land with appurtenances in the vill and territory of
Merton, of which one acre and 3 roods lie in the west field in le
Howes in a strip between the land of Sir John de Faucumberge
and the land of Stephen Hauteyn, and extends in length from the
headland (*forera*) of William de Estthorp on the east to the
boundary on the west, and one rood which lies in width between
the land of the said Sir John and Stephen on both sides and
extends in length from the little mere (*marra*) to Westmere; in
the east field lies an acre at Subrioutgang stretching in length
from the headland of John de Hedon to the ditch of Fosshame,
and in width between the lands of the same John de Hedon on
both sides; and half an acre lies near the church of the said vill,
in length from le Kyrkedale to le Westmere, and in width between
the lands of the said Sir John de Faucumberge and the land of
the said Stephen; and half an acre lies in length in one strip
extending from the side of Lambwath to Estmar, and in one
butt extending from the headland of Stephen Hautayn to le
Estmar, and in width between the lands of Sir John and Stephen
on both sides. He also grants 2½ acres of meadow in Merton, of
which one acre and a rood lie in the east field of the same vill,
that is, in the marsh of Buretre, half an acre, in Milnemar and
Blasyke on the south of the spring there, one rood, and in the
west part of Oustmar and Lambcothill in a strip opposite Dame-
oubrioutgang, half an acre, and in the west field in Braythemar
beginning at le Howes on the north, lie an acre and a rood; he
further grants pasture for one large beast (*ad unum grossum
auerum*) in le Frithes of Estmerton; to hold to Stephen Storme,

---

[1] Seal: green wax, oval, 1¼ × 1 in.; a small device like the petals of a
flower; S' ROB AUTAINE.

Matilda and Simon for their lives and for the lifetime of the survivor, of the grantor and his heirs, paying yearly at the Nativity of St. John the Baptist one silver penny for all secular service. Reversion to the grantor and his heirs. Alternate seals.[1] Witnesses: William Hautyn, John of Gloucestre, John de Hedon, William de Estthorp, Robert Ernis. At Merton. (*Ibid.*, No. 350.)

306. Saturday after the Beheading of St. John the Baptist (Aug. 30), 1326. Attornment.[2] Isabel, widow of Ralph de Marton has become the tenant (*me su attorne*) of John, son and heir of William de Hedon and Margaret, his wife, to hold of the same John and Margaret and of the heirs of John, a bovate and a butt of land, an acre and a rood of meadow with appurtenances in Estmerton, paying 1*d.* yearly at St. John the Baptist for all manner of services; which bovate, butt of land, acre and rood of meadow Isabel holds as dower, of the assignment and of the heritage of Richard, son and heir of Ralph de Merton, formerly her husband. Richard has granted that the reversion of the said lands which should revert to him after Isabel's death shall remain to John de Hedon and Margaret, his wife, and the heirs of John, as contained in the charter which Richard has made to John. Alternate seals.[3] At Merton. Witnesses: John Hauteyne, John of Gloucester, John du Four, William de Estethorp, Stephen Storme. (*Ibid.*, No. 351.)

307. Friday after the Apostles Simon and Jude [Oct. 29], 1333. Indenture of Attornment.[4] Stephen Storme of Marton has become the tenant of John de Hedon, son and heir of William de Hedon, in 4 [acres] of land and 2½ acres of meadow with appurtenances in Marton, likewise in pasture for one large animal, for 1*d.* rent payable yearly at St. John the Baptist for all services; which 6½ acres of land, meadow and pasture Richard son and heir of Ralph de Marton leased to Stephen Storme, Maud (*Mahaude*), his wife, and Simon their son, for the term of their lives, as is more fully contained in the indenture made between Stephen and Richard; which land, meadow and pasture and 1*d.* rent John de Hedon has of the demise and feoffment of Richard, son and heir of Ralph de Marton after the death of the said Stephen Storme, Maud and Simon. Alternate seals. At Marton. (*Ibid.*, No. 352.)

308. Monday after the Apostles Peter and Paul, 47 Edward III [July 4, 1373]. Inspeximus by William de Esthorp and Isabel, his wife, of a release of John Smyth of Merton and Isabel, his wife, to Henry Botteler and Sybil, his wife, and their assigns, of

---

[1] Tags for three seals: two, of red wax, remain—(1) a bird with a human head; above it . . . . NSU; (2) diam. 1 in., apparently an ape on a donkey.

[2] In French.

[3] Fragment of seal of yellow wax; device not clear; ✠ PRI . . .

[4] In French.

a messuage, 4 bovates of land and 3 crofts with appurtenances in Merton, which the said John and Isabel held of William de Esthorp for the term of their lives by a charter (*scriptum*), as follows:

Release by John Smyth of Merton and Isabel, his wife, to Henry Botteler and Sybil, his wife and their assigns, of all right and claim in a messuage, 4 bovates of land and 3 crofts of herbage with appurtenances, which John and Isabel hold of William de Esthorp and Isabel in the vill of Merton for the term of John and Isabel's lives or the lifetime of the survivor; to hold to Henry and Sybil and their assigns for the term of the lives of John and Isabel, or for the lifetime of the survivor. Witnesses: Thomas Disney, William de Hedon, Thomas son of Isabel de Marton, Nicholas de Lyrholm. At Merton, Sunday after the Apostles Peter and Paul, 47 Edward III [July 3, 1373]. William de Esthorp and Isabel ratify and confirm this release and further grant to Henry and Sybil and John son of [Robert *inserted above the line*] Mathewman, the reversion of the said premises after the decease of John Smyth and Isabel; to hold to Henry, Sybil and John son of Robert Mathewman for the term of their lives and of the life of the survivor, and one year longer, of William de Esthorp and Isabel, his wife, paying yearly 42s. of silver at Whitsuntide and Martinmas in equal portions; the land and tenements to be returned in as good state or better than when taken over; Henry, Sybil and John to dig the earth of the tenements and carry soil to improve the land. Warranty. Sealing clause. Witnesses: Thomas Disney, William de Hedon, Thomas son of Isabel de Merton, Nicholas de Layrholm, John Palmar. At Merton. (*Ibid.*, No. 353.)

309. The Beheading of St. John the Baptist, 3 Henry V [Aug. 29, 1415]. Grant by Stephen Wright of Merton, chaplain, and Thomas Wade of Carleton to John Dysny of Fosham of a messuage and 2 bovates of arable land with appurtenances in the vill of Estmerton, which lie between the messuage of John Tomson on the south and the messuage of William Scotte on the north, which messuage and lands the grantors had of the gift of John Palmer; to hold to John Dysny, his heirs and assigns, for ever, of the chief lords of the fee. Warranty. Sealing clause.[1] Witnesses: John de Holme, Robert Haytfeld, Thomas Grymeston, Robert Garton of Garton, William, lord of Grymeston, William Esthorp of Merton, John Tomson of the same. At Merton. (*Ibid.*, No. 354.)

310. Nov. 20, 17 Henry VI [1438]. Grant by John Constable of Halsham, knt., John Warter, John Hedon of Kyngeston super Hull, chaplains, and John Elwyn of Hedon, to John Hedon of Merton and Margaret, his wife, of all their lands and tenements,

---

[1] Two seals of red wax; both badly broken.

rents and services with appurtenances in Merton, Preston and Hedon in Holdernesse which they recently had, among other things, of the gift and feoffment of the said John Hedon of Merton; to hold to John and Margaret, for the term of their lives, with remainder to the right heirs of the said John for ever. Sealing clause.[1] Witnesses: John Melton, William Twyer, Robert Haytefeld, Thomas de Grymeston, John Disney. (*Ibid.*, No. 355.)

311. Aug. 28, 14 Edward IV [1474]. Grant by John Hedon of Marton in Holderness to William Grymston of Burton Pydse and Thomas Grymston of Flynton in Holdernes, gents., of a messuage in Marton situate near the church of St. Leonard of Marton, and 4 bovates of land in the fields of the same vill which were lately in the tenure of John Kyrkeby; one part of the said 4 bovates is called le Grete oxgang; he also grants a messuage and 2 bovates of land with appurtenances in the vill and fields of Preston in Holdernes, now in the tenure of Thomas Barchard of Preston; to hold to William and Thomas, their heirs and assigns, of the chief lords of the fee. Warranty. Sealing clause.[2] Witnesses: John Constable of Halsham, John Holme of Pagilholme, Robert Twyer of Gaunstede, Walter Grymston of Grymston, James Heton of Weton near Welwik in Holdernes, esqs. At Marton. (*Ibid.*, No. 356.)

Masbrougb.

312. Saturday after St. Michael, 12 Henry VI [Oct. 4, 1410]. Grant by Simon Mersburgh to William Spendyng of Roderham, of an acre and half an acre of land and meadow lying in different places in the fields and territory of Mersburgh, of which the acre of arable land lies in a place called le Bellands, between the land of the abbot of Rughford on the south and the land recently belonging to John Pouay on the north; and the half acre of land and meadow lies divided, of which one parcel of arable land lies between the meadow of Thomas de Reresby on the north and the land of the grantor on the south, and abuts above the common way towards the west; and the meadow part lies towards the western end of the meadows of Mersburgh, and abuts above the land of the said Thomas towards the north; to hold to William, his heirs and assigns, freely etc., of the chief lords of the fee in perpetuity. Warranty. Sealing clause. Witnesses: Ralph Pouay, John Bollrome, John Dobson, John Wrauby. At Mersburgh. (*Duke of Leeds*, Hornby Castle Muniments, Rotherham, No. 1.)

---

[1] Four small seals of red wax: (1) badly broken; (2) a Latin cross standing on a base, a very small circle each side of the cross shaft; (3) a cross; (4) a lamb and flag.

[2] Seal: red wax, diam. 1 in.; a cowled head in profile; . . . . UARDI DE HEDON.

Menston

313. Thursday, SS. Simon and Jude [Oct. 28], 1281.[1] Grant by Walter son of Walter de Haukeswod . . . .[2] for the health of his soul and the soul of his wife Beatrice, to God, Blessed Mary and St. Leonard of Essold and to the nuns serving God there, of a toft with a croft and 7 acres of land and meadow, half with appurtenances in the place called Rodes in the territory of Mensington; also grants 4s. 4½d. annual rent from Thomas son of Simon de Rodes for a tenement which he holds of the grantor, payable at the two terms, namely, Whitsuntide and Martinmas; also grants 2s. 6d. from Robert Rufus and his heirs for a tenement held of the grantor and payable in like manner; also 15d. from William son of Simon de Rodes, with homages, wards, reliefs, escheats and suits of all tenants, and all other appurtenances within the vill and territories of Mensington; to hold of the grantor and his heirs in pure and perpetual alms, so that half (media pars) of all the gift both of the assize rents and rents of the said lands shall accrue in usefulness for the first common of the said house, that is in the hands of the prioress, and the other part for a pittance of the house on the day of the anniversary of Walter, and this is the allowance of the sub-prioress,[3] paying yearly to the grantor and his heirs a rose at the Nativity of St. John the Baptist for all services. Warranty. Sealing clause. Witnesses: Sir William de Lassel, Simon Ward, Alexander de Ledes, knts., Robert Wyerlay', John de Marelay, Matthew de Bramee, William de Midelton, Simon son of Thomas de Gyselay. (*Farnley Hall MSS.*, No. 48.)

314. Wednesday, St. Mark [April 25], 1341. Grant by Walter de Haukesworht to Walter, his son, and Elizabeth his wife, and their lawfully begotten heirs, of all his capital messuage of Mensington iuxta Otley, with all the lands, meadows, woods, rents and services, which he has in the same vill and territory; to hold freely in all courts, wards, reliefs, escheats and in fields, meadows, woods, pastures, waters, wastes, moors, marshes, turbaries, of the chief lords of the fee, paying yearly to the grantor a rose at the Nativity of St. John the Baptist. Should Walter and Elizabeth die without heirs, reversion to the grantor. Warranty. Sealing clause. Witnesses: Sir John Ward, knt., Peter de Marthelay, Ralph de Ilkton, William de Ilkton, Robert de Burghlay, Michael de Raudon, John de Carlton. At Hakesworht. (*Ibid.*, No. 49.)

---

[1] SS. Simon and Jude, Oct. 28, fell on Tuesday in 1281.

[2] Document torn.

[3] See Power, *Medieval English Nunneries*, pp. 323 *et seq.*, for a description of such pittances.

315. Jan. 20, 9 Henry V [1421–22]. Grant[1] by John Elenson of Menston to Thomas Hawkesworth, Robert Ottelay, chaplain, and John de Rodes, of all his lands, meadows and tenements in the vill and fields of Menston, which he had of the gift and feoffment of Henry de Merbek; to hold of the chief lords of the fee. Warranty. Sealing clause.[2] Witnesses: Nicholas de Bayldon, John de Rawdon, Walter Grauer, William Grauer, William de Brerhagh. At Menston. (*Ibid.*, No. 50.)

♏entborpe

316. Tuesday the Morrow of the Annunciation, ... 4 [Edward I] [March 26, 1276].[3] Grant by William son of Richard de Menthorpe, with the consent of John his elder brother, to John his younger brother, of a bovate of land with a toft and other appurtenances in the vill of Menthorpe; also confirmation of the gift in accordance with a charter which John, junior has of John, senior. Sealing clause. Witnesses: Robert de Osgoteby, Walter Page, John son of John of the same, Geoffrey Surflet of Southduffeld, John de Sadyngton of the same, Walter de Bubwythe, Richard del Flet of the same. At Menthorpe. (*Y.A.S.*, M[D] 183, No. 1.)

317. Monday after the Purification of the B.V.M., 49 Edward III [Feb. 5, 1374–5]. Lease by Robert Gouk of Othelingflet to John Dayuill of Hayton' of all his lands and tenements in the vill of Menthorpe, also of the ferry (*passagio*) which he holds in common with the said John, of the gift and feoffment of John Dayuill of Wytmore; to hold to John for the term of eight years from the date of this charter, paying to the grantor a rose [yearly ?] during the term of this lease. Sealing clause. At Othelingflet. (*Y.A.S.*, M[D] 182, No. 47a.)

♏itton

318. Friday, SS. Marcellinus and Peter, 24 Edward [June 8, 1296]. Appointment by Henry de Kyghelay, knt., of Roger de Stolbes to deliver seisin to Thomas le Morays, of all the lands, tenements, rents and services which he had in Mitton of the gift of Ralph de Mitton. Sealing clause. At Sutkypp' [?]. (*Farnley Hall MSS.*, No. 51.)

319. Sept. 20, 36 Edward III [1362]. Indenture between John Suthron of the one part, and Thomas, his brother and Isabel, his sister, of the other part, witnessing that John has received of Thomas and Isabel the following goods, namely,

---

[1] Grant and sale by the same to the same of all his goods, chattels and easements, dated Jan. 20, 9 Henry VI [1431]. (*Ibid.*, No. 50a.)

[2] Seal: red wax; the letter R beneath a crown.

[3] Date almost entirely erased, but the script appears to be late thirteenth century and the day falls correctly on a Tuesday in 4 Edward I.

11 oxen, 3 cows, and one bull, one heifer, one sow (*truye*), one boar, one pig, 5 bullocks called *Tuynters*,[1] 3 coverlets and the blankets (*tapits*), one embroidered [?] (*crosele*) coverlet, 4 pairs of sheets (*lyntheux*), 2 blankets, 3 shaloons (*chalons*), 2 pots for the fire [?] (*darisine*), 2 small pots (*posenets*) for the fire, one pail (*paiele*), 2 leaden pans (*plumbs*); concerning which John binds himself to render faithful account to Thomas and Isabel, when the debts of Thomas le Surreys, their father, shall be paid in full. Alternate seals. At Mitton. (*Ibid.*, No. 52.)

ﬅuston

320.   Thursday after the Conversion of St. Paul the Apostle [Jan. 25], 1334[-5]. Quitclaim by Emma Gynur in her pure widowhood and lawful power, for herself and her heirs in perpetuity, to Adam de Elmet, senior, of Muston, his heirs and assigns, of an annual rent of ½*d.* with all manner of dues and issues from an acre and a half of land in the fields of Muston, which Thomas de Bukton formerly held of the gift of Isabel, daughter of Walter Bonesire. Sealing clause. Witnesses: Roger Malbys, Robert de Bukton, John, son of Savyne, John Horegh, William Belle. At Muston. (*Archer-Houblon MSS.*, No. 370.)

321.   The Apostles Philip and James, 28 Edward III [May 1, 1354]. Manumission[2] by William Malbys, knt., of William de Raygat of Muston and of all his offspring born and to be born. Renounces all claim on the said William de Raygat and his offspring by reason of his being a serf, and they are to be quit of all services. At Scalton. (*Ibid.*, No. 371.)

322.   March 10, 2 Henry IV [1400]. Grant by William Rowclyff, rector of the church of Halneby and John Dawe, chaplain, to Elizabeth, widow of Adam de Beckewyth, of the manor of Muston, with all the lands, rents, services and all other appurtenances, also all the lands, tenements, rents and services in the vill and territory of Fyvelay[3] which they had of the gift of the said Elizabeth; to hold to her for the term of her life, of the chief lords of the fee, with remainder successively to, (1) William de Beckewyth, son of Elizabeth and his male heirs lawfully begotten; (2) John de Beckewyth, his brother and his male heirs lawfully begotten; (3) Ralph de Beckewyth and his male heirs lawfully begotten; (4) Katherine, wife of John de Kellowe, daughter of Elizabeth and sister of Ralph, and her heirs male lawfully begotten; (5) Elizabeth de Beckewyth, sister of Katherine, and her male heirs lawfully begotten; (6) Elizabeth Heryng,

---

[1] A steer of two winters (*Eng. Dialect Dict.*).

[2] Also confirmation thereof by Thomas son of William Malbys, dated May 3, 1354. (*Ibid.*, No. 372.)

[3] Filey.

daughter of Thomas Heryng and the heirs of her body lawfully begotten; (7) to the right heirs of Elizabeth widow of Adam de Beckewyth. Warranty. Sealing clause.[1] Witnesses: Robert de Twyre, Gerard Saluayn, knts., John Lassels, Thomas de Mapilton, John Boye of Ryghton, Henry de Gryndall of the same, John Paulyn of Humanby. At Muston. (*Ibid.*, No. 373.)

Newby Wiske

323. Friday, Morrow of St. Hilary [Jan. 14], 1311[-12]. Grant by John de Neuby to Robert de Neuby his son, of his manor of Neuby on Swale in demesnes and fees, in reliefs, wards and escheats, in reversions and with all homages and services of free tenants, and with all the land which Sir Henry Percy holds of him, the grantor, at farm in the vill of Neuby aforesaid, and with all other appurtenances in any way pertaining to the said manor of Neuby; he also grants to Robert 3½ acres of meadow with appurtenances which he, the grantor, has in the vill of Dalton near Topp'[cliffe], with a certain annual rent of 6 marks from John de Allwe . . . ., his heirs and assigns, at the two accustomed terms of the year, for a carucate of land which the said John holds hereditarily of the grantor in the vill of Aystanby[2] near Topp' [cliffe]; to hold to Robert of the chief lord of that fee hereditarily, paying yearly to the grantor during his lifetime 40 marks sterling at Whitsuntide and Martinmas in equal portions for all secular services. Warranty. Alternate seals.[3] Witnesses: William Darel', John Wayand, Robert de Foxoles, John Mansel, William de Eskelby, Alexander de Midelton', John de Balderby. At Neuby. (*Y.A.S.*, M^D 182, No. 47.)

324. Monday after St. Luke the Evangelist, 26 Edward III [Oct. 22, 1352]. Release and quitclaim by Thomas son of William de Holteby of Neuby, to Elizabeth Darelle, of all his right and claim in a bovate of land and the meadow pertaining to the same, which he had of the gift and feoffment of Roger de Holteby, in the vill of Neuby super Wisk. Warranty. Sealing clause. Witnesses: William de Lasseles, Thomas de Caberghe, Alan de Neusome. At Thresk. (*Ibid.*, No. 48.)

Newbay

325. Thursday before St. Peter in cathedra, 44 Edward III [Feb. 21, 1369-70]. Quitclaim by Isabel, widow of John Ceeyvill of Whitmore to John Cawode and Margaret his wife, of all right in all the lands, tenements, meadows, moors and services which

[1] Seals: two, of red wax—(1) not deciphered; (2) diam. ¾ in., two triangles on the same base.

[2] Aisenby.

[3] Seal: white wax, diam. 1^1/10 ins.; blurred.

she has in the vill and territory of Newhagh iuxta Hemyghburgh and Osgoteby[1] iuxta Barthelby.[2] Warranty. Sealing clause.[3] Witnesses: Robert Rabas, John de Sadygton, William de Hathelsay, John de Surflet, Robert Riuyle, Robert de Saxton, Henry de Stokbrig. At Newhagh iuxta Hemygburgh. (*Farnley Hall MSS.*, No. 53.)

Newland (Eastrington)

326. June 9, 14 Henry VI [1436]. Appointment[4] by Thomas Wryght of Beleby, son and heir of Richard Wryght of Gilberddyke, son and heir of William Wryght of the same, son and heir of William Brusor del Dyke and Agnes, daughter of John del Gare of Neuland, of William Hydwyn, citizen and merchant of York, as his attorney to deliver to Thomas Gare, citizen and alderman of York, full seisin and possession of 6 selions of land with appurtenances lying in the fields of Neuland, called Northchamberlandfeld, according to the form of a charter made by Thomas Wryght to Thomas Gare. Sealing clause. (*Archer-Houblon MSS.*, No. 397.)

Newton Rocheford

327. Thursday in the second week of Lent, 3 Richard II [April 12, 1380]. Release and quitclaim by Robert de Thorp iuxta Rudstan, John de Octon iuxta Thweng and Thomas de Ratelesden, to Joan daughter and heir of Sir Walbran de Rocheford, knt., of all right and claim which they have or may have in all the demesnes, lordships, lands, tenements, rents, and services of all manner of tenants, with villeins and their sequel and chattels, with appurtenances, all of which they lately had of the gift of the said Joan, in the vill and territory of Neuton Rocheford near Burton Flemyng. They renounce all right and claim for themselves and their heirs. Sealing clause.[5] Witnesses: Sirs John de St. Quyntyn, John Constable of Halsham, John de Siwardby, knts., Peter de Bukton, Thomas Dysne. At Neuton Rocheford. (*Ibid.*, No. 399.)

Ormesby

328. Jan. 14, 3 Richard II [1379–80]. Grant by John Bayhouse of Ormesby in Clyveland, to Thomas Howome, citizen and mayor of York, of a messuage with a croft and 2 acres of land in the vill and territory of Ormesby, where the messuage lies between

---

[1] Osgodby.   [2] Barlby.   [3] Seal of black wax, broken.

[4] Also quitclaim of the same lands by the same to Thomas Gare, dated June 12, 1436, and witnessed by John Portyngton, William Mouston, William de Thorp, Thomas Ute, John Soull'. At Neuland. Seal: red wax, a merchant's mark. (*Ibid.*, No. 398.)

[5] Tongues for three seals: on one a fragment of red wax; a shield of arms, blurred but possibly a cross charged with a pierced mullet.

I

the messuage of the abbot of Whytby on the south and the tenement of the prior of Gysburn on the north; to hold to Thomas, his heirs and assigns, of the chief lords of the fee. Warranty. Sealing clause.[1] Witnesses: Thomas de Hoton', John de Lasyngby of Marton', William Cloket, John Stormy of Dromondeby,[2] Robert son of Robert de Pynchonerthorpe.[3] At Ormesby. (*Miss A. Norfar.*)

Osgoðby (E.R.)

329.   Sunday after the Nativity of St. John the Baptist [June 26], 1384.   Quitclaim by John Quytemore of Selby to Agnes and Alice, daughters of John de Cawode, and the heirs of their bodies lawfully begotten, of all right in a toft in the vill of Osgoteby, which Henry the son of Gervase once of Novahaya[4] held; also of a selion of land lying in Wythis in the territory of the same vill; also of a rood of land lying between [the land] of Jordan son of Aylmer, and Walter son of Walter; also of 2 acres of meadow called Becsike; to hold to Agnes and Alice and the heirs of their bodies, with remainder to John son of David de Cawod, his heirs and assigns. Warranty. Sealing clause.[5] Witnesses: John de *marras*, Robert Renell, Robert de Saxton, Henry de Barlay, John Robertson of Wystowe. At Cawod. (*Y.A.S.,* Mᴰ 182, No. 48a.)

Osgooðby

330.   Monday after St. Agatha the Virgin [Feb. 8], 1315[-16]. To all sons of Holy Mother Church, from William de Buscy, knt., son of Oliver de Buscy, now with God, greeting. Following an inspection of the charters of his ancestors, he now grants and quitclaims, for himself and his heirs, to God, Blessed Mary and the abbot and convent of Byland (*Bellalanda*) and their successors, in pure and perpetual alms, all right which he has in all the lordship of the vill of Angoteby, by many called Osgoteby, and in all secular services, exactions and demands, also forfeits and escheats (*extrisfetis*), in all else touching the same lordship and in all other lands and tenements whatsoever which the abbot and convent had by gift and grant throughout his fee. Warranty. Sealing clause.[6] Witnesses: Sirs John de Barton of Freton,[7] Thomas de Coleville, John Malebys, Robert de Coleville, knts., John de Harnby, steward of the said abbot and convent, Robert de

---

[1] Seal: red wax, diam. ₁₀/₁₀ in.; in a cusped border a floral device; seal broken and legend undeciphered.

[2] Dromanby.   [3] Pinchinthorpe.   [4] Newhay.

[5] Seal: red wax, broken; merchant's mark; legend undeciphered.

[6] Seal: red wax, diam. 1 in.; shield of arms, a lion [?] rampant to dexter; legend . . . . DE BUSCI.

[7] Fryton, par. Hovingham.

Foxoles, William Wysbarne.   In the market place of Tresk. (*Farnley Hall MSS.*, No. 54.)

331. Oct. 20, 24 Henry VIII [1532]. Indenture between John, abbot of the monastery of Blessed Mary of Byland (*Bella-land'*) and the convent of the same place, of the one part, and Richard Askwyth of Osgoodby of the other, witnessing that whereas the abbot has granted and demised to Richard and Brian, his son, a third part of their grange called Osgoodby grange, with appurtenances, being in the tenure and occupation of the same Richard, from Martinmas next for 99 years, paying yearly to the grantor and his successors 6 *marks* 8s. 10½d. of legal English money at Whitsuntide and Martinmas in equal portions; the abbot now grants for him and his successors that Richard and Brian shall have sufficient *housebotte, fyerbotte, hedgebotte, ploughbotte and cartebotte* during the said term; and Richard and Brian agree that they will properly maintain and repair at their own cost the third part of the premises with all the houses and buildings constructed there, both the roofs with the straw (*stramine*) and the plastered walls (*muris luteis*), and hand them over in good condition at the end of the term. Alternate seals.[1]   (*Ibid.*, No. 55.)

Otley

332. Sunday before the Ascension [May 13], 1341. Grant by Matilda, daughter of Thomas Payllene of Ottelay to Dom. Robert Bonenfant, chaplain, his heirs and assigns, of a burgage with appurtenances in Ottelay, which she had inherited from Thomas Payllene, her father, and which lies between the burgage of William, son of Paul, on the west, and the burgage which Robert, the clerk, her grandfather, gave to Emma, her mother, on the east; she also grants an acre and a rood of land with appurtenances in the west field of Ottelay in the place called le Storch; also all her lands and pastures in Fernelay iuxta Ottelay in the place called Fernelay Fytts; also an acre and a rood in the same field lying between the land of Richard Ketyll of Ottelay on the east, and the land of William son of William son of Paul de Ottelay on the west; to hold to Robert, his heirs and assigns, in perpetuity of the chief lords of the fee. Warranty. Sealing clause.[2] Witnesses: Walter de Haukesworth, Walter, his son, Robert de Burlay, John de Carleton, senior, Hugh de Horsford, Adam, rector of Ottelay, Nicholas Bonenfant of the same, Henry, his brother, Hugh Tannator, Thomas son of William the clerk. At Ottelay. (*Ibid.*, No. 56.)

---

[1] Seal: red wax, broken; part of the seal of Byland Abbey. Reverse, two small seals, blurred. See Vol. V, p. 5. Part of the legend remaining reads . . . ERIUM ✠ DE B . . . .

[2] Seal, dark green wax, blurred.

333. June 7, 2 Richard II [1379]. Release by Adam Rid-
dynges to Nicholas son of John Adamson de Ottlay, of all right
in all manner of actions, real and personal, which he has against
him by reason of a bond entered into between them. Sealing
clause.[1] At York. (*Ibid.*, No. 57.)

Ousefleet

334. Grant by William son of Richard son of Ranulph de
Useflet to John Gouk of Athelingflet, Alice his wife, and the heirs
and assigns of the said John of a piece (*placeam*) of land with
appurtenances in Useflet, a perch in width and extending in
length from the highway in Useflet to the middle of the water
of the Use (*ad filum aque de Use*), lying between the toft of the
said John on one side and a piece of land belonging to Agnes,
the grantor's sister, on the other side; to hold of the chief lords
of the fee. Warranty. Sealing clause. Witnesses: Walter son
of Robert de Useflet, Thomas de Whyten,[2] William son of Hilard,
John son of William de Useflet, Thomas Peper. (*Archer-Houblon
MSS.*, No. 400.)

335. Release and quitclaim by Walter son of Richard son
of Ranulph de Useflet to John Gouk of Adlingflet, Alice his wife
and their heirs and assigns, of all right in a certain selion lying
in the field of Useflet called Colmanriges between the land of
William Torel on one side and le . . . klandik on the other. Sealing
clause. Witnesses: Nicholas Haukesgarthe, Robert de Haldanby,
Walter son of William de Useflet, Thomas de Whiten, William
son of Hilard. (*Ibid.*, No. 401.)

336. Release and quitclaim by Thomas son of Richard son
of Ranulph de Useflet to John Gouk of Athelingflet and Alice his
wife, their heirs and assigns, for ever, of 6*d.* of the annual rent of
2*s.* which John and Alice were accustomed to render for the lands
and tenements which they had of the gift and feoffment of Robert
brother of the said Thomas son of Richard son of Ranulph, in
Useflet. Thomas renounces all right for himself and his heirs in
the said 6*d.* per annum and in the right to take any other services
for the lands and tenements except 18*d.* per annum. Sealing
clause. Witnesses: Sir Gerard de Useflet, Walter son of Robert,
Thomas de Whyten', William son of Hilard, Thomas Peper.
(*Ibid.*, No. 402.)

337. Martinmas [Nov. 11], 1314. Lease by William Thorel
of Useflet, Alice his wife and William their son, to John Gouk
of Adlingflet and Alice, his wife, of a selion of land with appurtenances in Useflet in the field called Burricroft, which lies in length
and breadth between the land of Roger Hurtquart on the east

[1] Seal of green wax, broken; a floral device, legend undeciphered.
[2] Whitton, Lincs.

and that of Richard son of Ranulph on the west; to hold for the term of their lives or for the lifetime of the survivor, paying yearly from the day of the making of this deed for 12 years a rose at the Nativity of St. John the Baptist for all services, and thereafter 20s. yearly in equal portions at Whitsuntide and Martinmas. Warranty. If John and Alice should die before the end of the 12 years, remainder to their heirs and assigns until the completion of the said term. William, Alice, and William their son, have sworn on the Gospels (sacrosanctis) to uphold this grant. Alternate seals.[1] Witnesses: William son of Hilard, Thomas Peper, Thomas Cornwall, John son of Christiana, William Ben. If any expenses are placed on these lands for the building of the church at Whytegeft or for making the ditch at Estoft, William and Alice and their son, William, will acquit John and Alice for the said selion during the said term. At Useflet. (*Ibid.*, No. 403.)

Oxspring

338. Grant by Robert son of Henry del Clay to Thomas the shepherd (*bercario*) of Thurkeland, his brother, and his heirs or assigns in return for a sum of money which Thomas gave him as a fine (*in gressuma*) for two assarts with appurtenances in the territory of Oxpring, of which one lies on the east side of Kotes and is called le Heyefeld and which remains entirely in length and breadth, without reservation, as Henry del Clay held it; and the other assart lies between Molgerode on the north and the land of Richard del Mers on the south, and abuts at one end above the assart of the said Richard, called le Stonirode, and the other above le Storyebroc, with all the meadow and a grove adjoining the same assart, also as held by Henry del Clay; he further grants a broad path through Molgerode and Coppicstorye, with free entry and exit for the carrying of the crops pertaining to the assart at all times of the year with the carts and their loads, also for the animals driven to the assart for pasture; to hold of the grantor and his heirs, to give, lease, sell, or assign should they wish, with all liberties and easements, paying yearly to the grantor a rose at the Nativity of St. John the Baptist for all suits and secular services. Warranty. Sealing clause.[2] Witnesses: Gerard de Thurkerland, Thomas Yrland, Matthew de Oxpring, Adam de Kotes, Roger the smith (*fabri*), of the same, Richard de *marisco*, John son of John de Estfeld, Dom. Robert de Berfeld, chaplain. (*Farnley Hall MSS.*, No. 58.)

339. Grant by John son of Robert de Oxpryng, to Elias the clerk, dwelling in the vill of Oxpryng, of a piece of land lying

---

[1] Tongues for two seals of which one remains: small, green wax; device undeciphered; CREDE MIHI.

[2] Seal: green wax, vesica shaped, $1\frac{1}{4} \times \frac{9}{16}$ in., device of leaves; ROBERT: CLE .

within the confines of the vill in a place called Longgelay, within the land of Elias; to hold of the chief lords of the fee. Sealing clause. Witnesses: John de Burghland, Richard Danyol, Matthew his son, John son of Adam Cotes, John Pogge, Richard de Marisco, smith (*fabro*). (*Ibid.*, No. 59.)

340.   Wednesday before St. Catherine the Virgin [Nov. 24], 1333. Grant by Elias the clerk of Oxspring to John, his son, and his heirs, of all his lands, tenements, meadows and woods with appurtenances in the vills of Oxspring, Thurgerland and Holand-swayn; to hold to John, his heirs and assigns, of the chief lords of the fee, freely [*etc.*], in perpetuity. Warranty. Sealing clause. Witnesses: Sir Nicholas de Wortelay, knt., Henry de Rockelay, John de Thurgerland, Matthew Daniel of the same, John son of Roger de Cotes, John son of Adam of the same. At Oxspring. (*Ibid.*, No. 60.)

341.   Thursday after the Annunciation [Mar. 28], 1342. Grant by Adam Poger of Cotes to John son of Elias the clerk, of 3 acres of land with appurtenances lying in the territory of Oxpring in the place called Heghfeld; to hold to John and his heirs and assigns of the chief lords of the fee. Warranty. Sealing clause.[1] Witnesses: Richard, lord of Oxpring, Ralph de Estfeld, John Naleson of Cotes, John son of Roger of the same, John son of Adam of the same. At Oxpring. (*Ibid.*, No. 61.)

342.   The Morrow of St. Swithin, 16 Edward III [July 16, 1342]. Grant by Adam son of John Poger of Cotes, to John son of Elias the clerk, of 5 acres of land with all the wood in Lobanks as far as Rumlun [?] water on the south, and a piece of the afore-said land and wood called Barherse in Oxpring; to hold to John, his heirs and assigns, of the chief lords of the fee. Warranty. Sealing clause. Witnesses: Ralph de Estfeld, John son of Siale [?] of Cotes, John son of Roger of the same, Robert del Clay, John son of Adam of Cotes. At Oxpring. (*Ibid.*, No. 62.)

Pollington

343.   Sunday before Epiphany [Dec. 31], 1342. Quitclaim by Henry de Arnethorp' of Polyngton' to John de Metham, his heirs and assigns, of all right in an annual rent of 3s. from lands and tenements which William Kay and Alice his wife, and Thomas del Twayt recently held of the grantor in Polyngton, payable at the four terms decreed in the soke of Snaithe, and as the grantor received, which rent John shall have by demise of the grantor at the close of the year. Warranty. Sealing clause.[2] Witnesses: Sir Thomas de Metham, knt., William de Wynteworth, Robert

---

[1] Seal: black wax, undeciphered.
[2] Seal: brown wax, diam. $\frac{7}{10}$ in.; probably a fleur-de-lis.

son of Alexander of Balne, John Tempelman, William Benet, Thomas de Layburne, and John Stansfeld, clerk. At Polyngton. (*Y.A.S.*, M^D 182, No. 49a.)

344. Oct. 20, 10 Richard II [1386]. Grant by Adam Vendilok of Goldale to Richard de Houke of Goldall and Alice his wife, of all the land which the grantor has on the day of making this deed in the fields of Polyngton' called Westfeld, Midelfeld, Estfeld and le Thwayt, with 6*d.* annual rent from a tenement of William Baille in Polyngton with appurtenances; to hold to Richard and Alice and the heirs and assigns of Richard of the chief lords of these fees. Warranty. Sealing clause. Witnesses: John de Roghshagh, John Scot of Polyngton, William Child, Richard Dowenyng, William Broun. At Polyngton. (*Ibid.*, No. 49.)

345. Vigil of St. Dionysius, 21 Richard II [Oct. 8, 1397]. Grant by John Daunay to William de Burgoyne of an annual rent of 40*d.* which John Benet of Polyngton' pays yearly to the grantor, an annual rent of 2*s.* 4*d.* which Alexander Storrour and Richard Storrour pay to the grantor in the same [vill], and an annual rent of 12*d.* which John Child of Polyngton' pays to the grantor in the same vill. Warranty. Sealing clause.[1] Witnesses: Thomas Dilcok, Richard Locster, Adam Benet, William Child, Robert Chereholme. At Polyngton. (*Ibid.*, No. 50.)

Rawcliff (Snaitb)

346. Sunday after the Deposition of St. Wilfrid the Bishop [Oct. 17], 1344. Release by Adam Wouderofe of Rouclyf' to Richard de Neusome, clerk, his heirs and assigns, of all his right and claim in an annual rent of 4*d.*, for an acre of moor lying in the territory of Rouclyf' in Inclesmore, which rent came to the grantor by inheritance after the death of John Wouderof', his father, and which acre of moor Richard had of the gift and feoffment of John, son of Henry de Tempelhyst, with all commons and easements belonging to the said acre of moor. Warranty. Sealing clause. Witnesses: Adam de Beltone, John de Gryngelay, Thomas de Hillum, clerk, John Hunter, William Godeknave. At Rouclyf'. (*Ibid.*, No. 51.)

Reedness

347. Grant by Thomas son of Adam de Rednesse to Warin, son of Nicholas, his heirs or assigns, for his homage and service, of the whole tenement with appurtenances in Rednesse, which he holds of the gift of Walter son of Robert de Rednesse; to hold to Warin, his heirs or assigns, of the grantor and his heirs freely and quietly in fee and inheritance, paying yearly to the grantor and his heirs 12*d.*—6*d.* at Whitsuntide and 6*d.* at Martinmas—for

---

[1] Seal: red wax, oval; a head to the sinister.

all services. Warranty. Sealing clause. Witnesses: Robert son of Ang'r, William son of Robert, Robert le Baylol, John son of Thomas, Ranulph son of Thomas, John son of Stephen, Walter son of Geoffrey. (*Archer-Houblon MSS.*, No. 404.)

348. Saturday in the feast of St. John ante portam Latinam, 30 Edward III [May 7, 1356]. Grant by Joan, widow of John de Bekyngham of Redenesse to Richard son of William de [C]rull of Swynflet, his heirs and assigns, of 10 acres of land with appurtenances in Redenesse, of which one acre lies in a field called Ryhyllcroft, and one and a half acres and half a rood lie in a field called Engbyk, and one acre and a half and half a rood lie in a field called Ryefeld, and one acre lies in a field called le Langfeld, and 3 acres and 3 roods lie in a field called Stokfeld, and one [acre] in a field called Newbrek; to hold to Richard, his heirs and assigns, of the chief lords of the fee. Warranty. Sealing clause.[1] Witnesses: William Gattnyst, John Aung', William de Swynflet, Thomas de Lathum, William de Swynflet, William Raynald, John son of James Aung'. At Redenesse. (*Ibid.*, No. 405.)

349. Oct. 4, 1390. Grant by John Kyrkeby of Cotenesse, Richard Dayuyll, and Hugh de Horsyngton of Athelyngflete to Robert Cussette of Redenesse, of a messuage, 17 acres of land with appurtenances in the vill and territory of Redenesse, of which 10 acres formerly belonged to Thomas Bekyngham of Redenesse and the other 7 acres to William Altofts of the same vill; to hold to Robert and the heirs of his body lawfully begotten, of the chief lords of the fee; remainder in default of lawful issue, to John Gouke of Athelyngflete and his heirs for ever; to hold of the chief lords of the fee. Alternate seals.[2] Witnesses: Thomas Aung' of Redenesse, Roger Stanfeld of the same, William Aung', Thomas de Halton, Robert Aung' of the same. At Redenesse. (*Ibid.*, No. 406.)

350. Three weeks after Easter, 11 Henry VI [May 3, 1433]. Final concord at Westminster between John Cerff, *quer.*, and William Scargyll, esq., *deforc.*, concerning a messuage, 4 tofts, 6 acres of land and 2½ acres of meadow with appurtenances in Redenesse. William quitclaims the said messuage and lands to John and his heirs for ever. John gives 100 marks of silver. (*Ibid.*, No. 407.)

Reighton

351. Grant and confirmation by Alice daughter of Benedict de Ricton to Simon de Cokefeld, his heirs and assigns, of 3 bovates of land with appurtenances in the territory of Ricton, lying

[1] Small dark green seal: oval, chipped; a bird vulning itself above a nest containing three small birds; legend not deciphered.
[2] Seal: small fragment of white wax.

towards the west of those 8 bovates of land which the grantor sought to obtain (*quesivi*) from Simon de Hal before the justices itinerant at York; she further grants 2 tofts lying in the vill of Ricton between the toft of William de Ergum, which Richard brother of Grene holds of the said William, and the road which leads to the church; in which tofts Robert, son of Hugh, and Warin formerly lived; to hold freely, quietly and peacefully of the grantor and his heirs, in ways and paths, in meadows and pastures and all other easements pertaining to the said vill, doing such forinsec service as pertains to 3 bovates of land of the same fee where 14 carucates make a knight's fee. Warranty. Sealing clause. Witnesses: Robert de Buterwic, Robert de Killinghom, Walter de Grendale, William de Hastorp, William de Ergum, Robert de Munceus, William de Neuill, William de Wyern, Geoffrey the butler (*pincerna*) of Hund', John Gerebric. (*Ibid.*, No. 413.)

352. Grant and confirmation by Hawys, daughter of Daniel de Righton, to Dom. Nicholas,[1] perpetual vicar of Righton, of a toft with a croft and an acre of land, with appurtenances, in the vill and fields of Righton; which toft lies between the toft of John Hyrnyg and the toft which belonged to Robert Sayer, and the croft lies between the croft of the said John and the croft which belonged to Walter son of Herbert; half of the acre of land lies in le Southdaylis between the land of the said Walter and the land which Ingram de Hale holds, and the other half lies in le Medelkiruis between the lands of the said Walter and Ingram; to hold to Dom. Nicholas, his heirs and assigns, freely and peacefully of the chief lord of the fee, in perpetuity. Warranty. Sealing clause.[2] Witnesses: John de Speton, Nicholas de Hale, William Gens', Ingram de Hale, Robert Hyngam. (*Ibid.*, No. 408.)

353. Grant and confirmation by William, son of Hawys, daughter of Danyel de Rychton, to Juliana, daughter of Richard son of Ralph de Rychton, of half a toft and croft, on the east, and half an acre of land, namely, one rood in le Medilkirwes and one rood in le Suthdayles, on the east and south, with the appurtenances in Rychton, which toft and croft and land the grantor had of the gift of the said Hawys, his mother; to hold the said half toft and croft and the half acre of land of the grantor and his heirs with all appurtenances, liberties and easements to the same tenement belonging for the term of her [Juliana's] life, paying yearly to the grantor and his heirs 1*d.* at Christmas for all secular services, exactions and demands. Warranty. Sealing clause. Witnesses: Nicholas de Hale, John de Speton, Dom.

---

[1] Nicholas de Swarby, vicar 1294–1325.

[2] Seal: white wax, small, diam. ⅞ in.; undeciphered.

Nicholas, vicar, John de le Hil, Robert Sayer, Ingram de Hale. (*Ibid.*, No. 409.)

354. Grant and confirmation by Adam son of William de Poclingeton to Richard de Hale and his heirs or assigns of half a toft in the vill of Ricton, namely, that half which lies near the toft of Robert le Neucomene on the west; also of half a bovate of land in the territory of the same vill, which lies near the land of the said Robert le Neucomene on the west; and of a rood of land which abuts on the ditch of Barbeldal, which lies near the land of the said Robert on the east; also of all right and claim in a toft and land which formerly belonged to Malger son of Augrym. Richard and his heirs and assigns to hold freely, quietly and peacefully, paying to the grantor and his heirs 22*d*. yearly—11*d*. at Whitsuntide and 11*d*. at Martinmas—and 5*d*. to the chief lords of the fee for all services, customs, exactions, and demands, suit of courts, liberties and easements, within the vill and without, pertaining to the said land and toft. Warranty. Sealing clause. Witnesses: Sir Ralph de Hale, knt., Peter de Monceus de Ricton, Gilbert Draitvil, Walter son of Hubert, John son of Ingram, John de Barbeldal of the same. (*Ibid.*, No. 410.)

355. Grant and confirmation by Thurstan de Matu[m] to Walter son of Warin de Ricton and his heirs of 9 bovates of land in Ricton, to be held in fee and hereditarily of the grantor and his heirs, in return for an annual rent of 7*s*. 6*d*., payable as follows: at Whitsuntide 22½*d*., the like sum at the feast of St. Peter Advincula, the like at the feast of St. Martin, and the like at the Purification of the B.V.M.; the lands to be quit of all other services and customs. Witnesses: Robert son of Mag[er], his brother Geoffrey de Hergum, Geoffrey Aguillun, Henry Siluer, Eustace de Muncel, Ralph his brother, Malger son of Geoffrey de Hergum, Simon his brother, Robert Talun, William de Bouint[on], Ralph, chaplain of Hergum, William, chaplain of Fleinesburg, Eustace de Ricton and three of his sons, Gilbert de Speton and his brother. (*Ibid.*, No. 411.)

356. Grant by Thurstan de Matham to Gilbert Beusyre of Ryhton of 13 bovates of land with appurtenances in the territory of Ryhton, to be held hereditarily to the same Gilbert, his heirs and assigns, with all appurtenances in meadows and feedings, in all places within the vill and without, and with all liberties, free customs and easements to the same pertaining; paying 10*s*. 10*d*. at four times in the year, in equal portions, namely, at the Purification of the B.V.M. 2*s*. 8½*d*., at Whitsuntide 2*s*. 8½*d*., at St. Peter ad vincula 2*s*. 8½*d*., and at Martinmas 2*s*. 8½*d*., for all secular services, exactions and demands. Warranty. Sealing clause. Witnesses: Robert son of Mauger, Geoffrey his brother, Geoffrey Ageyllun, Henry Sylver, Eustace de Munceus, Ralph

his brother, Malger son of Geoffrey de Hermyn, Symon his brother, Robert Ealun. (*Ibid.*, No. 412.)

357. Quitclaim by William son of William son of Walter the clerk of Rycton, for himself and his heirs, to Ingram de Hale, of all right and claim which he has or may have in the vill of Rycton, namely, in all the lands, tenements, tofts, crofts, rents, meadows, pastures, with all liberties, easements and escheats which either William his father, or Walter his grandfather, at any time held in the vill of Rycton of the fee of St. John of Beverley. Sealing clause.[1] Witnesses: Sir Ralph de Hale, knt., Peter le Mounceus de Rycton, Robert Sayer of the same, William de Ergom, Ernald de Hoketon, William of the same, John de Marton, Stephen, the clerk. (*Ibid.*, No. 414.)

358. Grant and confirmation by William son of Walter de Ricton to Stephen son of Thomas de Flixton of a piece of meadow on the east side of the grantor's croft, which contains in width 5 perches 3 feet and extends in length 22½ perches, and lies near the croft of Walter . . . h . . . i on the west; to hold of the grantor and his heirs to Stephen and his heirs and assigns freely, quietly and in peace, paying yearly to the grantor and his heirs 1*d.* at Easter for all services and demands. Warranty for said land with free entry and exit. Sealing clause. Witnesses: Sir Nicholas de Hale, Peter de Muncell, Richard de Hale, Gilbert son of William, Walter son of Hubert, Ralph son of Richard. (*Ibid.*, No. 415.)

359. Morrow of St. Matthew the Apostle [Sept. 22], 1330. Grant and confirmation by Alice sister and heir of Nicholas, son of Ingram de Hale, to John de Speton, senior, of 2 tofts, 2 bovates and 8 acres of land called forland, in Righton, and all rents and services in the same vill which descended to her by hereditary right after the death of her brother Nicholas. John de Speton, his heirs and assigns, to hold the tenements, rents and services .freely, quietly and peacefully of the chief lords of the fee in perpetuity. Warranty. Sealing clause.[2] Witnesses: Dom. Benedict, vicar of Righton, Richard Randolf, Nicholas de Hale, William Beausire, William del Hill, William le Hird, Thomas de Thirnum. At Righton. (*Ibid.*, No. 416.)

360. Feb. 24, 1331[-2]. Acquittance. Isabel, widow of Ingram de Hale of Righton and Alice her daughter and heir of Nicholas son of the said Ingram (*Alicia filia et heres Nicholai filii dicti Ingelrami*) have received from John de Speton, senior, from March 1, 1330[-1] to March 1, 1331[-2], four quarters of corn and maslin (*mixtilionis*), half a quarter of malt, a thousand turves

---

[1] Seal: yellowish-brown wax, diam. $1\frac{1}{10}$ ins.; four wedges arranged saltirewise; FIL WILLV . . . .

[2] Tag, but seal missing.

and 6s. 8d. in which he was bound to them by certain indentures. Sealing clause. At Richton. (*Ibid.*, No. 417.)

361. Wednesday the vigil of St. James the Apostle [July 24], 1336. Grant and confirmation by John de Speton, senior, to John de Sutton of Seterington and Alice, daughter of Ingram de Halle, his wife, of a toft in the vill of Righton, namely, that toft which Alice formerly leased of the grantor and which is enclosed by a ditch to the north; to hold for the term of their lives or for the lifetime of the survivor, paying yearly to the grantor or his heirs a rose in the season of roses for all services. After the deaths of John and Alice, reversion to the grantor and his heirs. Alternate seals.[1] At Righton. Witnesses: Dom. Benedict, vicar of the church of Righton, Nicholas de Halle, William Beausire, William del Hille, William le Hird, Thomas de Thirnam. (*Ibid.*, No. 418.)

362. Wednesday the vigil of St. James the Apostle [July 24], 1336. Grant and confirmation by John de Speton, senior, to John de Sutton of Seterington and Alice, daughter of Ingram de Halle, his wife, of 2 tofts [*as described in* No. 359]; to hold to them and their lawfully begotten heirs, and should they die without such heirs, reversion to the grantor and his heirs. Warranty. Sealing clause. Witnesses: Dom. Benedict, vicar of the church of Righton, Nicholas de Halle, William Beausire, William del Hill, William le Hird, Thomas de Thirnum, Richard Randolf. (*Ibid.*, No. 419.)

363. Invention of the Holy Cross [May 3], 1348. Grant and confirmation by Benedict, perpetual vicar of the chapel of Ryghton, to Nicholas de Hale of Ryghton, Margaret, his wife, and the heirs of their bodies lawfully begotten, of 5 bovates of land in the field of Ryghton, lying between the land of the abbot of Ryuauys on one side and the land of William Fraunces of Flaynburgh on the other; also of a messuage with 2 bovates of land which Robert son of Gilbert holds of the grantor in bondage, and one water mill newly built; to hold freely, quietly and in peace with all meadows and pastures and other appurtenances of the chief lords of the fee in perpetuity. If Nicholas and Margaret die without heirs of their bodies lawfully begotten, reversion and remainder to the true heirs of Nicholas. Warranty. Sealing clause.[2] Witnesses: Sir Marmaduke de Gryndall, Sir George Saluan, knts., John de Speton, Henry Malbis de Fyuele, William Beusir de Ryghton, William del Hylle of the same, John de Sutton of the same. (*Ibid.*, No. 420.)

---

[1] Seals: two of white wax, small, round; legend and device obliterated.
[2] Seal: red wax, round, diam. 1₁/₁₀ ins.; a sixfoil; ✠ CAPVT CERV[I] D[EI] . ✠.

364. Wednesday after St. Peter ad vincula [Aug. 5], 1349. Grant[1] and confirmation by Nicholas de Hale of Ryhgton to Benedict, vicar of Ryhgton, chaplain, and Thomas de Speton, senior, chaplain, and Thomas de Speton, son of John de Speton, chaplain, of all his capital messuage, except only his hall, and all the lands and tenements which he had by hereditary right after the death of his father; also a water mill, which he had of the gift of John de Speton, in the vill and territory of Ryhgton, with all the appurtenances, commodities and easements within the vill and without; to hold to them, their heirs and assigns, freely, quietly and peacefully in perpetuity, rendering to the chief lords of the fee the due and accustomed services. Warranty. Sealing clause. Witnesses: Sirs Marmaduke Conestable, Thomas de Sywardeby, Marmaduke de Grindale, knts., William de Bucton, John de Bucton, Thomas de Carthorp, Henry Malbish, John de Cawod. At Ryghton. (*Ibid.*, No. 421.)

365. Dec. 27, 10 Richard II [1386]. Lease by Thomas de Ryse of Beverley to John Ras of Ryghton, junior, of 2 pieces of ground and 2 bovates of land with le Gret Forland and all other appurtenances in the vill and territory of Ryghton, situate in manner and form as lately held by John de Sutton; John Ras and his assigns to hold the lands for the term of the life of Thomas de Ryse, paying yearly to Thomas or his assigns 8s. in equal portions at Whitsuntide and Martinmas. John to maintain the buildings in good repair during this period against wind and rain at his own cost and to return them in as good condition as when he received them, damage by fire or tempest (*igne alieno ac infortunio aerio*) excepted. If the rent is in arrears in part or whole for the space of forty days after the fixed terms, it shall be lawful for Thomas to distrain. Warranty. Alternate seals. At Ryghton. (*Ibid.*, No. 423.)

Rigton

366. [1301.] Indenture whereby it is stated that since an agreement had been sought between Ralph de Skreuyne of the one part and brother R, abbot of Fountains[2] and the convent of the same and Robert de Furneaus of the other part, by a writ of novel disseisin at York before John de Mettingham and the justices of the king's bench in the third week after Easter, 29 Edward son of Henry [1301], concerning the reasonable estovers in the woods of Ryggeton and Stayneburne which pertained to Ralph's free tenements in Wytheton[3] and Houby[4]; now it is agreed in the following manner, namely, that Ralph quit-

---

[1] Also, same day, appointment of John de Speton as attorney to deliver seisin. Seal: brown wax, diam. $\frac{7}{8}$ in.; two animals passant to dexter. (*Ibid.*, No. 422.)

[2] Robert Bishopton, 1290–1310.

[3] Weeton, par. Harewood.   [4] Hewby.

claims for himself and his heirs all rights and actions which he has in the same woods pertaining to his tenements, saving only to himself, his heirs or to the occupier of his tenements, one oak for all estovers of oak in Ryggeton yearly in perpetuity for *husbote*, and this with the concurrence of the foresters of Robert and the abbot, and with reasonable notification if they wish to be there, or without view of foresters but with due notice if they do not wish to be present. Alternate seals. Witnesses: Sirs John de Kirkeby, Henry de Boys, knts., Henry de Skreuine, William Faukes of Newall, William de Castelay, William de Farnelaye. (*Farnley Hall MSS.*, No. 63.)

Ripon

367. Monday, St. Andrew. 15 Edward son of Edward [Nov. 30, 1321]. Grant by Robert son of Simon de Ilkley to Alan his brother, of that burgage in the street of All Saints in Ripon, which lies between the burgage which once belonged to . . . .[1] and the burgage once belonging to . . . .; to hold to Alan and his lawfully begotten heirs, and should he die without heirs, reversion to grantor. Warranty. Sealing clause. Witnesses: Nicholas Hubert, esq., John Skayf, Peter de Malton, Richard Bercar', Robert de Slyngesby. At Ripon. (*Bramley MSS.*, No. 22.)

Roos

368. Wednesday after the Assumption of the B.V.M., 40 Edward III [Aug. 19, 1366]. Grant by Margaret le Skynnare to Walter *of the* Pole, of a messuage with appurtenances in Rosse which lies between the land of John le Steor on one side and the land of John Deye on the other and extends from the path leading to the church of Rosse towards Brompton as far as the land of William Gadde; to hold to Walter, his heirs and assigns, of the chief lords of the fee in perpetuity. Warranty. Sealing clause. Witnesses: Thomas Selyman, Thomas le Shephurde, William Graas, Richard Tolle, John Deye. At Rosse. (*Y.A.S.*, M^D 242, No. 2.)

Rotherham

369. Saturday the vigil of the Nativity of St. John the Baptist [June 23], 1347. Grant by Philip Cradok, son and heir of Richard Cradok, to William de Bradelay and Agnes his wife, of a selion of arable land with appurtenances lying in the fields of Markesburgh, between the lands of Cristiana called Litester, and abutting at one end on one Flete and at the other on the second Flete; to hold to William and Agnes, their heirs and assigns, freely, in fee and hereditarily in perpetuity; paying yearly to God and the Service of the Blessed and Glorious Virgin

---

[1] Deed very stained in parts. A copy of the original document, and notes relating to other deeds, on the back.

Mary of the church of Roderham a halfpenny at the Assumption for all secular services and demands. Warranty. Sealing clause. Witnesses: John son of John de Mappels, Simon Litester, John Menewot. At Roderham. (*Duke of Leeds*, Hornby Castle Muniments, Rotherham, No. 2.)

370. Wednesday after Trinity Sunday [June 7], 1363. In the name of God, Amen. I, Simon de Mersburgh make my testament in this manner. First I commend my soul to God, Blessed Mary and all the saints and my body to buried in the churchyard of Blessed Mary of Roderham, and my best mortuary. Item: to the neighbouring convent (*convocat'*) 30s. on the day of my burial. Item: to be distributed among the poor, 40s. Item: 12 lb. of wax and candles. Item: to any one of the altars of the church of Roderham 12d. Item: for the fabric of the same church one mark. Item: for the chapel of Holy Trinity, Roderham, 3 marks. Item: to any one of the chaplains of the church of Roderham, 12d. Item: to the chaplain of the parish of the said church 18d. Item: to the clerk, 6d. Item: to the gild of Holy Trinity of Roderham 5 marks. Item: to Dom John, vicar of Roderham one mark. Item: to Richard, my brother, one quarter of rye and one quarter of oats. Item: to the brethren of Tekil,[1] 20s. Item: to Beatrice, my daughter, 2 quarters of rye and 2 quarters of oats and 20s. Item: to Lettice, my daughter, 2 quarters of rye and 2 quarters of oats and one mark. Item: to John Symon and Robert and John, son of Deb', 4s. each. Item: to Richard Arter 4s. Item: to Simon Cristanson, one quarter of rye. Item: to the chaplain at Selby for a service for my soul, 14 marks. Item: to . . . . el de Roucliffe, 2s. and the remainder of my goods to the monastery of the same [?] for the health of my soul, according to the wishes of my executors, namely, Agnes, my wife, John, my son, Adam, my son whom I now appoint. At Mersburgh. (*Ibid.*, No. 3.)

371. St. Mary Magdalen, 9 Richard II [July 22, 1385]. Quitclaim by John de Marsburgh of Roderam to Adam his brother, of the same, and Alice his wife, and their lawfully begotten heirs, of all the tenements and the buildings thereon which belonged to Paul Hanson in the vill of Roderam, in le Briggate between the tenement of Richard de Palden on the north and the tenement which once belonged to John de Whistan on the south; he also quitclaims all right in the lands and tenements with appurtenances which he had of the gift of William Bugg, clerk, and William Wikyn in le Brokegate of the same vill between the said tenement of Paul on the west and a tenement called le Impezerd on the east; remainder to the right heirs of Adam and Alice should they die without lawfully begotten heirs. Sealing clause. Wit-

[1] Tickhill.

nesses: John de Palden, Thomas Bakster, William Wykyn, Richard de Palden. At Roderam. (*Ibid.*, No. 4.)

372. Whitsunday [June 4], 1430. Grant[1] by John Wraby of Roderham to Richard Lyster otherwise Dolfyn, of the same, his heirs and assigns, of a tenement in a street called Pontis between the tenement once belonging to Robert Lyster on one side and the road leading to the water of the Don on the other and abutting at one end on the highway and at the other on a certain wood of yew and hawthorn (*taxum et sinum arbores*) and Milnegrene; to hold to Richard, his heirs and assigns, of the chief lords of the fee. Sealing clause.[2] Witnesses: John Birlay, draper, John Bolom, William Wolhius, John Kyrk, bailiff, John Dolfyn, baker. At Roderham. (*Ibid.*, No. 5.)

373. Trinity Sunday [June 12], 1435. Indenture whereby John Mersburghte of Roderham grants and demises to the abbot and convent of Rufford a messuage in Roderham lying between the house of the rector of a moiety of the church on one side and the messuage of St. Mary on the other; to hold to the abbot and convent and their successors or assigns from Whitsuntide next for the full term of 17 years following, free of rent; during which term and at the conclusion thereof John agrees to pay all expenses and to maintain and repair the buildings whenever necessary. Warranty. Alternate seals.[3] At Roderham. (*Ibid.*, No. 7.)

374. Nov. 20, 38 Henry VI [1459]. Be hit knowyn to all Crysten peple that wee Thabott[4] of Rufford, lorde of Rodurham, John Clarell of the parysh of Rodurham, squyer, Thomas Wortlay of Rodurham, squyer, Sir William Kelenvyker of Rodurham, Sir Richard Belgh of the same towne, chauntere preste of the Holy Crosse, Sir Richard Galbert, proketor of the Kyrke of Rodurham, Sir William Dolfyn of the same towne, chauntere preste of oure Lady, Robert Dolfyn, baxter, John Dolfyn, lytster, John Dolfyn, rasursmyth, Robert of the hyll, fysher, William Walker, walker, John of the hyll, lytster, William of Burlay, vyntener, John Sylvester, baylyff of the same towne, Richard Wylock, the kynges baylyff, William Gurre, yoman, William Harryngton, fysher, William Swathe, spycer, John Ullay, sherman, Thomas Smyth, corveser, Richard Bokkyng, glover, Richard Ullay, sherman, John Pye, barker, Robert Berker, berker, John Bocher, iren-monger, Thomas Parker, draper, Ralph Wylbram, hardewareman,

---

[1] Quitclaim of the same by John Povay of Barbotthall to Richard Dolfyn, *lyster*, dated St. Barnabas [June 11], 1430, and witnessed by John Baddes-worth, William Wolhouse, John Birlay, draper, John Merkesburgh, John Bolom. (*Ibid.*, No. 6.)

[2] Seals: four, of black wax, on two tongues; undeciphered.

[3] Seal: blob of red wax.

[4] The abbot.

Laurence Fernlay, mercer, John of Byrlay, bocher, Richard Faukener, yoman, and Henry Tayler, mercer, all of the same towne of Roderham, in depressyng of wrong and enforsyng of right knolage, certefye and here wytnes that one, John of Marsburgh, sumtyme called John of Marsburgh thelder, was saysyd of certen lande and tenements in the townes and feldes of Rodurham and Marsburgh in his desmesne as in fee, and so seised of the same landes enfeffed William Kynwelmirsh and Thomas Smyth, clerkes, and one John of Marsburgh then called John of Marsburgh the yonger, cosyn to the forsaid John of Marsburgh thelder, that is to say, son to Adam of Marsburgh, brother to the forsayd John, thelder, to the use and profyte of the said John of Marsburgh the yonger, be a dede and seisin lyuered ther uppon, be force of which feffement the said William Kynwelmarsh and Thomas Smyth and John Marsburgh the yonger, were seised of the hole landes that were to the said John of Marsburgh thelder; and of ij meses in Rodurham, parcell of the forsaid landes, wherof thaton is set be twix a mese that longes to the chauntere of oure Lady on the west partie and a mese that is parcell of the personage of Rodurham on the este partie, and that on hede buttes upon the Kyrkyerde of Rodurham, and that other hede upon the hie way, and that other mese is set in Brokegate betwix a mese that longes to the chauntere of the holy Crosse on the Este partie and the broke on the west partie, and thaton hede buttes upon a mese of the abbottes of Rufford, and that other hede on the hye way; the said John of Marsburgh the yonger, cosyn to the said John of Marsburgh thelder, contenned pesible possession withowte enterupcon of any person or persons all his lyfe tyme and had issue, John of Marsburgh that nowe is, and dyed, aftre whos deth the said John of Marsburgh that nowe is, as son and heir to John of Marsburgh the yonger, entered and contenned possession . . . .[1] for more clere evidence and notyce to . . . . credence be . . yeven that this premysses be true, Wee the forsayd [names as above] and Iche of hus syngulerle to this present oure wrytyng haue sette oure seales.[2] Yeven the xx day of November the yere of the reign of Kyng Henry the sext aftre the conquest xxxviij. (*Ibid.*, No. 8.)

375. Sept. 20, 14 Henry VIII [1522]. Quitclaim by Robert Bate of Rotherham to Anne Lister, of all right in all those lands and tenements with appurtenances in Rotheram, Brynsforth and Marsburgh in co. York, which he recently had and claimed by right of Elizabeth, late his wife, and which once belonged to John Marsburgh. Sealing clause.[3] (*Ibid.*, No. 9.)

[1] Holes in the deed.

[2] Tongues for seven seals, three blobs of red wax on No. 3.

[3] Seal: fragment of brown wax: the letter B.

J

376. St. Martin the Bishop, 21 Richard II [Nov. 11, 1397]. Grant by John Brompton of Roderham to Thomas Bolloke of Graynhyll in the parish of Norton, of a piece of land with buildings thereon in Roderham in le Brygegate, with gardens and all other appurtenances; to hold to Thomas, his heirs and assigns, of the chief lords of the fee, freely etc., in perpetuity. Warranty. Sealing clause.[1] Witnesses: John Mersburgh, John Bolom, William Wollhaws, Ralph Pouey, John Wrauby. At Roderham. (*Ibid.*, No. 10.)

377. Friday before SS. Simon and Jude [Oct. 27], 1402, 4 Henry IV. Bond by John Paldene, chaplain, son of Richard de Paldene of Roderham, to John Wrauby, or his attorney who shall show this paper, in 20 marks to be paid at Roderham at the following Easter. Sealing clause.[2]

Condition: if John Wrauby shall hold and enjoy a messuage with buildings thereon, the bond to be void. (*Ibid.*, No. 11.)

378. Monday before the Exaltation of the Cross, 6 Henry V [Sept. 12, 1418]. Grant by Thomas Bullok of Grenehill to Richard Dolfyn of Roderham, dyer (*tinctor*), of a parcel of his toft which lies in Roderham in the street called Pont' between a tenement of John Povay on the east and a place called Mylnegrene on the west, and abutting at one end on the highway towards the north and at the other on the grantor's toft towards the south, which toft the grantor had with all his other lands and tenements in the territory of Roderham of the gift and grant of Thomas de Wombwell; to hold to Richard, his heirs and assigns, freely [*etc.*], paying yearly to the grantor and his heirs and assigns 2*d.* at the usual terms for all secular services. Warranty. Sealing clause.[3] Witnesses: Ralph Povay, John Mersburgh, bailiff of Roderham, John Bolome, John Wrauby. At Roderham. (*Ibid.*, No. 12.)

379. St. Peter ad vincula, 1 Henry VI [Aug. 1, 1423]. Grant by John Anabyll of le Halgh[4] to Thomas Clarell, junior, esq., and John Marsburgh of Roderham, of all his lands and tenements with appurtenances in co. York; to hold to them, their heirs and assigns, of the chief lords of the fee. Warranty. Sealing clause. Witnesses: John Bolom of Roderham, John Wraby of the same, John Palden of Grysbroke, William Zhole once of le Halgh, John Carter of the same. At le Halgh. (*Ibid.*, No. 13.)

380. Aug. 20, 1 Henry VI [1423]. Quitclaim by Simon Mersburgh to John Mersburgh, his kinsman, of all right in a messuage with appurtenances in Roderham lying between the messuage belonging to the Service of Blessed Mary on the west

---

[1] Seal: red wax; gem; the letter R.

[2] Seal: yellow wax, diam. $\frac{7}{8}$ in.; two interlaced triangles enclosing a leopard's head.

[3] Seal: red wax, small; the letter R.

[4] Haugh.

and the messuage once belonging to the house of the rector of Roderham on the east and abutting at one end on the churchyard of the church of Roderham, and at the other on the highway. Warranty. Sealing clause.[1] Witnesses: John West, John de Byrley, John Dolfyn, William Wolhous, John Bolom. At Roderham. (*Ibid.*, No. 14.)

381. St. Giles [Sept. 1], 1429. Indenture by which Richard Dronfeld and Richard Bete, chaplain, grant to John Wraby and Agnes, his wife, a messuage in the street called Pontis in Roderham and 3 acres of land lying in divers places in the fields of Mersburgh, and a parcel of garden once belonging to Stephen del Karr, with free entry and exit through a messuage once belonging to the same Stephen, which John Wraby recently acquired from Stephen; and the messuage lies between the messuage of John Mersburgh on one side and the messuage of Richard del Abdy on the other, and abuts at one end on le Ympezerde and at the other on the highway; and the parcel of garden lies between the barn once belonging to the said Stephen and le Ymperzerd and abuts on the land of John Mersbergh and on the said garden [*sic*], which contains 8 ells in breadth from its boundaries; and of the 3 acres, one lies above Mouselay near Morewodestabill' between the land of Thomas Rerysby, knt. on one side and the land of John Robynson on the other and abuts on the highway at one end above the land of the said Thomas, and another acre lies between the land of Thomas on both sides and abuts on Mersburghmore at both ends, and the third acre lies above Hertlay between the land of Thomas Rerysby and the land recently in the tenure of Simon Mersburgh and abuts at one end on le Keryng and at the other on the land of the said Thomas; to hold with all appurtenances to John and Agnes for the term of their lives of the chief lords of the fee; and after their deaths remainder in default of issue successively to the following and their lawfully begotten heirs: Joan their daughter; John son of John Wraby; Alice daughter of John Wraby for the term of her life; John son of Alice; Agnes daughter of Alice; Joan daughter of Alice; the right heirs of John Wraby in perpetuity. Warranty. Sealing clause.[2] Witnesses: John Kyrk, bailiff, John Mersburgh, John Bolom, William Wolhous, John Birlay, draper. At Roderham. (*Ibid.*, No. 15.)

Scaggletborpe

382. Friday after St. Catherine the Virgin [Nov. 26], 1406, 8 Henry [IV]. Grant by William de Garton of Ellerburn to Philip Barker of Malton and Margaret, his wife, of 2 messuages with appurtenances in the vill of Scakilthorpe, of which one messuage

---

[1] Seal: black wax, broken; part of a shield of arms in a cusped border; undeciphered.

[2] Seals: two, of red wax, both bearing the letter R.

lies between the tenement of Ralph, Baron de Graistock on the south and the tenement of William Wetwang on the north, and the other lies between the grantor's tenements on both sides; he also grants all his lands in the territories of Scakilthorpe and Rillyngton; to hold to Philip and Margaret for the term of their lives or for the lifetime of the survivor, rendering the accustomed services to the chief lords of the fee; after their deaths remainder to, (1) William Barker, their son, and his lawful heirs, and in default of lawful issue in each case to, (2) Thomas Barker, brother of William, (3) John Barker, brother of Thomas, (4) the right heirs of John Palmer. Warranty. Sealing clause.[1] Witnesses: Thomas Foxoles of Setryngton, William Lokton of the same, John Rawlynson of Rillyngton, Richard Redenesse, Hugh Filay of the same. (*Y.A.S.*, M^D 117, No. 2.)

Sedbergh

383. Thursday the morrow of St. John the Baptist, 14 Edward son of Edward [June 25, 1321]. Bond.[2] Walter de Hurworthe, rector of a moiety of the church of Sedbergh, Thomas de Faghside, William de Brig, Thomas son of Thomas, and William Blaykeling hold themselves bound to Thomas de Thornton and William de Siggeswik, their heirs and executors in 4 sacks (*sakes*) of good wool *e uette* which is called *Schapman War*, to be paid to Thomas and William, or to one of them, at Sedbergh in Lonesdale, one at Trinity next and one each year thereafter at Trinity until the 4 sacks be paid. Sealing clause. Witnesses: William de Clapham, Adam de Doubiging, Richard de Burgh, Gregory de Burton, Thomas de Lund. At Sedbergh in Lonesdale. (*Farnley Hall MSS.*, No. 64.)

Sessay

384. Inspeximus by Marmaduke Darelle lord of Ceszay of a charter of William Darelle, his ancestor, by which he granted for himself and his heirs to John de Hoby of Hetoun, Thomas Maunselle of the same, and Richard Bygot' of the same and their heirs, common pasture from the north part of Butrelle strete as the road goes from beyond Butrelle strete between Hetoun and Daltoun, and from the said road to the water called Iselbeck; he [William Darell] also granted to the same John, Thomas and Richard, their heirs and assigns, for himself and his heirs, that after the corn and hay had been taken in the field of Ceszay, on the northern side of the vill and Ceszaybeck towards Hetoun, they should have common pasture for themselves, their heirs and men, for all manner of their animals; and that they should have common in the meadow called Paddocker in time of *warancie*[3]

---

[1] Seal: brown wax, diam. ½ in.; letter R between two stars.

[2] In French.

[3] *Warancia*, a warren; *warrencio*, to place land in the status of a warren.
          —*Med. Latin Word List.*

and in other times after the hay had been lifted; and that they should have common in the meadow of Walterker after the hay had been lifted; he also granted to them and their heirs for himself and his heirs that they might go anywhere between the meadow of Walterker and Lestlyngthorne without any impediment just as in their own common at all times and hours without prohibition (*defensio*) there, except where corn or hay was growing; and for this grant John, Thomas and Richard, their heirs and men, paid for their animals' herbage, namely for each large beast (*grosso bestio*) 1*d.*, and for 5 sheep 1*d.*, yearly at the Feast of Holy Trinity to William and his heirs for ever, and should do for William and his heirs one boon work for one day yearly in the autumn, and should also provide for William and his heirs their ploughs twice yearly, namely, for one day's ploughing at the winter sowing and another at the spring sowing, and with their harrows in like manner to harrow twice yearly; and they should have one other day of work for the said William and his heirs: and the said John, Thomas and Richard, their heirs and men, should grind the corn growing on their lands of the fee of Ey at the grantor's mill at Ceszay to the 7th measure (*vas*), and do all the aforesaid services which pertain to the manor of Ceszay in no other place; and if the said mill was not able to grind through lack of water, then it should be lawful for them to grind their corn elsewhere, without contradiction by William or his heirs, during the lack of water: and if any of these liberties had not been fully used he granted for him and his heirs that these might be enjoyed without contradiction; and if John, Thomas and Richard or their heirs or men should suffer any distraint by which they incurred loss or damage, it should be lawful for them to withdraw their services until they had full amends. Which charter of the aforesaid William Darelle . . . .[1] (*Y.A.S.*, M^D 182, No. 52.)

385. Saturday after Epiphany [Jan. 13], 1358[-9]. Grant by William de Mapilton', rector of Ceszay, to Marmaduke Darelle and Alice, his wife, of 2 messuages with gardens and crofts, in the vill and territory of Ceszay, and with the dovecots belonging to the messuages; he also grants common pasture for their animals in all the pastures of Ceszay except le Ragarthe; also a reasonable supply of wood (*racionabilia estoveria*) from the woods of Ceszay for burning, lighting and repairs on the messuages, as decided by the foresters; which messuages the grantor had of the gift and feoffment of Marmaduke; to hold of the chief lords of the fee. Warranty. Sealing clause. Witnesses: John Darelle, John de Malton', William Attewelle, John de Stapilton', John Courper. At Ceszay. (*Y.A.S.*, M^D 153, No. 11.)

386. April 18, 14 Henry VI [1436]. Indenture witnessing grant and confirmation by Edmund Darelle of Cessay, knt., to

---

[1] Bottom of deed cut off.

George de Etton', William Willesthorp', esq., Henry Wyllestorp', clerk, William Darelle of Mowegrene and Robert Crosse, esq., and William Barry, esq., of his manors of Cessay, Eldmere, Dalton, Thurkylby and Broddesworth with appurtenances; and all other lands which the grantor has in Crakhalle, Heton', Middilton', Catton' on Swale, Harlesay and Thornton' on the Moor near Allerton, and elsewhere in co. York; he also grants all lands, tenements with appurtenances in the city and suburbs of York; to hold to George, William, Henry, William, Robert and William, their heirs and assigns, of the chief lords of the fees. Warranty. Sealing clause.[1] Witnesses: Richard Pykering, knt., Laurence Baxby, Walter Calverlay, John Willisthorp'. (*Y.A.S.*, M[D] 182, No. 54.)

387. Feb. 26, 15 Henry VI [1436-7]. Appointment by Isabel, widow of Edmund Darelle, knt., of William Crauford, knt., as her attorney to take seisin from the sheriff of York, of a third part of two manors, 60 and 10 messuages, 2 water mills, 80 and 24 and 4 acres of land, 123 acres of meadow, 50 and 6 acres of wood, 1,100 acres of pasture, 30s. and 4s. and 9d. rent,[2] with appurtenances in Sessay, Broddisworth and Heton', all of which she receives by deed of gift in the king's court, wherefor she shall hold nothing against Henry Willisthorp', clerk, William Darelle of Mowgrene, Robert Crosse and William Barre, by the judgements of the same court. Sealing clause.[3] (*Ibid.*, No. 55.)

388. 17 April, 17 Henry VI [1439]. Grant by John Colynson' son and heir of Edmund Colyn of Longnewton, to John Coupeland of Sessay, of 3 acres of land and appurtenances in the territory of Sessay; to hold to John Coupeland, his heirs and assigns, of the chief lord. Warranty. Sealing clause.[4] Witnesses: Robert Skelton', William Colynson of Sessay, John Smyth of the same. At Sessay. (*Y.A.S.*, M[D] 153, No. 12.)

389. Oct. 20, 20 Henry VI [1441]. Appointment by Ranald Paron and Emma, his wife, of John Heton and Ranald Thomlyson as their attorneys to deliver full and peaceful seisin to Isabel Darelle, widow of Edmund Darelle, knt., of all the lands, tenements, rents, services with appurtenances which Ranald and Emma have in the vill and territory of Sessay; with their agreement and goodwill to whatever the attorneys shall do in their name. Sealing clause.[5] Witnesses: William Barre, Henry Maunselle, William Chilton' of Dalton, Thomas Ka of the same, Thomas Thomlynson of Heton. (*Ibid.*, No. 13.)

---

[1] Seal: red wax; a cowled head to the sinister.

[2] 1 *li.* written above the line.

[3] Seal: red wax, not deciphered.

[4] Seal: red wax, diam. ½ in.; a dog's head to the dexter.

[5] Two seals of red wax: (1) possibly the letter W surrounded by a circlet of leaves; (2) octagonal, undeciphered.

390. Monday before SS. Simon and Jude, 20 Henry VI [Oct. 23, 1441]. Release by William Colynson' of Yarome[1] to Dame Isabel Darelle, widow of Edmund Darelle, knt., of all right which he has in all the lands, tenements, rents, services with appurtenances which recently belonged to Edmund Colynson', his father, in the vill and territory of Sessay; neither the said John nor his heirs, nor any of his name to have any claim to the lands. Sealing clause.[2] Witnesses: [*as to the preceding deed*]. At Sessay. (*Y.A.S.*, M^D 182, No. 56.)

391. Feb. 6, 23 Henry VI [1444–5]. Quitclaim by Christopher Boyntone and John Coupland and their heirs to Dame Elizabeth Darelle, widow of Edward Darelle, knt., of all right which they have in 3 acres of land with appurtenances in the fields and lordship of Sesay, which 3 acres once belonged to Edmund Colynson of Longfeseton'. Warranty. Sealing clause.[3] Witnesses: Richard Weltden', Hugh Forster, William Pikeryng, John Danby, chaplain. At Sadbery.[4] (*Y.A.S.*, M^D 153, No. 14.)

392. Aug. 9, 26 Henry VI [1448]. Grant by Thomas Smythe of York, chaplain, to Robert Skelton' of Cessay, *husbandman*, of all his tenement and 4 acres of land and meadow in Ceszay, which tenement lies between the land of George Darelle on both sides, and lengthways from the highroad to Ceszay in front to the close of William Barre at the back; to hold to Robert Skelton, his heirs and assigns, of the chief lords of the fee. Warranty. Sealing clause. Witnesses: George Darelle, William Barre, knts., John Richardson, John Robynson, William Mitlawe, *yeomen*. At Ceszay. (*Ibid.*, No. 15.)

393. Aug. 22, 2 Henry VII [1486]. General release and quitclaim by Robert Foster of Cessay in co. York, yeoman, to Thomas Darelle, esq., of all actions, quarrels, demands [*etc.*]. Sealing clause. (*Y.A.S.*, M^D 182, No. 57).

Settrington

394. The first Sunday in Lent, 1312 [Feb. 13, 1312–3]. Lease by Adam son of Alexander Calm of Seterington to Hugh Palmer of Seterington, his heirs and assigns, of a toft in the vill of Seterington, which lies between the toft of Roger del Frith and the toft which belonged to Richard Dorant; also all the land which the grantor has, with a meadow in the territory of the same vill, namely, 5 roods lying in that part (*loco*) of the fields which is called le Graes, in length from the cultivated land of

---

[1] Yarm.

[2] Seal: red wax; crossed lines.

[3] Seals: two of red wax: (1) broken; (2) diam. ⅞ in.; possibly an eagle or hawk.

[4] Sedbury, par. Gilling.

Henry de Rillington as far as Cliffe[1] (*ad cliffum*), and one rood above Cliffe (*super cliffum*), and 5 roods on the *assylandes* and half an acre of land in Cliffe (*Cliffo*); to hold to Hugh, his heirs and assigns, freely [*etc.*] of the chief lords of the fee, paying yearly to them 21*d.*, half at Whitsuntide and half at Martinmas, for all secular services, exactions and demands. Warranty. Sealing clause. Witnesses: Robert de Bucketon', Clement *super* Grene, Wilfrid Stull', Thomas ad Molendinum, William Chaumberl', Henry de Rillington, Thomas Witeheued. At Seterington. (*Y.A.S.*, M[D] 117, No. 1.)

Sberburn (E.IR.)

395. Sunday after St. Catherine the Virgin [Nov. 27], 1345. Quitclaim by Thomas son of Robert Birkebayn of Schirburn in Harfordelyth, his heirs and assigns, to Dom. Richard Hardyng of Wynteringham, chaplain, of all right in a toft with appurtenances in Schirburn, which lies between the toft of Adam de Everingham on the north side and the common lane on the west, and between a toft which the grantor holds of the Brethren of the Hospital of St. John of Jerusalem on the south as far as the common way on the west [east ?]. Warranty. Sealing clause.[2] Witnesses: Thomas Brete of Brumton, William Duchty of Schirburn, Thomas his son, Robert called Storor, Richard de Neuham. At Schirburn in Harfordelyth. (*Y.A.S.*, M[D] 118, No. 1).

396. Wednesday after St. Agatha, 1357 [Feb. 7, 1357–8]. Grant[3] by Richard de Wynteringham, rector of the church of Langton, to John Poly, his heirs and assigns, of a toft [*as in the preceding deed*]. Warranty. Sealing clause.[4] Witnesses: William Brett' of Brumpton, Thomas Dowghti of Schirburn, Richard de Newham, Thomas de Barkendale, William Barker of the same. At York. (*Ibid.*, No. 2.)

397. Thursday in Easter week [April 14], 1379. Grant by Robert Birkebayne of K . . . u[5] to John Poli of Schirburne in Herforhtlith of a toft with appurtenances in Schirburne which lies between the toft of Sir William Latimer on the north and the toft of Robert Toller on the south; to hold to John, his heirs and assigns, of the chief lords of the fee; he also grants to John an acre of meadow with appurtenances within and without the vill

---

[1] It is not clear whether in the first two instances " the cliff " is meant, or the locality Cliffe, as in the third.

[2] Seal: reddish brown wax; two interlacing squares enclosing a device, undeciphered.

[3] Quitclaim of the same to the same by Richard son of Robert de Neuton, nephew of Richard de Wynteringham, dated Feb. 11, 1357–8. An oval seal of black wax, undeciphered. (*Ibid.*, No. 3.)

[4] Seal: black wax; broken.

[5] Probably Kekham, as in No. 400; Kirkham ?

of Schirburne, lying towards the sun (*sole*) next to the meadows of Ralph, Baron de Graystoc and extending from the ditch called Hengedic to the water of Derewent. Warranty. Sealing clause.[1] Witnesses: Peter Ledelady, Richard Hydon, John Lacy, Robert Golde, John Smyth, William Barker, Adam Barker, John Lefe. At Schirburne. (*Ibid.*, No. 4.)

398. Whit Sunday [May 13], 1380. Grant by Robert Moller of Schirburn in Herfordhlith, son of William Moller, to Thomas son of Ellen de Schirburn, of a messuage and buildings thereon, with appurtenances in Schirburne, which the grantor once had of the gift and feoffment of William Moller, his father, and which extends in length from the common way in Schirburne towards the south, as far as the land of St. John of Jerusalem towards the north, and in breadth between the land of Lord de Latymer on the west, and on the east partly adjoining the land of the same lord and partly along that of Robert de Schirburn; to hold freely [*etc.*] of the chief lords of the fee. Warranty. Sealing clause.[2] Witnesses: Robert de Schirburne, Thomas Dughty, John Puly, Peter Ledelady, Richard Ython. At Schirburn' in Harfordhlith. (*Ibid.*, No. 5.)

399. Mar. 19, 1395[-6], 19 Richard II. Grant by Thomas son of Hugh de Snaynton to John Tekill of Schirburn, of all that messuage with buildings thereon, with appurtenances which he had of the gift and feoffment of Thomas son of Ellen de Schirburn', and which lies [*as described in preceding deed*]; to hold freely [*etc.*] of the chief lords of the fee. Warranty. Sealing clause. Witnesses: Henry Thomson, John Dughty, John Poly, Robert Toller.· At Schirburn. (*Ibid.*, No. 6.)

400. Friday before St. Gregory the Pope, 1395 [Mar. 10, 1395-6]. Grant by John Poly of Kekham to Richard Poly, his son, of Schirburn' in Herforthlyth, of a toft with appurtenances in Schirburn', which lies between the toft of Lord de Nevell' on the north side and the toft of John Tekell on the south; also grants an acre of land [*as described in grant 2, No.* 397]; to hold of the chief lords of the fee. Warranty. Sealing clause. Witnesses: Robert Laundmot, William Toller, Robert Brett of Brunton, William Barnby, Robert Toller. At Schirburn'.

401. April 30, 22 Henry VI [1444]. Grant by Robert Faweder son of John Faweder of Shirburne to Richard Cusson of the same, of a toft which lies between the toft of Lord de Nevell on the north and the toft of William Lutte on the south, and an acre of land [*as in grant 2, No.* 397]; to hold freely [*etc.*] of the chief lords of the fee. Warranty. Sealing clause. Wit-

---

[1] Seal: red wax, diam. $\frac{7}{10}$ in.; a bird surrounded by, and with a spray of leaves in its beak.

[2] Seal: brown wax, diam. $\frac{1}{2}$ in.; three figures, possibly the Crucifixion with the figures of the B.V.M, and St. John; or the Transfiguration.

nesses: Robert de Malton, John Shirburn, John Landemott, junior, Richard Smyht, senior, Richard Smyth, junior. At Shirburn. (*Ibid.*, No. 8.)

402. Jan. 10, .. 9 Edward IV [1469-70].[1] Grant by Richard Cusson of Scherburn' to John Lawmlay of [*the lands described in the preceding deed*]. Warranty. Sealing clause. Witnesses: John Westile, John Pulle, John Welburn, Alan Maltton, John Buesse, senior, Thomas Screyssenar. At Scherburn. (*Ibid.*, No. 9.)

403. June 24, 21 Edward IV [1481]. Quitclaim by John Lute, citizen of London to William Malton, of all right in all that messuage with appurtenances in Shirburn which lies between the land of Sir Richard . . . .[2] Gloucester on the east, and the tenement of St. John of Jerusalem on the west, and from the highway in front towards . . . . of the vill as far as the land of Richard Shirburn towards the north at the back. Warranty. Sealing clause. Witnesses: Richard Sherburn', John Forthe, Robert Otway, Thomas Watson, Christopher Gray. At Shirburn'. (*Ibid.*, No. 10.)

Snaith

404. Quitclaim by Agnes widow of Peter son of Thomas de Snayhte in her widowhood and own right, to John son of Matilda of the same, his heirs and assigns, for a certain sum of money given to her in need, of all right which she has in that toft and croft which was her dower after the death of Peter, in the vill of Snayhte, lying between the toft of the said John towards the east and the toft once of William, son of Juliana. Warranty. Sealing clause.[3] Witnesses: John son of Thomas the clerk of Snayht, Thomas son of Adam the tailor (*cissor*), John son of Thomas son of Nicholas, Edmund the tanner (*tanator*), John Gilmain. (*Y.A.S.*, M[D] 153, No. 17.)

405. Quitclaim by Agnes widow of Peter son of Thomas de Snayhte, in her widowhood and own right, to John son of Matilda de Snayht, his heirs and assigns, for a sum of money given for entry, of all right which she has in respect of her dower in a third part of a selion of land lying in the west field of Snayht, between the land of Adam son of Adam Joice and the land of Richard son of Peter son of Thomas, and abutting on the land of the said Adam and on the toft of the said John. Warranty. Sealing clause. Witnesses: John son of Thomas the clerk, William son of Thomas the clerk, Thomas son of Adam the tailor, John son of Thomas son of Nicholas, Edmund son of William the tanner (*tanator*), Hugh son of Alan. (*Ibid.*, No. 18.)

406. Quitclaim by Agnes widow of Peter son of Thomas de Snayht, in her widowhood and own right, to John son of Matilda

---

[1] The deed is badly rubbed.
[2] Document rubbed in places.
[3] Seal: oval brownish white wax, blurred and undeciphered.

de Snayht, his heirs and assigns, for a sum of money given to her in her need, of all right in respect of her dower following the death of Peter son of Thomas, in a third part of that toft with buildings upon it which Peter sold to Peter de Saltmarsh, which lies in length and breadth in the vill of Snayhte, between the toft of the same John and the toft which once belonged to William son of Juliana. Warranty. Sealing clause. Witnesses [*as to the preceding deed*]. (*Ibid.*, No. 19.)

407. Easter Eve, 4 Edward son of Edward III (*sic*) [April 7, 1329–30]. Grant by Thomas son of John le Littester of Snaythe to John Lely of Carleton', clerk, and Joan, his wife, and Geoffrey son of the same John and Joan, their heirs and assigns, of a messuage with appurtenances in Snaythe, which lies between the messuage of John son of John le Warner on one side and the messuage once of Adam the tailor (*le taillur*) on the other, and extends in width next to the king's highway for 2½ perches and 2 feet, and in the middle for 2½ perches and 2 feet, and at the end towards the south for 1½ perches and 1 foot, and in length for 10½ perches and 3½ feet, and 3½ feet in width in one direction from the said messuage as far as the broad way between the messuages of the said John le Warner and Adam; to hold to John, Joan and Geoffrey, their heirs and assigns, of the chief lords of the fee. Warranty. Sealing clause. Witnesses: Lawrence de Heck, John de Snaythe, William his brother, Thomas the tailor of Snaythe, William Parheued of Couwyk, Adam son of Hugh de Carleton, Thomas son of Henry de Cowyk, William Mons of the same. At Snaythe. (*Ibid.*, No. 16.)

408. Monday before Epiphany [Dec. 30], 1332. Grant by John Haliday of Snaythe and Amice, his wife, to Henry Dynthard of Snaythe, smith, of a toft with buildings upon it in Snaythe, which lies in length and breadth between the toft of Blessed Mary on the south and the common way called Bondegate on the north, and adjoins the common way which leads towards the marsh on the west and the toft once belonging to John Ryder towards the east; to hold to Henry, his heirs and assigns, of the chief lord of the fee. Warranty. Sealing clause.[1] Witnesses: John son of Thomas the clerk of Snaythe, William, his brother, Thomas son of Adam the tailor (*le Taylleur*) of the same, John son of Malkin of the same, John son of Thomas son of Nicholas of the same, John Warner, Edmund le Barker of the same. At Snaythe. (*Y.A.S.*, M^D 182, No. 61.)

409. Michaelmas [Sept. 29], 1333. Recites that whereas Thomas Emys having granted to William son of William the clerk of Couwyk 2 selions of land with appurtenances in the coppices of Snaythe which he held as is fully stated in the charter

---

[1] Seals: two, oval brown wax, ⅝ × 1¾ ins.; (1) S.JOH.HALIDAY; (2) undeciphered.

of feoffment; now William grants for him and his heirs . . . .[1] the 2 selions of land to hold for a term of 18 years; wherefor William and his heirs hold themselves bound to Thomas and his heirs in the sum of 40s. yearly until the end of the said term. Sealing clause.[2] At Snayth. (Ibid., No. 62.)

410. [1341] Indenture[3] witnessing demise by William son of John de Couwyk to William Mons of Couwyk of half of his messuage in the vill of Snaythe and all his lands, tenements, rents and appurtenances in the vill and territory of Snaythe; which lands [etc.] he held for a period by an indenture of Richard, the late son of Adam, the bailiff (attesche) of Snaythe. To hold to William Mons, his heirs and assigns, from St. Peter in cathedra, 1341, for the term of 41 years next following, rendering to the chief lord of the fee the due and accustomed services. Warranty. Alternate seals. Witnesses: Henry Fiter of Snaythe, John Dennyson of the same, William Jacob, Adam Manbryd, Adam Paynott'. (Ibid., No. 63.)

411. Friday, St. Nicholas [Dec. 6], 1342. Grant by Nicholas de Mar, chaplain, to William Mons of Couwyk and Agnes, his wife, of all his lands, tenements, rents and moors with appurtenances, which he had of the gift of the said William, in Snaythe and Couwyk; to hold to William and Agnes, their heirs and assigns, of the chief lord of the fee. Warranty. Sealing clause.[4] Witnesses: John de Snaythe, William Gateryst, Alexander de Cridelyng', John le Warner, Thomas Godard of Couwyk, clerk. At Snaythe. (Ibid., No. 64.)

412. Sunday after St. John the Baptist [June 27], 1344. Grant by John Dynthard of Snaythe to Henry son of John Ferre' of Snayth and his lawful heirs, for a certain sum of money, of a selion of land lying in the west field of Snaythe, between the land of Margaret Rycard of Snaythe on the east and the land once of Joice Radde of Snaythe on the west and abutting on the footpath to Moreland at the southern end, and in the broadway which leads towards Dor to the north, and contains in length 2 roods; to hold to Henry and his lawful heirs of the chief lord of the fee. Warranty. Sealing clause. Witnesses: Simon Ferre' of Snaythe, John Warner of the same, John Godard of the same, Edmund Barker. At Snayth. (Y.A.S., M⁰ 153, No. 20.)

413. Oct. 20, 1345, 20 Edward III. Grant by Richard son of Richard del Hille of Snaythe to John de Neuton and Joan his wife, of one dole of land and meadow, in width from both sides of the head of a rood (latitudinis ad utrumque caput unius

---

[1] Document stained and writing obliterated.
[2] Seal: on tongue cut from document, yellow wax, undeciphered.
[3] In French.
[4] Seal: brown wax, undeciphered.

perticate), with appurtenances in Snaythe, lying in the northern meadows of the vill, and extending from the fence (*sepe*) of the field called Estfeld on the southern headland to the water of the Ayr on the northern headland, between the land and meadow which belonged to Alice de Dor on one side and Denise (*Dionisie*) le Toller on the other; to hold to John and Joan, and the heirs and assigns of John, from the Michaelmas preceding for 41 years. Warranty. Alternate seals. At Snaythe. Witnesses: John son of Richard del Hille, John de Saltmersk, John de Gardelby, Adam Dikesson, Richard Alkok. (*Y.A.S.*, M^P 182, No. 65.)

414. Sunday before St. Martin [Nov. 6], 1345. Grant by Henry son of Peter de Snaythe and Alice, his wife, to Richard son of Alexander de Whitelay, his heirs and assigns, of a strip of land and meadow with appurtenances, containing in length one rood and lying in the northern meadows of Snaythe at Le Fordols, between the land and meadow of John de Snaythe on the east and the land and meadows of Robert de Snaythe of York on the west, and abutting on the land of Henry le Sagher on the south and on the meadow of the abbot of Selby of Rouclif on the north; to hold of the chief lords of the fee. Warranty. Sealing clause. Witnesses: John de Snaythe, Alexander de Crideling', John de Mora, Thomas Godard, Geoffrey Wale. At Snaythe. (*Ibid.*, No. 66.)

415. [1348.] Grant by Adam son of John son of Randulf, to Henry son of Robert Forster of Snaythe, of an acre of land lying in the west field of Snayth between the land of John Niffe on the east and the grantor's own land on the west, and abutting on the road which leads towards Dor on the south and on the road below . . . .[1] *pibus* of the same vill on the north; to hold to Henry, his heirs and assigns, from Michaelmas 1348 for 51 years. Warranty. Sealing clause.[2] Witnesses: Alexander de Credeling, Richard son of William de Snayth, William Friere. (*Ibid.*, No. 67.)

416. Saturday after St. Peter ad vincula, 25 Edward III [Aug. 6, 1351]. Grant by Richard son of Walter de Wrangle,[3] to John son of Andrew Anisthy of Leek, his heirs and assigns, of all his lands and tenements with appurtenances which he has or may have in the vill of Stneythe; to hold to John, his heirs and assigns, of the chief lord of the fee. Warranty. Sealing clause.[4] Witnesses: Richard Harald, Alan Newe, of the same, John Baldewyn of the same, Richard Hermyn of the same, Alan son of Robert de Wrangle. At Wrangle. (*Ibid.*, No. 68.)

[1] Hole in document.

[2] Seal: yellow wax, round, diam. 1¼ ins.; undeciphered.

[3] Wrangle and Leake, adjoining parishes in the wapentake of Skirbeck, co. Lincoln.

[4] Seal: oval, white wax; undeciphered.

417.   Indenture by which John son of William Lyholf' of
Snaythe demises to William the smith (*fabro*) of Snaythe, and
Alice, his wife, their heirs and assigns, all the lands, meadows and
tenements, with moors, pastures, commons with appurtenances in
the vill and territory of Snaythe and Couwyk, namely, those
which John holds by hereditary descent in the soke of Snaythe
following the death of William Lyolf, his father, except a certain
tenement, built upon by William son of the clerk of Snaythe,
near to the tenement of a certain William of Lincoln; to hold
from Michaelmas, 1321, for 51 years.   Et quod predicti Willelmi
et Alicie erant . . . . de dicto . . . . [all crossed out]. (*Ibid.*, No. 69.)

418.   Indenture witnessing that Dom. Thomas le Smythe of
Snaythe, chaplain, grants and demises to Henry son of Robert
of the same all the messuages, lands, meadows, moors and pastures with the appurtenance which descended to Thomas by
inheritance after the death of William Smythe, his father,'which
the same William held for a term of years by the demise of John
son of William son of Peter Lyolf, lying in the vills of Snayth
and Cowyk and in the territory of the soke of Snayth, the bounds
of which more fully appear in an indenture made between John
Lyolf and William Smyth; and also of all the right which ought
to descend by inheritance to the grantor in the lands and meadows
with appurtenances called Babbeland, which Geoffrey of Lincoln
held when the terms of the then tenants have elapsed; to hold
from Monday after Holy Trinity, 1358, to the end of the term
contained in the indenture of John Lyolf, namely, from the feast
of St. Michael, 1357,[1] for 25 years, of the chief lord of the fee;
saving to Alice Smythe of Snaythe, sister of Thomas, an acre of
land lying . . . . west of Snaythe, and Thomas wishes and grants
for the said acre of land so demised that the aforesaid Henry
[2] . . . . acre of land . . . . all others . . . . the same Alice . . . .
should demise . . . . it shall be lawful for the said Henry to enter
and hold peacefully; and if the said Dom Thomas or his heirs
. . . . (*Ibid.*, No. 70.)

419.   Thursday after Easter, 25 Edward III [April 21, 1351].
Grant by Roger Paynot of Snaythe to John Neuton' and Joan,
his wife, of one and a half acres of land with appurtenances lying
in the east field of Snaythe, between the land of Thomas Rudde
on the east and the land of Robert son of William de Snaythe
once belonging to John le Toller on the west, and adjoining the
land of John de Neuton' at Coksty towards the south, and on
the hedge of the aforesaid field on the north; to hold to John
and Joan and their heirs and assigns of the chief lord of the
fee.   Warranty.   Sealing clause.[3]   Witnesses: Richard son of John

[1] 1347: see preceding deed.
[2] Document stained and writing faded.
[3] Seal: brown wax, oval, 1 × 1⅓ ins.; Virgin and Child; AVE MARIA
GRACIA.

de Snaythe, Robert son of William de Snaythe, Thomas Godard, John of the Moor (*de mora*), John son of William de Couwyk, Henry son of Joyce de Couwyk. At Snaythe. (*Ibid.*, No. 71.)

420. Friday after SS. Peter and Paul [July 1], 1375. Indenture witnessing lease by William Ketyl of Rouclif', near Snaythe, and Katherine, his wife, and William de Ingoldesby of Santoun in co. Lincolnn, and Marjory (*Marioria*) his wife, to Thomas de Knottynglay of the same and Henry del Brigg of Snaythe, of all those lands, tenements, meadows, rents and pastures with appurtenances which belonged by inheritance to Katharine and Marjory within the soke of Snaythe, following the death of William son of Matilda de Snayth, their brother; and other land also [belonging] to the same William, William, Katharine and Marjory and their heirs and assigns living in Inglesmor; to hold the said lands [*etc.*] for the term of eight years from the Feast of St. Michael the Archangel, 1375, for a sum of money. Warranty: Thomas and Henry to perform the due and accustomed services. Alternate seals.[1] Witnesses: Richard de Snaythe, Henry son of Robert de Snaythe, John Long, John Edmund of Snaythe, John Marshalle, Henry de Rednesse, William de Hatfield of Rouclif. At Rouclif'. (*Ibid.*, No. 73.)

421. Sept. 12, 1380. Grant by John de Fryston' chaplain, William de Hathelsay, John Saunderson and Thomas Dylcok to Thomas Adam of Snaythe and Alice his wife, of 4 acres of land and meadow lying in the northern meadows of Snaythe on the east side del Stathe, and 5 acres of land and meadow lying in le Fremanhagge, and an acre and a half of land in the west field in Overoxnhaghe abutting on the highway which leads towards Dor and upon Mideloxnhaghedyk; to hold to Thomas and Alice and the heirs and assigns of Thomas. Sealing clause. Witnesses: Richard le Drax, John Long, John Frere, Henry Joce, Peter de Crulle. At Snaythe. (*Ibid.*, No. 74.)

422. Monday after Michaelmas, 5 Richard II [Sept. 30, 1381]. Indenture by which John Jepson of Snaythe grants to Thomas Paynot of Snaythe and Alice his wife, half an acre of arable land in the west field of Snaythe between the land of Geoffrey Fox on the west and the land of Thomas Payuot on the east, and abutting on the highway leading to Dor on the north and upon Brocaithirne on the south; to hold to Thomas and Alice, their heirs and assigns, from Michaelmas, 1382, for 24 years. Warranty. Witnesses: William Gibson' of Cowyk, John Long, Henry Joceson, John . . ondirhille.[2] (*Ibid.*, No. 75.)

---

[1] Seals: two of brown wax on tongue cut from bottom of document; undeciphered.

[2] Seal: dark brown wax, diam. 1 in.; blurred, probably the Virgin and Child.

423. Friday in Easter Week [March 27], 1383. Indenture by which Marjory, widow of John Bogher of Snayth, leases to Henry Bogher, living in Rouclif, a messuage lying in Snaythe between the messuage of John Spenser towards the east and a tenement of John Frere to the west, and abutting on the highway to the north and on the field of Snaythe on the south; to hold to Henry, his heirs and assigns, during the lifetime of Marjory, of the lord of the fee; paying yearly to the lessor or her attorney 3s. 4d. of silver at the four terms in equal portions, namely, St. Michael, St. Andrew, Palm Sunday, and St. John the Baptist; the first term of payment to begin on the Feast of St. Michael next following. If the said rent should be in arrears either wholly or in part after any of the terms by 20 days, then it shall be lawful for Marjory to re-enter, distrain [etc.] until satisfaction be made. Warranty. Sealing clause.[1] Witnesses: Thomas de Snaythe, John Frere, John Longe of Snaythe, John Mareschalle, William de Hathsek' of Rouclif. At Snaythe. (Y.A.S., M^D 153, No. 21.)

424. Thursday after Michaelmas, 7 Richard [II]   [Oct. 1, 1383.] Grant by John Rodgeer of Lofthouse to John de Lynlay, keeper of the park of Fyppyn, of a messuage and 5½ acres of land and meadow with appurtenances in Snaythe; to hold to John, his heirs and assigns, of the chief lords of the fee. Warranty. Sealing clause.[2] Witnesses: Thomas Elys, William Denyas, John Long of Snaythe, William Baille of the same, Richard de Metham, Richard Butler, John Culpoun. At Snaythe. (Y.A.S., M^D 182, No. 76.)

425. Morrow of St. Laurence [Aug. 11], 1390. Grant by John, son of Adam le Spenser of Rouclif' near Snaythe, to John Friston, chaplain, living in Snaythe, son of Richard de Friston, his heirs and assigns, of a moiety of a toft built upon in the vill of Snaythe, which lies in length and breadth between the toft which John Litster holds on the east, which toft formerly belonged to John de Cowyk, and the toft which William Bougher holds on the west, which formerly belonged to Adam, son of William Bougher, and which abuts on the king's highway of the said vill on the north and on the highway passing below the vill on the south; with free entry and exit to the said moiety by that road which lies between the toft formerly belonging to Adam Bougher and the toft formerly of Richard, son of James Hers; he further grants to John a butt of land with appurtenances in Snaythe, lying between the garden formerly of Adam Bougher and the land which John Litster holds on the east and a certain lane which once belonged to the said Adam and Richard Spenser on the west, and which abuts on the common way at the southern end and

---

[1] Seal: white wax, diam. ₁⁷₀ in., undeciphered.

[2] Seal: black wax, diam. ⅘ in.; the letter P surrounded by sprigs of leaves.

on a garden formerly of the said Adam at the northern end, and which contains in length 10 perches (*perticatas*); to hold of the chief lord of the fee. Warranty. Sealing clause. Witnesses: John Culpoun, Hugh Bladeworthe, John Longe, Thomas de Crulle, John Edmund. At Snaythe. (*Ibid.*, No. 77.)

426. Tuesday after St. Hilary [Jan. 18], 1390[-1]. Release and quitclaim by Simon de Hek to John de Pykburne of Pontefract and John son of William de Hek, their heirs and assigns, of all right and claim in all those lands and tenements, rents and services, with all meadows, grazings, pastures and woods, with appurtenances which John and John had of the gift and feoffment of Simon de Hek within the soke of Snayth or elsewhere in co. York. Warranty. Sealing clause. Witnesses: Adam de Wynteworthe, Thomas Dylcok, William de Hek, John Robynson, John atte Oke. At Lytelhek. (*Ibid.*, No. 78.)

427. Christmas Eve [Dec. 24], 1392. Indenture by which Cecily, daughter and heir of John Orr of Snaythe, demises to John Litster of Snaythe and Matilda his wife, their heirs and assigns, 2 acres of land lying scattered (*divisim*) in the east field of Snaythe, of which one acre lies between the land of Thomas Manbrid on the west, and the other acre lies between the land of John Gepson' on the east; and these 2 acres abut on Wrimor on the south and on the hedge of the field on the north; to hold to John and Matilda, their heirs and assigns, from Christmas 1392 for 20 years, saving the terms of the tenants of a certain length (*de quadam longitudine*) in the southern part of the said 2 acres if any terms remain incomplete, by doing therefor to the lord of the fee the services pertaining to the 2 acres, except that William Horn shall bear the burden of all service during the first 4 years. Warranty by Cecily and her heirs for a certain sum of money paid by John and Matilda. Alternate seals. Witnesses: Thomas Frere, William Writhe, John Gepson', Thomas Manbrid'. At Snaythe. (*Ibid.*, No. 79.)

428. Monday after St. Luke the Evangelist, 17 Richard II [Oct. 20, 1393]. Quitclaim by Adam son of Roger de Wentworthe of Snaythe to John Daunay of Escrik, his heirs and assigns, of that warranty (*warrantiam*) made to him, his heirs and assigns by the said John, in respect of a certain tenement in Snaythe with appurtenances in which John now lives; also in respect of another tenement in Cowyk lying between the tenement of Henry White and John Camyn', plasterer (*pargittour*); and of a third tenement in Walmegate, York, between the tenements of Nicholas Destorfolk and William de Aldeburghe, knts.; also of the ferry over the water of Derwent, and of a garden, croft and 2 acres and 6 meadows in the vill of Menthorpe lately belonging to Robert

K

son of John de Surflet, as laid down in quitclaim of John to Adam. Warranty. Sealing clause.[1] (*Y.A.S.*, M° 153, No. 122.)

Speeton

429. Gilbert de Gant, earl of Lincoln,[2] to his steward and to all his men as well French as English, greeting. Know that I have given and granted to Tero', son of Malger, half of Speeton, that is in tofts and crofts, finally and without restraint; [to hold] freely and quietly to him and his heirs, of me and my heirs. Know also that I warrant to him the said land against all men, and this with the consent (*concessione*) of Lambert the constable, whose daughter Tero has by the service of one part of a knight's fee (*cuius filiam Tero habet per seruicium de una parte unius militis*). Witnesses: Geoffrey de Gant, Robert de Gant, Baldwin de Gant, Ralph de Noua uilla, Henry de Willardeby, Walter de Grendale, Geoffrey son of Malger, William de Barewythe, Hugh son of Ralph, Gilbert de Lea, Alban de Bucheton, Peter de Bernebia, Ralph Pilat.[3] (*Archer-Houblon MSS.*, No. 462.)

430. Friday after St. Luke the Evangelist [Oct. 20], 1346. Will of John de Speton, senior. He leaves his soul to God and Blessed Mary and all saints and his body to be buried in the church of Blessed Mary of Bridlington, near Joan formerly his wife. Item: for his mortuary fee his best animal, and in wax to burn about his body for four tapers two . . . .[4] for the distribution of bread and herrings (*in pane et allece*) to the poor on the day of his burial 2 marks; to the sacristan of Bridlington for the church (*ad opus ecclesie*) 20s.; to the convent of Bridlington for a pittance 20s.; to the prior and convent of the order of friars preachers of Scarburg' 20s.; to brother John de Hakenes of the same order and convent 20s.; to the friars minor of Scarburg' 6s. 8d.; to the friars of Mount Carmel of Scard[eburg'] 6s. 8d.; to the chapel of Speton 6s. 8d.; to the parochial chaplain of Bridlington 2s.; to the parochial chaplain of Grendal 2s.; to Dom. Benedict, vicar of Righton, 6s. 8d.; to Nicholas de Hale 6s. 8d. Item: to Elizabeth his daughter 13s. 4d. and to Joan her daughter 13s. 4d.; to Isabel his daughter 20s.; to Joan his daughter 13s. 4d.; to Margaret his daughter 30s.; to Margery his daughter 20s.; and to his three young boys, Ralph, William and Ace, to each 20s. Item: to a chaplain to celebrate for his soul 60s. His executors to distribute the residue of his goods as may seem best for the

---

[1] Seal: red wax, diam. 1½ ins.; in a cusped border a heater-shaped shield bearing a chevron between three leopards' heads erased; SIGILLU: ADE: DE: WYNTWO . . . .

[2] This appears to be a copy in a fifteenth-century hand; the limits of date are 1147-56 (*Early Yorks. Charters*, ii, p. 434; and *cf.* page 429 for the first four witnesses).

[3] On the dorse of the document are certain names and sums of money, all very faint.

[4] A word which appears to be *patras*.

good of his soul. He appoints as his executors Dom. Thomas his son, chaplain, and Dom. Benedict vicar ot Righton, and Nicholas de Hale and brother John de Hakenes to superintend the will (*superintendentes*). Sealed[1] with his seal and the seals of his executors, and with the seal of the dean of Dikering whom he has procured as a witness of the truth (*et sigillum decani de Dikering apponi procuravi in testimonium veritatis*). At Speton.

Item: *do et lego Thome fratri meo capellano et Thome filio meo* [crossed out]. He leaves to Margaret his daughter his great chest (*cista*); to Thomas his brother his robe of . . . .[2] of the prior of Bridlington; to Thomas his son his Flemish chest (*cistam meam Flandr'*); to John his son and heir his long chest of oak; to Ace his son a corslet (*corset*); to Richard his servant a red robe; to John de Shafthow all his clothes of velvet except a hood and a tabard (*collobium*) which he leaves to his brother Thomas. Item: to Robert son of Robert de Harpham a tunic of motley (*unam tunicam mixtam*); to Margaret Adelard a supertunic with a hood. Item: to Thomas his brother and Thomas his son, chaplains, the manor of Twynlynge[3] with the lands and tenements in Righton pertaining which he had of the grant and demise of the abbot and convent of Rievall, for a certain term, as more fully appears in a certain writing made between them, in order that the said Thomas and Thomas shall cause to be celebrated, or one of them shall celebrate, during this term for the soul of Robert de Wyern' and the soul of Amice his wife and the souls of John de Speton and Joan his wife.

Dorso: Proved before William, archbishop of York, Nov. 14, 1346, at his manor of Cawode, and administration granted to Dom. Thomas, chaplain, son of the deceased, and Dom. Benedict, vicar of the church of Ryghton, executors named in the will. Sealing clause. (*Ibid.*, No. 463.)

431. Thursday after Easter, 36 Edward III [April 21, 1362]. Grant by John [L]ourance of Bukton, chaplain, and William his brother, chaplain, William Hoiy of Hundemanby, chaplain, John de Hadthelard, chaplain, and John de Shirburn, chaplain, to John de Speton and Christiana, his wife, of the manor of Speton with appurtenances; to hold to John and Christiana for the term of their lives with remainder to Thomas Rise of Beverley and Margaret, his wife, and the heirs of their bodies, and in default

[1] Seal: Fragment of a fine seal of red wax. At the top under an elaborate pinnacled and traceried canopy, a Virgin and Child; below, the lower halves of two standing figures; at the bottom, the kneeling figure of a mitred ecclesiastic holding a cross, on each side of which has been a shield of arms, only one shield still intact, bears ten torteaux, 4, 3, 2, 1. The other shield may have borne a similar charge.

[2] This word not deciphered, apparently *liba . . ce*, possibly from *liberata*, a gift.

[3] Thwing.

of such issue successively to, (1) the heirs of the body of Margaret, (2) Elizabeth, sister of Margaret and one of the daughters of the said John de Speton, (3) the lawfully begotten heirs of Elizabeth, (4) the right heirs of John de Speton; to hold of the chief lords of the fee. Warranty. The part of the indenture remaining with John de Speton and Christiana sealed with the seals of the said chaplains and of Thomas de Rise and Margaret, his wife; to the part remaining with Thomas and Margaret, John, Christiana and Elizabeth and the said chaplains have placed their seals; and to the part remaining with the said chaplains, John and Christiana and Elizabeth as well as Thomas and Margaret have placed their seals.[1] Witnesses: Marmaduke Conestable, William de Erghum and Robert de Boynton, knts., John de Bukton, Robert de Bossale, Walter de Staxton. At Speton. (*Ibid.*, No. 464.)

432. April 22, 1455. Confirmation by Walter de Grymeston, John Haldenby and Robert Portyngton, esqs., William Hode, chaplain, and Thomas . . . . ,[2] to John Portyngton, esq., and Alice, his wife, of all the lands and tenements . . . . rents, with appurtenances in Speton, Righton, and Neuland super Ayre which the confirmors lately had of the demise of the aforesaid . . . . to hold all the lands, tenements, rents, services, mills, woods and moors with appurtenances to John [and Alice] for the term of their lives and the lifetime of the survivor, of the chief lords of the fees. Appointment of Walter . . . . as their attorney to enter the premises and deliver seisin. Sealing clause.[3] Witnesses: Thomas Metham, Brian Stapilton, knts., Robert Constable, Peter Bukton, ... William Mapilton. (*Ibid.*, No. 465.)

433. Oct. 8, 4 Edward IV [1464]. Confirmation by Thomas Portyngton, clerk, and Edward Saltmersh, to Alice, widow of John de Portyngton, knt., of their manor of Speton near Brydlington, and all the lands, tenements, rents and services in Speton and Ryghton with appurtenances, which manor [*etc.*] belonged to Margaret, late wife of the said John; to hold to Alice for the term of her life; warranty by Thomas and his heirs. Appointment of John Vauasour, William Vauasour and William Goldesburght as their attorneys to enter the premises and deliver seisin. Sealing clause. (*Ibid.*, No. 466.)

434. June 19, 12 Edward IV [1472]. An agreement[4] made in the manor of Lekyngfelde before the Right Noble and Right

---

[1] Five seals: (1) small round seal of white wax, a bird—(2) seal missing—(3) two small seals of white wax, both round but chipped; device on the upper seal blurred, apparently two animals; the lower undeciphered—(4) white wax, broken; on a heater-shaped shield three feathers—(5) a small round seal of red wax; an equestrian figure with drawn sword facing to the sinister.

[2] The left margin of the deed is badly torn away.

[3] Three seals of red wax: (1) apparently a bull's head couped; (2) the letter T; (3) the letter W.

[4] In English.

Worthy lord Henry Percy, earl of Northumberland, between Dame Alice, late wife of Sir John Portington, knt., and master Thomas Portyngton, clerk, brother and heir of Sir John, of the one part, and Sir Robert Constable, Sir William Eures, Sir Walter Gryffyth, knts., Marmaduke Constable, Robert Constable, esqs., John Somerby and Thomas Pratt of Bridlyngton, Robert Barett and Isabel Veele, widow, of the other part, touching all the lands and tenements, rents and services with appurtenances in the towns of Speton and Righton, which were lately in the possession of the said Sir John Portyngton: it was settled that Sir Robert Constable [and the other members of the second party] shall release all their right and claim in the said premises to Dame Alice and Thomas Portyngton and to the heirs of Thomas, and that Dame Alice shall enter and occupy the premises and take the rents and profits of the same, for which Dame Alice and Thomas shall pay to the said Robert Barett 23 marks in form following, namely, 11 marks 6s. 8d. at the delivery of the said release, and 11 marks 6s. 8d. at the feast of St. Peter ad vincula next following the date of this present writing. In witness whereof that part of this indenture tripartite remaining with Dame Alice and master Thomas is sealed[1] as well by the said Earl as by the said Sir Robert Constable [etc.].[2] (Ibid., No. 467.)

Stainburn

435. Grant by Elias son of Knut de Stainburn, to Agnes daughter of Ingerode his sister and her children by Hugh the chaplain, for her homage and service and for 28s. paid to him, of a toft in Stainburn of half an acre, namely the toft which lies between the lessor's toft and garden and the house of William Fraunces, also 4 acres of arable land and half an acre in the fields of the same vill, with all appurtenances, that is, an acre and a half which Arkill holds of the grantor in Northbugerude, and half an acre in Gillerude adjoining to the south, and an acre in Suthbugerud which extends towards Wranglandewath next to the land which belonged to William the crossbowman (arbalistarus) towards the north, and half an acre which lies in Laisingrode between the bovate of land which the monks of Fountains hold of Thomas de Foreston and the bovate of land which the said monks hold of William the crossbowman, and an acre in the cultivated land of Laisingrode towards the east; and if she shall

---

[1] Five tongues: (1) a blob of red wax, badly broken; (2) two small round seals of red wax; the top seal bears a device of a bird facing to the dexter, the second a small flower ; (3) two small seals of red wax, the upper badly broken; the lower bears a stag's head cabossed ; (4) two small seals of red wax; the upper bears the letters IS as a monogram; device on lower one not deciphered; (5) two small round seals of red wax; the upper bears a mark of some kind, the lower one the letter T under a crown.

[2] Also, Quitclaim by Robert Constable, etc., to Thomas Portyngton and Dame Alice, dated the following day, June 20th. (Ibid., No. 468.)

lack any acre there in the same cultivated land then she shall have land given to her in Lepthhil de Stainhoblandes; to hold of the grantor and his heirs in fee and hereditarily within the vill and without, in woods, plains, meadows and pastures, and with all easements pertaining thereto; and she and her children and their heirs shall have pasture for 100 sheep and their young for 3 years and similarly pasture for 10 cows and their young, and also for 12 sows (*sues*) and their young for one year, paying yearly to the grantor and his heirs 2*d*. at the Nativity for all services. Warranty. Witnesses: Nigel de Plumpton,[1] Peter his son, John his son, William de Marton, Matthew de Bram', Walter de Stokkeld, Robert son of Uckem' de Plumpton, Walans, chaplain of Stainburn, Robert son of Henry de Sikkelinghale, Robert Bongrant, Gilbert Lardin', Henry de Screuin, Adam son of Gregory de Stainburn.[2] (*Farnley Hall MSS.*, No. 65.)

436. Wednesday after the Purification of the B.V.M. [Feb. 6], 1319–20. Quitclaim by Agnes, widow of Adam son of Gilbert de Stanneburne, to Thomas de Craven and his heirs, of all actions, quarrels and covenants, rights and claims relating to a messuage with appurtenances in the vill and territory of Stanneburne, of which messuage Thomas was enfeoffed by her charter to him; and if any new covenant should be brought about on her part or in her name against Thomas, with the exception of the following, namely, that Thomas holds himself bound to her in the sum of 7 marks sterling to be paid at certain terms within one year, then she will pay 20*s*. to the master and brethren of the Hospital of St. John of Jerusalem each time such a claim is made against him. Sealing clause.[3] Witnesses: Robert le Page, Richard de Fekesby, Adam de Fekesby, John de Adell, Thomas de Screuinne. At Stanneburne. (*Ibid.*, No. 66.)

437. Translation of St. Thomas the Martyr [July 7], 1326. Grant by Thomas de Craven of Staynburn to John son of Robert de Staynburn of a toft with buildings and half a rood of land which he had of the gift of Agnes, daughter of Robert the miller, in exchange for a rood of land lying in a place called Stonelandes between the land of William Fayrebarn on the south and the land of Walter son of Wilfrid on the north; to hold to John, his heirs and assigns, freely [*etc.*], of the chief lords of the fee, and performing all services pertaining to the land except the taxation of the king and the tax of the vill for ploughing and making gardens (*jactura gardinorum*). Warranty. Sealing clause. Witnesses: William de Castelay, senior, William de Castelay, junior,

---

[1] As Nigel de Plumpton was dead in 1213–14 the date of this deed would be late twelfth or early thirteenth century.

[2] Fragment of large brown seal.

[3] Seal: brown wax, diam. 2 ins.; mailed equestrian figure to the sinister. ✠ SIGILLVM HENRICI . . . . . T.

William Mohaut of Lethelay, Fulk de Lindelay, Walter de Brotes. At Ottelay. (*Ibid.*, No. 67.)

438. Friday, Nativity of the B.V.M., 14 Edward III [Sept. 8, 1340]. Grant by Lawrence son of William de Castelay to Adam son of Robert del Cote of Staynburn and Margaret his wife, and the heirs of Adam, of a toft with appurtenances in the vill of Staynburn, which lies in length and breadth between the messuage of the rectors of the church of Kyrkeby on one side and the land of the abbots of Fountains on the other; to hold to Adam and Margaret and the heirs of Adam, freely, with all liberties and easements, hereditarily of the chief lords of the fee. Warranty. Sealing clause.[1] Witnesses: William de Mohaud, Walter de Kereby, William de Lyndelay, Patrick de Marton, John le Vauasour of Castelay, William son of William de Castelay, William de Skreuyn of Staynburn. At Staynburn. (*Ibid.*, No. 68.)

439. Sunday after clausum Pasche, 18 Richard II [Apr. 25, 1395]. Grant[2] by John de Esshe of Rigton and Agnes his wife, by mutual agreement and for the health of their souls, to Thomas Trump', provost of the chapel of Staynburne, and to his successors in that office in perpetuity, of a toft and a croft with appurtenances which lie in length and breadth between the land of the abbot of Fountains on the east and the land of St. Leonard on the west; to hold with all easements within and without the vill of Staynburne, paying yearly to the said abbot 1*d.* for all secular services. Warranty. Witnesses: Robert Swetyng, John Webster, Roger de Craven, Robert Cest, John Thomson of Craven, Stephen Trump', Walter de Qwellious. At Staynburne. (*Ibid.*, No. 69.)

Sutton=under=Whitestonecliff

440. Quitclaim by Brother Imbert de Peraut,[3] humble Master of the Knights of the Temple in England, with the counsel and consent of the Easter chapter in London, to the abbot and convent of Byland, of all right in that pasture which the abbot and convent recently enclosed near their ber . . . .[4] [sheepfold ?] of Wythstanklyf, saving that if any of the animals belonging to their [the Templars'] men of Kereby should stray into the enclosure by reason of faulty fencing they should not be . . . . [harmed ?] but driven back without detention, this quitclaim

---

[1] Seal: red wax, gem, the letter W.

[2] Quitclaim of the same, described as held by Thomas Trump', to Robert Sothern by Agnes, in her widowhood, dated Saturday before the Annunciation [Mar. 24], 1402–3, and witnessed by Thomas Lyndelay, William Wade, chaplain of Staynburne, John . . . . te, Robert Hessay, John Sothern. (*Ibid.*, No. 70.)

[3] Imbert de Peraut and William de Merden, the last witness, both occur *c.* 1270 (*Cal. Pat. Rolls*, 1266–1272, p. 541, and *V.C.H., Yorks.*, iii, 537).

[4] The deed is illegible in places.

notwithstanding. Sealing clause.[1] Witnesses: Brothers Ralph, chaplain, Richard son of John, William le Englys, Roger de Akeny, Robert Scropp', Ranulf de Bremesgrove, William de Merden, preceptor of York. (*Ibid.*, No. 70.)

Swanland

441. Sunday before Christmas, 13[3]2. Quitclaim by John son of Roger Ligiard of Anlovi[2] to Joan, widow of Walter son of Peter of Swanland, of all right in 4 acres of arable land in the field and territory of Swanland, which Joan had of the gift of Dervorgulia her mother; he renounces all claim for himself and his heirs. Sealing clause. Witnesses: Peter de Anlovy, William Ligiard of the same, Nicholas son of John of Swanland, Richard Bradan and John Franceys of the same. At Swanland. (*Archer-Houblon MSS.*, No. 488.)

Terrington

442. St. James [July 25], 1325. Grant by Joan, daughter of John Tornay of Tyverington, in her pure virginity, to Agnes, daughter of Robert le Archer, of a toft with a croft and a bovate of land with appurtenances in the vill and territory of Tyverington, all of which she had by inheritance after the death of her mother. The said toft and croft lie between the land of Peter Aspolyon on both sides and the bovate lies towards the west between the grantor's land on one side and the land of Matilda, widow of Robert the carpenter of Old Malton (*ueteri Malton'*) on the other; to hold with all liberties, easements [*etc.*], within and without the vill, to Agnes and the heirs of her body, of the grantor and her heirs, rendering yearly a clove gillyflower at the Nativity if demanded, and performing the due and accustomed services to the lords of the fee. Should it happen that Agnes die without heirs of her body, reversion to the grantor and her heirs in perpetuity. Warranty. Sealing clause. Witnesses: Thomas de Vespont, John Latymer, Stephen de Tyverington, William his son, John de Cliffe, James de Galmethorpe. At Tyverington. (*Y.A.S.*, M[D] 153, No. 28).

443. Thursday after St. Catherine the Virgin, 38 Edward III [Nov. 28, 1364]. Quitclaim by Edmund de Firtheby to John de Bulmer, rector of the church of Bulmer, of all right which he has in a messuage and 2 bovates of land, and in a toft with buildings upon it, with appurtenances in the vill and territory of Teverington, which land and tenement once belonged to Robert de Firtheby, the grantor's father. Warranty. Sealing clause.[3] Witnesses: Thomas Gouer, Richard Bernard, George de Naulton', Henry de

---

[1] Seal of green wax; Paschal Lamb; ✠ SIGILLUM TEMPL . .

[2] Anlaby.

[3] Seal: brownish wax, diam. ¾ in.; an armorial shield; undeciphered.

Olesby, John de Strensale, William Lilling, William de Stokton'. At Edilthorpe. (*Ibid.*, No. 29.)

444. Sunday after the Ascension [June 4], 1329. Indenture by which John le Latimer of Tyverington and William Barton' of the same give and deliver to Thomas de Barton', Edmund de Stauelay and Dom. Hugh de Houingham, chaplain, executors of the will of Dom. John de Barton' of Friton, deceased, goods and chattels to the value of 20 marks sterling, namely, 60 and 16 sheep (*bidentes*), 4 oxen, 2 mares (*jumentas*), one black horse, and the crop (*uesturam*) of 20 and 3 acres of corn to be chosen from 4 bovates of land which William de Barton' has sown in the field of Tyverington, that is 11½ acres of wheat, and 11½ acres of oats, barley (*ordei*) and pease, and this by the will of the above executors in part settlement of a debt of 24*li.* in which John and William are bound to the executors; and if death or any other unforeseen disaster overtake any of the said animals during the fifteen days before St. John the Baptist next following this indenture, then John and William to bear all loss and make it good according to the estimation of true and lawful men. Alternate seals. Witnesses: John de Westerdale, William Menour, Thomas Vepont. At Tyverington. (*Y.A.S.*, M^D No. 155.)

445. 19 Nov., 15 Henry VII [1499]. Quitclaim by John Russell to Thomas Fenton' of Crake and his heirs and assigns of all right in 3 messuages and 4 bovates of land with appurtenances in Teryngton', in co. York, which lands he recently had of the gift and feoffment of John Kirkby and John Cocsper, chaplain. Sealing clause.[1] Warranty. (*Y.A.S.*, M^D 182, No. 97.)

Thirkleby (N.R.)

446. Notification[2] to the archbishop of York, the chapter of St. Peter and all sons of Holy Church by Gilbert del Meinil of Turkillebi, with the assent of Stephen, his eldest son and heir, and Idonia, his wife, of his grant to God and St. Mary of Byland and the monks serving God there, of all his cultivated ground which the monks have cleared in the lands of Turkillebi towards Angotebi in accordance with (*per*) those boundaries and divisions which Walter del Meinil, the grantor's father, had surveyed; he also grants a clearing from the breadth of the said cultivated land towards the east, in length as far as he, his heirs and his men of Turkillebi shall extend by assarting; to hold in pure and perpetual arms free of all secular services and demands in perpetuity, for the health of his soul and the souls of his wife, father and mother, ancestors and heirs. Warranty. Witnesses: William Darel, Philip, the grantor's wife's brother, Stephen, the grantor's

---

[1] Seal: red wax, diam. ½ in.; a boar facing to the dexter; undeciphered.

[2] For the full text, description of the seal and some notes, see the Appendix; illustrated in the Frontispiece.

son, Peter, the grantor's brother, Walter, the canon, cellarer of Newburgh, Oliver son of Vincent de Tresc, Simon, the grantor's steward, Robert the clerk, son of Robert de Busci. (*Farnley Hall MSS.*, No. 71.)

447. Apostles Peter and Paul, 12 Henry IV [June 29, 1411]. Grant by Robert de Thurkylby, son and heir of William Clerkson of Thurkylby, to Katherine de Sowreby, of a messuage, half an acre of land and half an acre of meadow with appurtenances in the vill and territory of Thurkylby, which the grantor had of the gift and feoffment of William Clerkson; to hold to Katherine, her heirs and assigns, of the chief lords of the fee, and finding yearly for the safety of the soul of Stephen de Menille and of his ancestors two lamps to burn in the church of All Saints at Thurkylby at the office of all principal feasts, and for three nights yearly, namely, All Saints, Christmas and Good Friday, for the aforesaid messuage [*etc.*]. Warranty. Sealing clause.[1] Witnesses: Marmaduke Darelle of Sezay, Henry Maunselle, Peter de Multon, John de Knayton, John Stelle. At Thurkylby. (*Y.A.S.*, M^D 182, No. 98.)

448. St. Lawrence, 12 Henry IV [Aug. 10, 1411]. Quitclaim by William Atkynson of Thurkylby to Katherine de Sowreby, daughter of William de Sowreby, her heirs and assigns, of all right and claim in all the lands, tenements, rents and appurtenances in the vill and territory of Thurkylby, which he once had of the gift of Robert de Thurkylby, son of William Clerkson' of the same. Warranty. Sealing clause.[2] Witnesses: Henry Maunesalle, Peter de Multon, John de Knayton, John Scott, William de Bagley. At Thurkylby. (*Ibid.*, No. 99.)

Tbiⱦendale

449. Lease by Sir Gerard Saluayn to John le Daye and Joan his wife of a messuage and 2 acres of land with appurtenances in Sixendall which the said John held of Sir Gerard; to hold for their lives and the lifetime of the survivor, paying yearly to Sir Gerard and his heirs 3*s.* 4*d.* at Whitsuntide and Martinmas in equal portions. Warranty. Alternate seals. Witnesses: William de Wetewang, William Dounby, Walter Towers [?], John de Hunkelby, Andr[ew] de Sixendall. (*Archer-Houblon MSS.*, No. 489.)

Tburgoland

450. Release by John son of Robert del Clay, to Alan son of Thomas the shepherd, of Thurgerland, his heirs and assigns, for a sum of money, of all right in an annual rent of a rose which John used to pay to him for two pieces of land with wood growing thereon in the territory of Hoxspryng, one of which lies in the place called Hehefeld and the other in Henrerode. Warranty.

---

[1] Seal: fragment of small round seal of red wax bearing letter I.

[2] Seal: brown wax, letter R with a sprig of leaves on its sinister side.

Sealing clause. Witnesses: John le Laysseres of Thurgerland, Richard Danyel, Robert de Oxspryng, Roger the smith of Cotes, John de Byham, Elias the clerk. (*Farnley Hall MSS.*, No. 72.)

451. Wednesday after Corpus Christi, 33 Edward III [June 26, 1359]. Bond by John son of Richard de Hundersshelff, John de Salforth, Thomas de Salforth and John de Snodenhill, to Richard son of William Warde of Thurgerland in the sum of 4*li.*, in respect of measures [of corn] (*mittu'*) received from him; to be paid to him or to his attorney in Thurgerland at Michaelmas next, at Easter, and at the Michaelmas following in equal portions. Sealing clause. At Thurgerland. (*Ibid.*, No. 73.)

452. Friday, April 10, 34 Edward III [1360]. Indenture witnessing that whereas Robert Pye of Bircheworth and Isabel, his wife, Thomas son of John de Salforth and John son of Elias the clerk of Oxpring, hold themselves bound to Robert son of Elias the clerk of Thurgerland in 6*li.* 13*s.* 4*d.*, to be paid to Robert or his attorney at Thurgerland at the feast of the Nativity of Blessed John the Baptist next following, now it is agreed that if Robert shall hold for himself and his heirs all the lands with appurtenances in Thurgerland which he had of the gift of Robert Pye and Isabel for the lifetime of Isabel, without impediment from her or anyone acting in her name, then this obligation to be null and void; otherwise to stand in full strength. Sealing clause.[1] (*Ibid.*, No. 74.)

453. Wednesday after SS. Peter and Paul [June 30], 1367. Release by Robert, son of John son of Elias the clerk of Oxspring, to Robert son of Elias the clerk, dwelling in Thurgerland, his heirs and assigns, of all right in all the lands and tenements with appurtenances in Thurgerland, which Robert son of Elias the clerk held by hereditary right, after the death of Henry, brother of Robert. Warranty. Sealing clause.[2] Witnesses: William de Thurgerland, Robert de Estfeld, Robert Mokeston of Thurgerland. At Thurgerland.[3] (*Ibid.*, No. 75.)

454. Aug. 22, 1476. Release[4] by Elizabeth, widow of John Wrath of Heghfeld in the vill of Oxspryng, to John Elyson of Cootys, his heirs and assigns, dwelling in the capital messuage of the same John Elyson in Thurgerland, of all right in a broad footpath in her close, called Hadland, extending in length from the meadow belonging to John called Magotcroft as far as another close belonging to John called Brodrode, and in breadth as far

[1] Fragments of three seals of white wax.

[2] Seal: white wax, undeciphered.

[3] On the dorse is written in a later hand: A Release which showes howe all oure Ancestors came to the lande in Oxspringe.

[4] Also an indenture granting the same, dated March 8, ... Edward IV, in a bad state of repair, and torn away at bottom corner. (*Ibid.*, No. 76a.)

as the other for the distance of 5½ ells, where it is situated near the hedge growing on the west side of the same path; which path is to be made and kept up at the cost of John and his heirs in perpetuity, with the exception of two gates at the ends of the same hedge, which the grantor and her heirs made at their own cost, and which abuts on the southern end above the entrance in the hedge of Magotcroft, and at the northern end above a gate in the hedge of Broderode; to hold to John, his heirs and assigns dwelling in the said messuage, with free entry and exit for their carts, wagons, carriages, animals and all other goods and chattels. Warranty. Sealing clause. Witnesses: John Makeson of Holandswayn, Robert Cudworth of Thurgurland, John Holand of the same. At Thurgurland. (*Ibid.*, No. 76.)

Weavertborpe

455. Sunday after the Purification of the B.V.M., 5 Richard II, 1381 [Feb. 3, 1381–2]. Grant by William Phylippe of Barkyndale and Emma, his wife, to Dom. John Sowreby, vicar of Wyuerthorp, of all that half toft and croft with appurtenances in Wyuerthorp, which extends from the highway towards the south as far as the land of William de Wyuerthorp towards the north, and in breadth from the toft and croft of William Dogylby towards the east as far as the land of Lord de Brewse to the west; to hold to John, his heirs and assigns, of the chief lord of the fee. Warranty. Sealing clause. Witnesses: William de Wyuerthorp, John Marschall, William Clerk. At Wyuerthorp. (*Y.A.S.*, M^D 120a, No. 10.)

South Wbeatley

456. Monday before St. Thomas the Apostle, 20 Edward III [Dec. 18, 1346]. Grant by John de Imworthe to John de Warmesworthe of a moiety of a messuage with appurtenances in South Wheteley, which John had of the gift and feoffment of John de Warmesworthe, to hold from the feast of St. Thomas the Apostle, 20 Edward III [Dec. 21, 1346], for one year, paying to the grantor, his heirs or executors, 13s. 4d. at Easter and Michaelmas in equal portions. Warranty. Alternate seals.[1] Witnesses: John Hardneth, William son of Adam, Roger Coteron, John son of Elias (*Elie*), William de Whetlay. At South Wheteley. (*Y.A.S.*, M^D 182, No. 95.)

Wmestead

457. Grant by Henry de la Berthon' with the assent of Clarice, his wife, to William Avenel of Wrockeshal'[2] as the marriage portion of his daughter Agatha, of a fardel (*ferdellum*) of land with a messuage, a yard and all else pertaining thereto, which Henry de Wintred once gave to the grantor as the marriage portion of

---

[1] Seal: dark yellow wax, diam. ⅞ in.; rather blurred, but possibly two birds facing each other.

[2] Roshall, lost by inundation.

his daughter Clarice, in the vill of Wintred; to hold of the grantor, his heirs and assigns, to William and the lawfully begotten heirs of William and Agatha, freely, peacefully [*etc.*], in perpetuity, with all liberties and easements and customs in ways, paths, woods, plains, meadows, pastures and grazings, paying yearly to the chief lord of the fee a pair of spurs worth 6*d.*, or 6*d.* at Michaelmas, for all services, suits, exactions and secular demands which are the obligation of the grantor and his heirs, saving only that royal service which pertains to a fardel of land freely held in the same fee. Warranty against all men, and should it happen that the grantor or his heirs are not able or do not wish to warrant the land to William and his heirs, then he grants that William and his heirs shall have and hold in perpetuity an equal portion of the grantor's lands of la Berthon'[1] in whatever part they shall choose. Sealing clause. Witnesses: Henry Lonesest, Adam Malherbe, Hugh Malherbe, Henry Simund', John Wale, Robert Harlewine, Thomas Mogge. (*Y.A.S.*, M[D] 242, No. 1.)

Woodhall (E.R.)

458. Wednesday, St. Wilfrid, 36 Henry VI [Oct. 12, 1457]. Indenture by which Thomas Pertryk of Woodhall grants to Gregory Pertryk son of Gregory Pertryk, his son, all his lands, tenements, rents and services with meadows, pastures, grazings, woods and waters with all appurtenances in the vill and territory of Woodhall; to hold to Gregory and his lawfully begotten heirs of the chief lords of the fee; and for the provision and maintenance of five candles to burn before the image of Blessed Mary of Hemmyngburgh on the days when *Gaude Virgo salutata* or *Ave Regina*[2] are sung after mass in the same church, a messuage, one dole of meadow and an annual rent of 1*d.* and 14 selions of land given to Joan, late daughter of Thomas Pertryk, the grantor's grandfather, for the provision of the said candles, by the same Thomas, as is more fully described in his charter to her. Should Gregory die without lawfully begotten heirs, remainder to Richard Pertryk, chaplain, the grantor's son, to hold to him for his lifetime, paying yearly to Elizabeth, Isabel, Alice and Agnes, the grantor's daughters, 13*s.* 4*d.* for the provision of the candles during his life. After Richard's death, remainder to the grantor's daughters and their lawfully begotten heirs, to hold of the chief lords of the fee by the accustomed services, and providing the said candles. Should one of them wish to alienate her part of the said lands, rents [*etc.*], power to do so if to one of her sisters, but not to any other person. Should one of the sisters die without heirs,

---

[1] Burton Pidsea.

[2] *Ave Regina* was the antiphon sung after mass from the Purification to Maundy Thursday. *Gaude Virgo salutata* has not been traced, but the second verse of *Ave Regina* begins *Gaude Virgo gloriosa* and it is possible that this may be meant.

her portion to remain to the other sisters. Should they all die without heirs, remainder to the right heirs of the grantor in perpetuity. Warranty. Sealing clause. Witnesses: Robert Babthorp, esq., Thomas Hagthorp, Robert Portyngton, William Lawton, Richard Knyght, Leonard Knyght, William Hathelsay, Thomas Underwod, Thomas Robynson. At Wodhall. (*Farnley Hall MSS.*, No. 77.)

Woodkirk

459. Grant by Robert Burnel for the health of his soul and the souls of his parents and ancestors, to God and the church of St. Mary de Wudekircha and the canons of St. Oswald[1] serving there, in pure and perpetual alms, of all his assart which lies between the path called Kirketh and the broad way which leads to the bridge of Ligulf' as the hedge surrounds it; except that his wife shall hold 3 acres of the land of the church, paying yearly to the church 3*d.* at the Assumption of the B.V.M. Warranty. Witnesses: Alan de Ped . . . ., Walter his son, Simon de Linthona, Alan the squire of Alan, Peter de Floketona, Randolph Cardinal, Adam de Haukeswrthe, Alan the clerk of Bedeforde, Robert de Thodteclive, William of York, Jordan his son, Ralph son of Thomas son of Swein, William son of Ricolot [*sic*], Robert son of Robert, Richard Loholdt of Batheleia, Adam son of William chaplain of Batheleia, Nicholas de Erdeslau. (*BramleyMSS.*, No. 22.)

Worsborough

460. Oct. 22, 26 Henry VIII [1534]. Indenture whereby Thomas Elison of Workesburgh grants to Richard Kexforth, gent., William Brodesworth, Ralph Greves and William Haukesworth, all his messuages, cottages, lands, tenements, rents, reversions, services and all other hereditaments, with appurtenances in Cotes, Workesburgh, Cawthorne, Silkestone, Usilthwate,[2] and Waldershelf and elsewhere in England; to hold of the chief lords of the fee according to the indenture made between Nicholas Marsden and the grantor on Oct. 20, 26 Hen. VIII [1534]. Warranty. Sealing clause.[3]

Dorso: Livery of seisin to the above-named by Thomas Elison on Oct. 28, 1534, in the presence of Thomas Rawson, Thomas Grinlyngton, chaplain, Thomas Seuyd, Henry Hollande, junior, William Fendy, John Percy, William Marsden. (*Farnley Hall MSS.*, No. 78.)

Walkington

461. Morrow of St. Martin, 42 Henry III [Nov. 12, 1257]. Final Concord made in the court of the provost of Beverley at Beverley before Henry de Percy, John de Oleton, Robert Danyel

---

[1] Of Nostell. [2] Husthwaite. [3] Seal: blob of red wax.

and Geoffrey Agwylam, justices, and other faithful then present, between Ellen, daughter of Hugh de Driffeld, *quer.*, and John de Curzam and Alice his wife *imped.*, concerning 8 bovates of land with appurtenances in Walkington. John and Alice recognise the land to be the right of Ellen as that which she had of their gift; to hold to Ellen and her heirs, of John and Alice and the heirs of Alice for ever, paying yearly 1*d.* at Christmas and performing to the chief lords of the fee for the said John, Alice, and the heirs of Alice all other services which pertain to the land. Warranty. For this recognition, warranty, fine and agreement Ellen gave to John and Alice 30 silver marks. (*Archer-Houblon MSS.*, No. 490.)

York

462. Grant by Thomas, son of Robert Benet' of Heworth to Mariota his sister, of a messuage with appurtenances in Munkegate in the suburbs of York, which lies between the grantor's land on one side and the land which Thomas Gayt' holds on the other, and which extends from the highway of Munkegate in front, as far as the land once belonging to John del Poll' at the back; to hold of the chief lords of the fee. Warranty. Sealing clause.[1] Witnesses: Nicholas de Flemang, mayor of York[2]; Thomas de Alwarthorp', Nicholas de Colonia, Richard le Toller, bailiffs of York; John de Beverley, Ralph de Monkegate, Roger de Wharroum, Nicholas . . . .[3] [John] de Hibernia, clerk. (*Y.A.S.*, M^D 6, No. 1a.)

463. Thursday before the Nativity of St. John the Baptist [June 21], 1313. Quitclaim by John son of Gaudin the goldsmith of York, to Gaudin the goldsmith, his heirs and assigns, of all right in 3*s.* annual rent from the lands of Robert de Heword' in Munckegate. Warranty. Sealing clause.[4] Witnesses: John de Hornyngton', William Carpentar, William Rudde, Nicholas Gaudyne, Henry the clerk. At York. (*Ibid.*, No. 1.)

464. Wednesday before St. Margaret [July 15], 1327. Grant by Alan de Furnes of York to John Curteys, skinner (*pellipario*) of York, of all that messuage in the street of Blessed Peter the Little in York, which he had of the gift and feoffment of Eve, widow of Hugh de Acastre, grandmother of John; to hold with appurtenances to John, his heirs and assigns, of the chief lords of the fee. Warranty. Sealing clause.[5] Witnesses: Nicholas de Langeton, mayor of York, John de Woume, William de Hothum, Nicholas de Scoreby, bailiffs, Thomas de Redenesse, Stephen de

---

[1] Seal: brown wax, diam. ⅗ in.; undeciphered.

[2] Nicholas Fleming was mayor of York in 1316.

[3] Stain on document.

[4] Seal: black wax, small oval; probably Virgin and Child and kneeling figure; legend undeciphered.

[5] Seal: light brown wax, oval, $\frac{7}{10} \times \frac{8}{10}$ in.; possibly a ship; GUALO

Setryngton, Adam Skipwithe, Hugh de Friston', John de Nonyngton, Simon Gower, Robert de Duresine, William de Fratribus,
Thomas Deyvile, clerk. At York. (*Y.A.S.*, M^D 10, No. 1.)

465. Thursday before St. Margaret [July 16], 1327. Indenture by which John Curteys, skinner of York, holds himself bound
to Alan de Furnes of York, in the sum of 20 marks of silver, to
be paid to Alan or his attorney at York at the Invention of the
Holy Cross, 1330, to which settlement, both in time and place,
he holds himself, his heirs or executors bound, also all his goods
according to the judgement of lay or ecclesiastical judges. Alan
agrees on behalf of himself and his heirs that if John or his heirs
and assigns shall enfeoff Alan and his wife before the said Feast
by a charter of enfeoffment with warranty clause, with the piece
of land with the house (*hospitata*), with a cellar and a dwelling
room (*solar*), being 46 feet in length and 16 in breadth, in the
southern part of that messuage in the lane of St. Peter the Little
in York, the expenses and upkeep to be the responsibility of John,
his heirs and assigns, which messuage John had of the gift and
feoffment of Alan; to hold to Alan and Alice his wife for the term
of their lives, or for the lifetime of the survivor, with free entry
and exit to the land through either part of the messuage of which
the land is a portion. Alan also agrees that if he and his wife
shall peacefully enjoy a dwelling room in the east part of the
messuage, towards the churchyard of the church of Blessed Peter
the Little, and all the rooms built on the same part, namely, from
the same dwelling room as far as the ancient kitchen of the messuage, then John, his heirs and assigns, shall be released from all
the said debt of 20 marks, and John agrees that if he fail in the
above agreement then Alan, his heirs or executors, may seek to
recover the 20 marks without hindrance. Alternate seals.[1] At
York. (*Ibid.*, No. 1a.)

466. Saturday after the Decapitation of St. John [Aug. 29],
1327. Indenture by which John Curteys, citizen and skinner of
York, grants to Alan de Furnes and Alice, his wife, 20*s.* annual
rent, for the term of their lives or for the lifetime of the survivor,
to be received half at Martinmas and half at Whitsuntide, from
a messuage with appurtenances in the street of Blessed Peter the
Little, and which once belonged to Eve, widow of Hugh de
Acastre, the grantor's grandmother, and which he had of the gift
of Alan, with the exception of a piece of land 46 feet in length
and 16 feet in breadth, in the southern part of the messuage; to
hold to Alan and Alice of the grantor and his heirs, and if the rent
should be in arrears at any time, in whole or in part, then Alan
and Alice may enter and remove whatever satisfies them in place

---

[1] Seal: white wax, round, diam. ½ in.; a bird to the dexter; legend
undeciphered.

of the rent and arrears. Warranty. Alternate seals.[1] Witnesses: Nicholas de Langeton, mayor of York, John de Woume, William de Hothum and Nicholas de Scoreby, bailiffs, Thomas de Redenesse, Stephen de Setrington, Adam Kyngeson, William de Fratribus, Hugh de Friston, Simon Gower, Robert de Molesby, John de Nonyngton, Robert de Doresine, Thomas Deyvile, clerk. At York. (*Ibid.*, No. 2.)

467. Wednesday in Whitweek [May 26], 1333, 7 Edward III. Indenture[2] by which Thomas son of William Gra of Skelton' near York leases to Robert son of Hamo de Harum and Alice, his wife, for their lives, or for the lifetime of the survivor, all his tenement with shops (*shopis*), cellars, upper rooms (*solariis*), buildings and other appurtenances in the street of Marketskire in York, which the lessor had of the gift and feoffment of Master Thomas Gra, doctor [?] (*fisici'*), and which lies in breadth between the land of Peter de Haxiholme on one side and the land once of Andrew de Bolingbrok' on the other, and in length from the highway in front as far as the water of Fosse at the back; to hold of the grantor and his heirs, paying yearly a rose at the Nativity if demanded, and performing the due and accustomed services to the lord of the fee. The land to revert to the lessor after the deaths of Robert and Alice. Warranty. Sealing clause.[3] Witnesses: Nicholas de Langeton', mayor of York, Henry Lorbatur', William Fisher, William de Estrington', bailiffs, Thomas Durant, Richard de Leycestre, William de Horneby, Hugh de Miton', Alexander de Wakefeld, Peter le Poleter, Thomas Deyvile, clerk. At York. (*Y.A.S.*, M^D 9, No. 1.)

468. Grant by Robert de Harum, son of Hamo de Harum, rector of the church of Acastre Malbys, of a toft and 4 bovates of land with appurtenances in the vill and territory of Bodelom,[4] which the grantor had of the gift and feoffment of John de Multon of Sutton under Twitestonecliffe: he also grants all those lands and

---

[1] Seal: as to No. 464.

[2] Also (a) Counterpart. Seals: brownish wax; (1) diam. ½ in., blurred, possibly crossed hands; (2) an animal to sinister with a staff behind it. (*Ibid.*, No. 1a.)

(b) Quitclaim by the same to the same dated the Circumcision [Jan. 1], 1334[-5], and witnessed by Henry de Belton', mayor of York, John de Bristow, William de Shirburne, John Caproun, bailiffs, Hugh Sturmy, William Starre, William de Sproxton, Richard de Pikryng, Peter Aspilon of Calueton [Cawton]. At Harum. (*Ibid.*, No. 2.)

(c) Quitclaim by the same to the same, also of an annual rent of a rose at the Nativity of St. John the Baptist, dated Jan. 11, 1334[-5], and witnessed by Henry de Belton, Wm. de Schirburne, John Caperon, William de Redenesse, Thomas Durant, Richard de Leycestre, Hugh de Miton, William de Horneby, Alexander de Wakefeld, Peter le Poleter, John de Seleby, spicer, William de Beverley, spicer, Thomas Deyvile of York, clerk. At York. (*Ibid.*, No. 3.)

[3] Seal: white wax, round, diam. ₇⁄₁₀ in.; in a cusped border a shield of arms; a chevron between three lozenges.

[4] Beadlam.

L

tenements which he had of the gift of Amandus Sourdeuále of Hemingholme which Gerard de Heythorpe once held in the vill of Bodelom, also a messuage in the vill of Harum which he had of the gift and feoffment of Adam Proudefote of Harum. He also grants a tenement in Marketskire [*as described in No.* 467] in York which he had of Thomas son of William Gra; to hold of the chief lord of the fee. Warranty. Sealing clause.[1] Witnesses: Sir William Malbys, knt., Thomas de Etton, Robert de Sproxton', William Stibbinge, John son of Peter de Bodelom, Simon de Yolton'.[2] (*Ibid.*, No. 5.)

469.   In the name of God Amen, the Thursday after St. Thomas the Martyr, namely 15 July, 1334. I, William de Abbathia, girdler (*zonarius*) of York, make my testament in this manner. First I bequeath and commend my soul to God, Blessed Mary and all the saints and my body to be buried in the church of St. Mary's Abbey, York, near the font, and for my mortuary, my best robe with the sleeveless tunic (*collobio*). Item: I bequeath to the sacrist of St. Mary for ten oblations in respect of my burial in the church 20s. Item: for two chaplains to celebrate the divine offices for one year for my soul and the souls of the departed 10 marks of silver, and 3s. 4d. for bread, wine and wax for the same, and I will that one of them shall celebrate in the church of St. Olave, and the other in the chapel of Blessed Mary. Item: for wax for burning around my body and for the making of the same 13s. 3d. Item: to the sacrists of the said Abbey for bell-ringing for my soul 12d. Item: to the convent of Blessed Mary of York for a pittance (*pictantiam*) 14s. 4d. Item: for the funeral rites on the day of my burial 40s., and for the distribution of bread to the poor 10s. Item: to Margaret, my wife a certain annual rent of 5s. from a rackhouse (*tentorio*) built in the parish of St. Margaret, and from the garden of the rackhouse, which I had of the gift and feoffment of Thomas de Thurkelby and his daughters, to hold to Margaret freely [*etc.*] for the term of her life, of the chief lords of the fee, and after her death to William, son of Andrew de Tang' and the heirs of his body lawfully begotten, and if William should die without heirs, I bequeath the said rent to Richard, his brother, his heirs and assigns, to hold of the chief lords of the fee. Item: to the prior and convent of the Monastery of Blessed Mary at York and to their successors for the performance of my anniversary services yearly for ever, all that tenement with buildings and appurtenances in St. Giles' Street in the suburbs of York, which lies in breadth between the tenement once belonging to Robert son of Lawrence de Bouthum on one side and the land

---

[1] Seal: red wax, diam. $\frac{7}{16}$ in.; a squirrel to the dexter within two interlocking squares; . . E . . E . . E . . E

[2] Appointment of Richard de Hamecotes of York and William de Lepington' as attorneys. Nov. 11, 23 Edward III [1349]. Seal as to the grant. (*Ibid.*, No. 6.)

once belonging to Nicholas Gaudyn on the other, and in length from the high street in front to the land once belonging to William le Vendour at the back, also that tenement with appurtenances in Bouthum which I had of the gift and feoffment of Thomas son of William de Ulveston, which lies in width between the land which once belonged to Thomas de Ulveston on one side and the land of Peter de Shuptone on the other, and lengthways from the highstreet of Bouthum in front as far as the land of the said Thomas at the back; to hold the two tenements to the prior and convent and their successors, of the chief lords of the fee, by the due and accustomed services. Item: to Adam de Byron a woollen (*burneto*) tunic. Item: to the Augustine Friars of York 6s. 8d. so that the chaplain on the day of my burial shall say one mass for my soul. Item: to the Friars Minor of York 2s., and to the Dominican Friars (*fratribus predicatoribus*) 2s., and to the Carmelite Friars 2s. Item: to the church of the Priory of the Augustinians of York a towel (*manutergium*) for the altar of Blessed Mary in the church. Item: to William son of Ellen, my daughter, 20s.; and I will that my executors shall expend whatever is necessary for his education. Item: to the chaplain of my parish 12d., and to the clerk of the parish 6d. Item: to poor clerks and widows 3s. Item: to the lepers of Clyfton 6d. Item: to the fabric fund of the church of St. Peter of York 5s., and 13s. 4d. in which Robert Ward is bound to me. Item: to William de Appelby, clerk, 5s. Item: to Richard, son of my daughter Ellen, 20s. Item: to my daughter Alice for one dress to be bought for her, 20s. Item: to John, son of Ellen, my daughter, 20s. for his studies. Item: to John de Conyngesbourgh' 5s. if he will be my executor. Item: to Alexander de Mounckgat, my executor, 5s. and one tunic of best wool. Item: to John son of Andrew de Tang', after the death of Margaret, my wife, the best pot in my house, one skin bottle and the best table with trestles. Item: to John de Lambelay and Agnes, his wife, my daughter, 6 silver spoons (*coclear'*) and a copper (*eream*) pot which once belonged to William le Brewester. All the residue of my goods in whatsoever condition or place they may be, I bequeath to Margaret, my wife. I ordain that these shall be the executors of my will: Margaret, my wife, Alexander de Mounckegate and John de Conyngesbourghe, that they will faithfully perform whatever the Most High shall inspire them for the health of my soul. Sealing clause.[1] At York. Item: I bequeath to Brother Elias of Catherton' 5s. Item: to the Augustinian Friars of York an additional 6s. 8d.[2] (*Y.A.S.*, M⁰ 6, No. 2.)

[1] Seals: (1) red wax, round, the letter T; (2) red and brown wax, broken, probably the figure of a saint; (3) brown wax, broken, a merchant's device, legend undeciphered; (4) brown wax, square, undeciphered; (5) black wax, square, probably a fleur-de-lis.

[2] Administration granted to the executors at York, 14 kalends of November [Oct. 19], 1334.

470. Monday before the Purification of the B.V.M. [Jan. 31], 1334[-5], 9 [8 ?] Edward III. Quitclaim by John son of John de Warthille of York, to Thomas son of William Gra of Skelton' near York, his heirs and assigns, of all right in all the lands, rents, tenements with appurtenances in the city of York or in the vill of Acom near York, namely, all that tenement with appurtenances in Marketskire in York which Robert son of Hamo de Harum had for the term of his life of Thomas; also all that tenement with appurtenances in Conyngstret in York, which Thomas son of William had of the gift and legacy of Master Thomas Gra, doctor [?] (*Fisici*), which lies between the land of William Sperri on one side and the land once of Master Thomas de Cave on the other; also in all other lands [*etc.*] in York which Thomas son of William Gra had of the gift and legacy of Master Thomas; he also releases 2 bovates of land in Acom which Thomas had of the gift and legacy of Thomas Gra. Warranty. Sealing clause.[1] Witnesses: Henry de Belton', mayor of York, John de Bristowe, William de Shirburn', John Caperoun, bailiffs, Richard Toller, Richard de Allerton', Nicholas Fouk, William de Friston, Thomas Durant, Richard de Leycestre, Hugh de Miton', John Durant, Robert de Daleby, Nicholas de Scoreby, Henry de Scoreby, William Sperry, John de Barneby, Thomas Deyville of York, clerk. At York. (*Y.A.S.*, M^D 9, No. 4.)

471. Monday after St. Peter in cathedra [Feb. 28], 1334[-5], 9 Edward III. Grant[2] by John Curtays, skinner of York, to Dom. Thomas Abel, rector of the church of Blessed Peter the Little, of the northern half of his messuage with buildings and appurtenances in the street of Blessed Peter the Little, which messuage the grantor had of the gift and feoffment of Alan de Fornes, and which lies in length from the said street in front as far as the land of Thomas de Moubray at the back, and contains in breadth towards the street four ells and three fourths of an ell, and three parts of a quarter of an ell, without the inches [*sic*], and in breadth towards the land of Thomas de Moubray at the back seven ells, one quarter and half a quarter of an ell, without the inches; to hold of the chief lords of the fee. Warranty. Sealing clause.[3] Witnesses: Henry de Belton, mayor of York, John de Bristowe, William de Shirburne, John Caperon, bailiffs, Stephen de Setrington, John de Nunyngton, Alan de Quixlay, Alan Bride, Robert de Sallay, John de Cliderhowe, clerk. At York. (*Y.A.S.*, M^D 10, No. 3.)

472. Monday after St. Peter in cathedra [Feb. 28], 1334[-5]. Sale by John Curtays, skinner of York, to Dom. Thomas Abel,

---

[1] Seal: white wax, oval, $\frac{7}{10} \times 1\frac{1}{10}$ ins.; an animal, possibly a lion, rampant to the dexter.

[2] Also duplicate of deed.

[3] Seal: dark brown wax, round, diam. $\frac{7}{10}$ in.; device, a bird to the sinister; legend undeciphered.

rector of the church of Blessed Peter the Little, for a certain sum of money, of all his goods and chattels in the northern half of the messuage granted by John to Thomas and more fully described in his charter. Warranty. Sealing clause.[1] At York. (*Ibid.*, No. 3a.)

473. March 18, 1334[-5]. Indenture by which Thomas Abel, rector of the church of Blessed Peter the Little, leases to John Curtays, skinner, and Lettice, his wife, the northern half of a messuage with buildings and appurtenances in the street of Blessed Peter the Little, which the lessor had of the gift of John and which lies [*as described in No.* 471]; to hold for the term of their lives, or for the lifetime of the survivor, paying yearly a rose in the season of roses if demanded, and performing the due and accustomed services to the lords of the fee. After the deaths of John and Lettice, remainder to John de Thorneton, citizen of York, and Alice, his wife, daughter of John Curtays, and their lawful heirs, and should they die without heirs, to the nearest of kin (*propinquatoribus*) of John Curtays. Alternate seals.[2] Witnesses: [*as to No.* 471]. At York. (*Ibid.*, No. 4.)

474. Friday after St. Matthew [Sept. 22], 1335. Quitclaim[3] by William Atte Water, citizen and merchant of York, and Mariota his wife, daughter of Guy, goldsmith of York, deceased, to Margaret, widow of William de Abbathia, girdlemaker of York, deceased, and the executor of his will, also to Alexander de Munckgate and John de Conynggesburgh, co-executors with the said Margaret, of all those debts which the said William de Abbathia, while living, owed to William and Mariota or their assigns, or to the said Guy, and which were either bequeathed by the will of Guy or existed apart from the will; also all actions, demands [*etc.*], real or personal, which the grantors held against Margaret, Alexander and John, from the beginning to the end of the world. Sealing clause.[4] Witnesses: William de Estryngton, Thomas, brother of the said William, of Burghbrigg, Andrew de Tange, William de Cotingwit, William de Appelby, clerk. At York. (*Y.A.S.*, M^D 6, No. 3a.)

475. Saturday after St. Barnabas [June 13], 1338, 12 Edward III. Grant by John Curtays of York, skinner, to Dom. Thomas de Loudham, chaplain, of a tenement with appurtenances in Peterlanelitel in York, that is, a certain entrance way with a well called le Drauwelle situated in the entrance, which lies between the grantor's tenement, which John de Lutryngton and Alice, his wife, the grantor's daughter, and their lawful heirs are to

---

[1] Seal: as to No. 471, on a tongue cut from the bottom of deed.

[2] Seals: (1) same as to No. 471; (2) brown wax, a floral device.

[3] Similar quitclaim by Richard de Tickhill and Isabel, his wife, daughter of Guy, and witnessed by William Attewater in place of William de Cotingwit. (*Ibid.*, No. 3b.)

[4] Seals: two—one red wax, one brown; undeciphered.

hold after the death of the grantor and his wife on the one side, and the tenement which William de Mallerstang and Agnes his wife, the grantor's daughter, and their lawful heirs are to hold after death of grantor and wife, on the other, and which contains [*as described in No.* 471]; also all his cellar, called le Malthous, with a piece of land and a washplace (*latrina*) which lie between the cellar and the aforesaid tenement, with remainder to William and Agnes; to hold to Thomas, his heirs and assigns, of the chief lords of the fee. Warranty. Sealing clause.[1] Witnesses: Nicholas de Langeton, mayor of York, Hugh de Miton', Robert de Skelton, Robert de Askby, bailiffs, John de Shirburne, Stephen de Setrington, Richard de Brignalle, John Randman, John de Rypon, Robert of York, clerk. At York. (*Y.A.S.*, M^D 10, No. 5.)

476.   Wednesday, the Feast of the Nativity of St. John the Baptist [June 24], 1338. Indenture[2] witnessing grant by Thomas de Loudham, chaplain, to John Curtays, skinner, and Lettice, his wife, of all that tenement in the street called the lane of St. Peter the Little in York, with the upper stories and eaves ? (*gettes et efsdropes*) and with all the other appurtenances, which lies from the highway of Peterlane in front over the upper room and toft as far as the grantor's tenement at the back, and contains in length 29½ ells, and in length above the upper rooms built thereon 30½ ells less two inches, and lies in breadth between the grantor's tenement and his well called le Drauwell on the north on one side and a lane which is next to the church of Blessed Peter the Little on the south, on the other side; also grants a certain chamber or upper room built over le Malthous with gutters (*grundis*) under the feet of the posts of the said chamber, with free entrance and exit for the repairing thereof whenever and so often as it needs repairs or rebuilding, and this chamber or upper room is situated between the tenements of the grantor and of Thomas de Moubray, and contains in breadth 7 ells and in length 7½ ells; *to hold to John and Lettice for their lives or during the life of the survivor, of the chief lords of the fee, and after their deaths remainder to William de Mallerstang and Agnes, his wife, and their legitimate heirs, and in default of issue remainder to John de Lotryngton and Alice, his wife, and if they should die without heirs remainder to the right heirs of John Curtays. Warranty. Alternate seals.[3] Witnesses: Nicholas de Langeton, mayor of York, Hugh de Miton, Robert de Skelton, Robert de Askby, bailiffs, John de Shirburne, Stephen de Setrington, Richard de Brignalle, John de Rypon, John Randman, John de Nunyngton, William de Dyghton, Hugh de

---

[1] Seal: white wax, broken and blurred.

[2] Also counterpart, two brown seals, undeciphered.

[3] Seal: whitish brown wax, oval, $\frac{9}{10} \times \frac{7}{10}$ in.; two figures facing, with a pitcher between them, and the head and shoulders of a third figure below. Legend undeciphered.

Friston, William Swetmouth, Richard de Heselyngton of York, clerk. At York. (*Ibid.*, No. 6.)

477. Sunday after the Nativity of St. John the Baptist [June 28], 1338. Indenture[1] by which Thomas de Loudham, chaplain, grants to John Curtays of York, skinner, and Lettice, his wife, a tenement with appurtenances in Peterlanelitel, namely, an entrance with a well, called le Drauwell, which lies between a tenement which is to belong to William de Mallerstang and Agnes, his wife, after the death of John and Lettice, on the southern part on one side, and the tenement to belong to John de Lotryngton and Alice, his wife, after their death, on the north on the other side, and being in breadth in the front of the tenement, without the entry, towards the street of Peter lane, one ell, three quarters of an ell and a fourth part of a quarter of an ell, and in length between the aforesaid tenement from the street of Peterlanelitel in front as far as the tenement of Thomas de Moubray at the back; he also grants the cellar called le Malthous with a piece of ground on which the stepladder [?] (*stepeleder*) is usually placed; also a washplace (*latrina*), which lies between le Malthous and the tenement, to belong to William de Mallerstang and Agnes. [*Remainder of deed as from * in the preceding deed.*] (*Ibid.*, No. 7.)

478. Thursday after Trinity, 19 Edward III [May 26, 1345]. Indenture by which Robert son of Hamo de Harum demises to Alan de Brathetwayt of York and Agnes, his wife, a messuage in Marketskire, Pavement, York, with all upper rooms, cellars and appurtenances; to hold for the term of their lives, paying yearly to Robert and his heirs, for the 16 years following, 8 marks 6s. 8d. of silver at Whitsuntide and Martinmas in equal portions; after the end of the 16 years for the remaining years (*per quemlibet ann'*) 20*li.* of silver at the same terms. Alan and Agnes agree that if the rent should at any time be in arrears in part or wholly then Robert may enter and distrain. Sealing clause.[2] Witnesses: John de Shirburne, mayor of York, William de Acastre, Robert de Selby and William de Houyngham, bailiffs, Richard de Leycestre of York, John Duraunt of York. At York. (*Ibid.*, No. 7a.)

479. May 21, 1346. Appointment by Walter de Osbaldwik, tanner (*allutar'*) of York, and Sara his wife, of William de Appelby, clerk, as attorney to deliver seisin to John Archebaud, citizen and merchant of York, and Ellen, his wife, their daughter, of a messuage in Munkgate in the suburbs of York, in accordance with their charter. Sealing clause.[3] Witnesses: John de Crayke, John

---

[1] Also counterpart of indenture with two seals of brown wax, undeciphered.

[2] Seal: red wax, diam. ⅜ in.; blurred.

[3] Two seals, of brown wax: (1) broken; (2) a hare couchant to the dexter.

de Moreby, *Irenmanger*, Richard de Tichill'. At York. (*Y.A.S.*, M^D 6, No. 4.)

480. May 26, 1346, 20 Edward III. Grant by Walter de Osbaldwike, tanner (*allutar'*) of York, and Sara his wife, to John Archbaud, citizen and merchant of York, and Ellen his wife, the grantor's daughter, of a messuage with appurtenances in Munckgate in the suburbs of York, which lies in breadth between the land of John Crayke on one side and the land once belonging to Simon Gouwer on the other, and lengthwise from the highway of Munckgate in front, as far as the land once belonging to William Clervaux at the back; to hold to John and Ellen and their heirs of the chief lords of the fee. Warranty. Sealing clause.[1] Witnesses: Henry le Goldebeter, mayor of York, John de Crayke, John de Moreby, *Irenmanger*, Richard de Tichill', Thomas son of Nigel de Menyngthorp', Robert del Wald', William de Wirkesale, John le Hatter, William le Waterleder. At York. (*Ibid.*, No. 5.)

481. Wednesday, St. Thomas the Apostle [Dec. 21], 1362. Grant[2] by John de Norton', clerk, advocate of the court of York, executor of the will of Dom. William de Harum, late rector of the church of Acastremalbys, to John de Crome, Ralph de Romundby, Geoffrey de Gedeney and John de Thornton', spicer, of all that tenement in York [*as described in No. 467*] which William de Harum left to be sold; to hold of the chief lords of the fee. Sealing clause.[3] Witnesses: John de Langeton', mayor of York, Robert de Pathoron, Robert del Gare and Simon Gouk, bailiffs, Hamo de Hessay, Hugh de Miton', John de Santon', Richard de Thoresby, John de Clayton', Robert de Cliburn, clerk. At York. (*Y.A.S.*, M^D 9, No. 8.)

482. Tuesday after St. Michael, 39 Edward III [Sept. 30, 1365]. Grant[4] by Avelyn de Aclom to Sir William de Aclom], *chevalier*, of two rooms and two upper rooms (*solers*) with a garden, near the fountain (*ffountayne*), which the grantor has of the gift of William son of John de Barton' of Naburn; to hold with free entry and exit the said rooms in the grantor's tenement in Walmegat and Fishergat, abutting on Noutgaile, for the term of one hundred years, rendering to the grantor a rose at the time of roses if demanded. At York. (*Y.A.S.*, M^D 182, No. 103.)

483. Friday after the Ascension [26 May], 1368. Quitclaim by Roger Archebald, son of John Archebald, late citizen and merchant of York, to John de Houeden' of York, merchant, and Juliana his wife, their heirs and assigns, of all right in all that

---

[1] Seals: as to the preceding deed.

[2] Quitclaim of the same to the same, dated Dec. 25, 1362; same witnesses. (*Ibid.*, No. 9.)

[3] Seal: red wax, diam. ${}^{8}_{10} \times {}^{9}_{10}$ in.; undeciphered.

[4] In French.

messuage with appurtenances in Munkgate in the suburbs of York, which lies in breadth between the land once belonging to John de Crayke on one side and the land once of Simon Gower on the other, and in length from the highway of Munkgate in front, as far as the land once belonging to William Clervaux at the back; which messuage Juliana had of the gift and bequest of John Archebald. Warranty. Sealing clause. Witnesses: Robert de Howome, mayor of York, John de Clayton', Roger de Moreton' and John de Esshton', bailiffs, John de Langton', William Gra, Roger de Houyngham, Roger de Selby, Robert del Gare, Thomas Siggeston, Thomas Kylpyn, Robert de Cleburn', clerk. At York. (*Y.A.S.*, M^D 6, No. 6.)

484. Wednesday after the Sunday on which is sung *Quasi modo geniti* [April 8], 1369. Grant[1] by Alice, widow of John Caperon of York, to Dom. William de Bruneby, chaplain, of two messuages with appurtenances in Munckgate in the suburbs of York, which lie in length from the highway of Munkgate in front, as far as le Jubericroft at the back, and in width between the tenement of Robert de Holme on one side and the tenement of the said Alice on the other; to hold to William and his heirs, of the chief lords of the fee. Sealing clause.[2] Witnesses: William Savage, mayor of York, William Couper, William de Burton' and Hugh de Haukeswell, bailiffs, Richard de Thursby, John de Scorby, bowmaker (*bouer*). At York. (*Ibid.*, No. 7.)

485. April 10, 1370, 44 Edward III. Indenture witnessing grant by William de Bruneby, chaplain, to Adam Myles of Heworth, *pynner*, and Ellen, his wife, of two messuages with appurtenances in Munkgate in the suburbs of York, which the grantor had of the gift and feoffment of Alice, widow of John Caprone of York, which lie in length from the high street of Munkgate in front, as far as le Jubirycroft at the back, and in breadth between the tenement of Robert de Howome on one side and that of the said Alice on the other; to hold to Adam and Ellen and the heirs of their bodies lawfully begotten; and in default of lawful issue remainder to Richard de Thoresby of York, *draper*, William de Tikhill of York and Master John de Roucliff, their heirs and assigns, of the chief lords of the fee. Alternate seals.[3] Witnesses: Roger de Selby, mayor of York, Henry de Ribstan,' Richard de Wagher', William Giry, bailiffs of the city, John de Langton', William Gra, Robert de Howome, John de Santon', Thomas Gra. At York. (*Ibid.*, No. 9.)

---

[1] Quitclaim by the same to the same, dated April 3, 1370, and witnessed by Roger de Selby, mayor, Henry de Ribstan, Richard Waghr' and William Giry, bailiffs, William Gra, Robert Howome, John Santon'. At York. Same seal. (*Ibid.*, No. 8.)

[2] Seal: red wax, diam. $\frac{3}{8}$ in. a shield of arms, blurred; ✠ SIGILL IOHANNIS CAPERUN.

[3] Seals: red wax; (1) a quatrefoil, legend undeciphered; (2) missing.

486. Tuesday, St. Matthew the Apostle, 2 Richard II
[Sept. 21, 1378]. Grant by John de Roucliff, clerk, and John de
Beverlay, citizen of York, to Roger de Moreton', John de Dernyngton',[1] Hugh Dunnok, John de Sheffeld, William de Tikhille
and William Durem, citizens of York, of a messuage with shop
(*shoppe*) annexed and appurtenances in Marketskyre, the Pavement in York, which lies in breadth between the land of John
de Berden' of York on one side and the land of Richard son of
John de Santon' and a certain common lane leading from the
water of Fosse on the other, and in length from the highway in
front as far as the water of Fosse at the back, which messuage
the grantors had of the gift and feoffment of William de Brouneby,
chaplain; to hold of the chief lords of the fee. Sealing clause.[2]
Witnesses: John de Berden', mayor of York, John de Wraneby,
Thomas Smythe, bailiffs, John de Acastre, John de Santon',
Richard de Thoresby, John de Patherorn, John de Quixlay. At
York. (*Y.A.S.*, M^D 9, No. 10.)

487. Jan. 12, 2 Richard II [1378–9]. Grant[3] by John Kenlay
of York to John de Berden, citizen and merchant of York, and
William Brunelay, chaplain, their heirs and assigns, of an annual
rent of 10*s*. sterling in equal portions at Whitsuntide and Martinmas, from that messuage with appurtenances which the grantor
had of the gift and feoffment of John de Kenlay, his father, in
Bouthum in the suburbs of York, and which lies in length from
the highway of Bouthum in front, as far as the garden of the
abbot and convent of Blessed Mary of York, called Aumerygarth,
at the back, and in breadth between the land once belonging to
Thomas de Ulueston on one side and the land of the nunnery
of St. Clement on the other. Power to John and William to enter
and distrain if the rent be in arrears, wholly or in part. Warranty.
And for further security the grantor delivers seisin of this annual
rent of 10*s*. by handing over 1*d*. Sealing clause.[4] Witnesses:
John de Sheffeld, Elias Littester, William de Tikhill, bailiffs of
York, Thomas Gra, John de Gysburn, Roger de Moretun, junior,
John de Pathorn, John de Brathwayt, John de Quixlay, William
de Cestria of York, clerk. At York. (*Farnley Hall MSS.*, No. 79.)

488. Memorandum of the will of Eleanor Milys, wife of Adam
Milys of York, *pynner*, who died on St. Bartholomew's Day [Aug.
24], 1387, and who commended her soul to God and her body

---

[1] Possibly a form of Darlington.

[2] Seals: red wax; (1) blob of wax, bearing a fleur-de-lis; (2) diam. ⅔ in.;
in a cusped border, on a shield engrailed, a fleur-de-lis. JO . . . . DE
BEVERLAC.

[3] Five letters of the first line make an attractively floreated heading to
this deed, O,S,K,N,H.

[4] Seal: red wax, diam. 1 in.; in a cusped border a shield of arms, a chevron
between three lions' faces. ✠ SIGILLUM : JOHANNIS : KENLAY.

to be buried in the churchyard (*cimitterio*) of Holy Cross. Item: she willed her best robe for her burial. Item: all her other clothes to be given to the poor for the good of her soul. Item: two tenements with appurtenances in Monkgate to the said Adam Milys, her husband, to be sold for his maintenance and for the payment of her debts, or for whatever else Adam desires. For the faithful performance of the same she appoints Adam her executor.[1] (*Y.A.S.*, M^D 6, No. 10.)

489. Aug. 8, 1388, 12 Richard II. Grant by Adam Milys, *pynner*, of York to Nicholas de Skelton of York, of two messuages with appurtenances in Monkgate in the suburbs of York, which lie in length from the high street of Monkgate in front, as far as le Juberie Croft at the back, and in breadth between the tenement of William de Garnby, *carpenter*, on one side and the tenement of John de Beverlay on the other; to hold to Nicholas, his heirs and assigns, of the chief lords of the fee. Warranty. Sealing clause.[2] Witnesses: William de Selby, mayor of York, Henry Weyman', William de Leversham, John de Stillyngton', bailiffs, Robert Holme, John de Sadyngton', Robert Gare, Nicholas de Lyndesay, Robert Fymmer. At York. (*Ibid.*, No. 11.)

490. Thursday before Michaelmas [Sept. 26], 1392, 16 Richard II. Grant[3] by William de Tikhille, John de Dernyngton and John de Sheffeld, citizens of York, to Richard Alne, citizen of York, and Robert de Elmeswelle, chaplain, of a messuage and a shop adjoining with appurtenances [*as described in No.* 486]; to hold of the chief lords of the fee. Warranty. Sealing clause.[4] Witnesses: Robert Sauvage, mayor of York, John de Crauen, John de Penrith and William Vesty, bailiffs, John de Berden, John de Thornton', William de Pountfreit, John de Quixley, John de Bernardcastelle, Thomas Werd, William de Chestre of York. At York. (*Y.A.S.*, M^D 9, No. 11).

491. Dec. 30, 1396. Grant by Robert de Elmeswelle, chaplain, of a messuage and a shop [*as described in No.* 486] to William Ottelay, William de Touthorpe, chaplain, John de Darnyngton, Richard de Alne, John de Quixley, John Stokwyth and William Celer; to hold of the chief lords of the fee. Sealing clause. Witnesses: William Frost, mayor, John del More, Thomas Houeden, bailiffs, Thomas Gra, Thomas Howome, Robert Sauvage, William Selby, Simon de Quixley, John Houeden, William de Helmersley of York. At York. (*Ibid.*, No. 13).

---

[1] Seal: fragment of black wax on tongue cut from bottom of deed; also another tongue cut for fastening.

[2] Seal: red wax, diam. ½ in.; blurred.

[3] Release of the same by Richard de Alne to Robert de Elmeswelle, dated Nov. 1, 1396. Witnesses as to No. 491. (*Ibid.*, No. 12.)

[4] Three seals of red wax: (1) broken; (2) blob of wax bearing a fleur-de-lis; (3) the letter W between two sprigs of leaves.

492. Oct. 3, 1396. Grant by John de Houeden', citizen and merchant of York, to Elizabeth, widow of Richard Basy of Bilburgh' and John de Lucton', chaplain, of that messuage with appurtenances which John Morpath', *walker*, holds and occupies in Munkgate in the suburbs of York, and which lies in breadth between the land once belonging to John de Crayke on one side and the land once of Simon Gower on the other, and in length from the highway in front as far as the land once belonging to William Clervaux at the back; to hold to Elizabeth and John, their heirs and assigns, of the chief lords of the fee, on the following conditions: that if the grantor, his heirs or assigns, or any person in his name, shall pay to Elizabeth and John, their heirs, executors or attorneys, 23*li*. in the following manner, namely, 115*s*. at Pentecost next following, or during the 15 days after the Feast, 115*s*. at Martinmas or 15 days following, 115*s*. at Whitsuntide next or during the 15 ensuing days, and 115*s*. at Martinmas or during the 15 days after, and if the 23*li*. shall be paid in the aforesaid manner, then this indenture shall no longer be valid but shall be returned to the said John de Houeden', his heirs or executors, and he shall be permitted to re-enter and hold the said messuage as in its original (*prefatum*) condition; but if John, his heirs or assigns, shall default in payment of the 23*li*. in part or in whole at any of the stated terms, then this charter to stand. Warranty. Alternate seals.[1] Witnesses: William Frost, mayor of York, John del More and Thomas de Houeden', bailiffs, Simon Quixlay, William Sauvage, Richard Gyffon', William del Bothe. At York. (*Y.A.S.*, M^D 6, No. 12.)

493. April 10, 1398, 21 Richard II. Quitclaim by Nicholas de Skelton', sergeant at arms of our lord the king, his heirs and assigns, to William de Towthorp', John de Munketon', Robert Paa, John de Brynysshton', Robert Mekee, Robert de Folton', and John de Feryby, chaplains, of all right in two messuages with appurtenances in Munkegate in the suburbs of York, which once belonged to Adam Miles of Heworth and Ellen, his wife, and which lie in breadth between the tenement once belonging to Alice, wife of John Capron', on the other, and in length from the highway of Munkegate in front, as far as le Jubirycroft at the back. Warranty. Sealing clause.[2] Witnesses: Thomas Gra, mayor of York, William Sallay, John Hewyk, sheriffs, William Seleby, Thomas Thurkyll, John de Quyxlay, Nicholas Warthill, John Cuthbert, William Popilton' of York. At York. (*Ibid.*, No. 14.)

494. July 20, 1398. Indenture by which Agnes, widow of Nicholas de Touthorpe, leases to William de Touthorpe, Robert

---

[1] Seals: two, red wax; (1) round, diam. ½ in., figure of St. Catherine beneath a canopy, ELISABIT; (2) gem, two heads facing, male to the sinister, female to the dexter.

[2] Seal: red wax; small armorial shield bearing a chevron between three mullets pierced; legend undeciphered.

de Yokeflete, chaplain, Thomas Thurkylle of York and John de Quyxlay of York, all the lands and tenements with appurtenances which she has in the city of York, except that tenement[1] in which she now lives, which lie in breadth between the lane called le Kyrkelane, in the parish of Blessed Peter the Little, on one side, and the land belonging to the chantry from (*per*) Robert Swetemouth, in the church of Blessed Peter, on the other side, and in length from the highway called Peterlanelytylle in front as far as the land once belonging to John de Acastre at the back; to hold to the lessees, their heirs and assigns, paying yearly 6 marks 6s. 8d. at Martinmas and Whitsuntide in equal portions, for the whole of the lessor's life: should the rent be in arrears after any of the terms for the space of 20 days, Agnes may enter, hold and retain the tenement notwithstanding this agreement. Warranty. Alternate seals.[2] Witnesses: Thomas Gra, mayor of York, William Sallay, John Hewyk, bailiffs, William Pountfreit, John de Thorneton, John de Doncastre, William de Braweby of York. At York. (*Y.A.S.*, M^D 10, No. 8.)

495. July 23, 1398. Indenture by which William de Touthorpe, Robert de Yokeflete, chaplain, Thomas Thurkylle of York and John de Quyxlay of York grant and demise to Agnes, widow of Nicholas de Touthorpe of York, all that tenement which she now holds in le Kyrklane next to the church of Blessed Peter the Little; to hold to Agnês, her heirs and assigns, for the term of her life, paying yearly to the grantors a rose in the season of roses, if demanded, for all secular services, etc., while the grantors agree to pay all proper costs (*sumptibus*) and repairs during the life of Agnes. Warranty. Alternate seals.[3] Witnesses [*as to preceding deed*]. At York. (*Ibid.*, No. 10.)

496. July 24, 1398, 22 Richard II. Indenture[4] by which William de Touthorpe, chaplain, and John de Quyxlay resolve to deposit in the custody of Thomas de Thurkylle of York all the charters and documents below mentioned: first, a charter of Alan de Fourneis of York and John Curteys, skinner of York, concerning the whole of a messuage in the street of Blessed Peter the Little. Item: a charter of John Curteys and Thomas Abelle, rector of the church aforesaid, concerning half the above messuage. Item: two indentures between John and Lettice, his wife, concerning the above half messuage. Item: one charter óf John Curteys to

---

[1] Grant of the tenement to the same by the same, dated the following day. Same witnesses. Seal: red wax, diam. 1 in.; Virgin and Child surrounded by sprays of flowers. AVE MARIA GRACIA. (*Ibid.*, No. 9.)

[2] Seals: red wax; (1) oval, ₁⁷⁄₁₆ × 1 in., standing figure with ears of corn at each side, legend undeciphered; (2) small gem, bearing a man's head; (3) small rectangle with a beaded edge and a monogram or merchant's mark; (4) small blob, with (possibly) a griffon to the dexter.

[3] Seals: as to preceding deed.

[4] Also counterpart of deed.

Thomas Abelle concerning the half messuage. Item: one indenture witnessing a bond between John Fourneis [Curteys ?] and Alan de Fourneis concerning 20 marks security for a cellar and upper story in the said lane. Item: two charters from John Curteys and Thomas de Loudeham concerning a tenement with appurtenances in Peterlanelitell. Item: four indentures of Thomas de Loudham and John and Lettice concerning the above tenement. Item: one indenture of John Curteys and Alan and Alice concerning an annual rent of 20s. for the above messuage. Item: two deeds concerning the movables of John and Thomas Abelle. Item: one deed concerning the movables of Thomas Abelle and John Curteys. All of which documents Thomas Thurkylle shall have in custody under the following conditions: that if Agnes, widow of Nicholas de Touthorpe, shall continue to receive 6 marks 6s. 8d. during her life for that land and tenement which William de Touthorpe, Robert de Yokeflete, chaplain, Thomas Thurkille and John de Quyxlay had of her gift and feoffment, then Thomas Thurkylle shall give up to William de Touthorpe and John de Quyxlay, their heirs and assigns, the charters and deeds, but if Agnes be not duly paid in the appointed manner, then Thomas shall return the charters to Agnes, her heirs and assigns. Alternate seals.[1] Witnesses: Thomas Gra, mayor of York, William Sallay, John Hewyk, sheriffs, John Brathewayt, William Pountfreit, John de Thorneton, Thomas Santon, William Rillyngton. At York. (*Ibid.*, No. 11.)

497. Oct. 31, 1398. Indenture[2] by which the Master and Brethren of the Hospital of Holy Trinity and Blessed Mary in Fossegate, York, on behalf of themselves and their successors, grant to Agnes de Thouthorpe and William de Thouthorpe, chaplain, that whenever it happen that the tenement in the street of Blessed Peter the Little, which Agnes lately held, shall by the king's licence be alienated in mortmain to the Hospital, then, after two years following the death of Agnes, the Master and Brethren and their successors shall give to the poor of the Hospital at the Nativity of the B.V.M. next following 5d. of silver, and each year thereafter, at the same feast, 5d. in perpetuity; also that, for the souls of Agnes and William, John Luteryngton, Richard Hesilyngton and Alice, once his wife, and for the ancestors of Agnes and William, masses be celebrated in the Hospital, and commemorative prayers be offered by the poor for their benefactors to the Hospital, and that they shall be held in perpetual memory; and if it happen that William lives during this period,

---

[1] Seals: (1) oval, $\frac{7}{10} \times 1$ in., figure with ears of corn at each side, holding a book and a cross, legend undeciphered; (2) small, round, a griffon or winged dragon.

[2] Also counterpart of deed, with two small seals, blurred.

then he shall receive yearly from the rent of the Hospital 100s. for the term of his life. Alternate seals.[1] At York. (*Ibid.*, No. 12.)

498. March 13, 1404[–5], 6 Henry IV. Grant by Robert de Yokeflete, chaplain, Thomas Thurkille of York and John de Quyxley of York, to Robert Paa, John Bolron, chaplain, John Braythwayt, Thomas de Santon, Richard Hawkeswelle and John Wylton', citizens of York, of all those lands and tenements with appurtenances which they recently had of the gift and feoffment of Agnes, widow of Nicholas de Touthorpe, which lie [*as described in No.* 494]; to hold to the grantees, their heirs and assigns, of the chief lords of the fee, paying yearly to the poor of the Hospital of Blessed Mary and Holy Trinity at the Nativity of the B.V.M. 5d. of silver in perpetuity, so that for the souls of [*as continued in the preceding deed*]. Sealing clause.[2] Witnesses: Adam del Bank, mayor of York; John Bedale, John Wyton, bailiffs; William Sallay, Richard de Santon, William del Lee, William Lyons, Laurence Leverton. At York. (*Ibid.*, No. 13.)

499. April 18, 7 Henry IV [1406]. Indenture by which Marmaduke Darelle of Cessay leases to Richard Carwour of York, Agnes his wife, and Alice his daughter, all that tenement and garden, with all buildings and appurtenances in which Richard dwells in Bowethom,[3] in the suburbs of York, which lie in breadth between the land of John de Langton' on one side and the land of William de Wandesford on the other, and lengthways from the highway to Bowethom in front, to the same lands at the back; to hold from Whitsuntide 1406 for the full term of 40 years next following, paying yearly to Marmaduke, his heirs or assigns, 20s. at Martinmas and Whitsuntide in equal portions, and paying also to William Selby of York and his heirs 5s. at the same times and in equal portions. If the rent shall be in arrears at any time, in part or in whole, for as much as 40 days, then Marmaduke shall be permitted to distrain, remove and take away the articles distrained and to hold them until fully satisfied by the payment of the rent and arrears, and if the rent be not paid for three months after any of the terms then it shall be lawful for the lessor to enter and occupy the premises without hindrance from Richard, Agnes and Alice; the lessees to maintain at their own expense and to do repairs to the property as often as and when necessary, also to support all other charges on the property during the specified term, but Marmaduke, his heirs or assigns, shall at

---

[1] Seal: red wax, oval, $\frac{7}{16}$ × 1 in.; Virgin and Child beneath a gothic canopy; SIGILLUM . . . . .

[2] Seals: three, of red wax; (1) diam. $\frac{3}{4}$ in., a figure with a shield and an animal, probably a dragon, beneath its feet; (2) diam. $\frac{1}{2}$ in., a swastika; (3) in a hexagon a shield of arms, on a cross, a cross fleurie between four roundels.

[3] Bootham.

their own cost renew boards and laths (*tabulas, lattes*) and all timbers, also bear the expense of carting them to the site of the tenement. At the end of the term, Richard, Agnes and Alice shall leave the property in the same good repair as they found it, in the estimation of true and lawful men. Marmaduke to hold himself faithfully to these agreements and to consider himself bound to Richard in the sum of 20*li*.; Richard, Agnes and Alice similarly bound to Marmaduke in the same sum. Warranty. Alternate seals.[1] At York. (*Y.A.S.*, M^D 182, No. 102.)

500. Oct. 5, 1409, 11 Henry IV. Grant[2] by Elizabeth, widow of Richard Basy of Bilburgh', to John Bolron' and Robert Pay, chaplains, of that messuage with appurtenances which the grantor and John de Lucton, chaplain, held jointly of the gift and feoffment of John de Houeden, late citizen and merchant of York, which lies in Munkegate in the suburbs of York, in breadth between the land once belonging to John de Crayke on one side and the land once of Simon Gower on the other, and in length from the high street in front as far as the land once belonging to William Clervaux at the back; to hold to John and Robert, their heirs and assigns, of the chief lords of the fee. Sealing clause.[3] Witnesses: Henry Weyman, mayor of York; John de Northeby and Robert de Gayre, bailiffs; Thomas Santon, merchant; John Moreton, Robert Gaunt, Robert Feryby, William del Bothe, clerk, John Butercram. At York. (*Y.A.S.*, M^D 6, No. 15.)

501. Aug. 4, 2 Henry VI [1421]. Indenture witnessing that whereas the Master and brethren of the Hospital of St. Leonard, York, and Thomas Sutton and William Relford of York, *gentilmen*, are bound to Edmund Darelle of Sezzay, esq., and John Smelt of the same, yeoman, in 40*li*. sterling, to be paid at Martinmas next after the date of these presents, as more fully appears in the bond; and though Edmund and John are bound to the Master and brethren in 40*li*. sterling to be paid at Martinmas next following, nevertheless the parties aforesaid grant that if the Master and brethren and John Smelt accept the judgement of Christopher Boynton and Thomas Warde as arbitrators chosen on behalf of the said Master and brethren, and Thomas Maltby and John Greve chosen as arbitrators on behalf of John Smelt, to bring about a settlement touching certain causes, quarrels, [*etc.*], between the parties, in such a way that the four arbitrators settle the causes, debts [*etc.*], before Michaelmas next following, then the aforesaid two obligations shall be of no value and effect; but if the Master and brethren on the one part or John Smelt on the other refuse to accept judgement of the four arbitrators, then the obligation

[1] Seals: three, red wax—1 and 2 broken; device on 3 the letter H.

[2] Appointment of Alan Maldon and William Ribstan, chaplains, to deliver seisin; same date. (*Ibid.*, No. 16.)

[3] Seal as to No. 492.

of that party who refuses to accept judgement shall remain. Alternate seals.[1] At York. (*Y.A.S.*, M^D 182, No. 101.)

502. April 7, 1440, 18 Henry VI. Grant[2] by John Bolron, chaplain, to John Loftehous, senior, and William Marsshall of Petergate, citizens and merchants of York, of all that messuage with appurtenances in Munkegate which lie in breadth between the messuage of William Roche, *Gentilman*, on one side and the messuage recently belonging to John Esyngwald, citizen and merchant of York, on the other, and in length from the high street of Munkegate in front to the land of John Clervaux, knt., at the back; which messuage the grantor and Robert Pay, chaplains, held jointly of the gift and feoffment of Elizabeth who was the wife of Richard Basy of Bilburgh'; to hold to John and William of the chief lords of the fee. Sealing clause.[3] Witnesses: William Girlyngton, mayor of York; William Holbek, Thomas Danby, sheriffs of the city; John Bolron', Richard Warter, Richard Bukden', Richard Shirwod, citizens and aldermen of the city. At York. (*Y.A.S.*, M^D 6, No. 17.)

503. April 14, 18 Henry VI [1440]. Grant[4] by John Loftehous, senior, and William Marsshall of Petergate, citizens and merchants of York, to Thomas Kyrke, citizen and merchant, of a messuage with appurtenances [*as described in the preceding deed*]; to hold to Thomas, his heirs and assigns, of the chief lords of the fee. Sealing clause.[5] Witnesses: William Girlyngton, mayor of York; William Holbek and Thomas Danby, bailiffs; William Bowes, alderman; John Thresk, Thomas Crathorn, William Blawfront, William Couper, *pynner*. (*Ibid.*, No. 20.)

504. April 24, 18 Henry VI [1440]. Release by William Holbek, citizen and merchant of York, one of the executors of the will of John Aldestanemore, late citizen of York, to Thomas Kyrke, citizen and merchant of the same, his heirs and assigns, of all right in the messuage with appurtenances [*as before*]. Warranty. Sealing clause.[6] Witnesses [*as before except William Holbek*]. (*Ibid.*, No. 23.)

505. Dec. 20, 1477. Recites that Thomas Kirk, late merchant of York, having bequeathed to Alice Kyrk, his wife, a messuage with appurtenances in Munkgate in the suburbs of York, for the

---

[1] Tongues for three seals; small fragment of red wax on third.

[2] Appointment of John Bolron, chaplain, and John Burnlay, merchant, to deliver seisin. Same day. (*Ibid.*, No. 18.) Quitclaim of the same to the same, dated April, 9, 1440. Same witnesses. (*Ibid.*, No. 19.)

[3] Seal: red wax, diam. ½ in.; a device between sprays of leaves.

[4] (a) Quitclaim of the same to the same, dated April 16, 1440. Same witnesses. (*Ibid.*, No. 21.)
(b) Quitclaim dated April 20, 1440, by the same in their capacity as executors of the will of Richard Thuresby. Same witnesses. (*Ibid.*, No. 22.)

[5] Seals: two, of red wax; (1) diam. 1 in., a small shield in a cusped border, blurred, ... LOFTUS; (2) diam. ½ in., a small armorial shield, undeciphered.

[6] Seal: red wax; small shield, pseudo armorial, with the grantor's initials.

M

term of her life, with remainder (1) to John Kirk, her son, and his lawful heirs, (2) to his brother Robert, (3) to his brother Nicholas; and that John, Robert and Nicholas have died without lawful issue and without executors, and the said Thomas having willed that in such case the messuage should be sold, and the money received therefrom should be used for the health of his soul, as is more fully laid down in his will; now Thomas Tubbac, citizen and merchant of York, executor of the will of Alice Kirk, the other executors being deceased, as are the executors of the will of the said Thomas Kirk, grants to John Tonge, John Gyliot, John Feryby, William Tod, Thomas Scotton, merchants of York, the said messuage, which lies between the tenement of William Roche on one side and that once belonging to John Esyngwald on the other, and from the high street in front to the land of Richard Clervax, esq., at the back; to hold of the chief lords of the fee by the due and accustomed services. Warranty. Sealing clause.[1] Witnesses: John Longe, mayor of York; Robert Ancok, William Spence, bailiffs; Richard York, Thomas Wrangwish, Henry Williamson, Nicholas Longcastre, John Beseby. At York. (*Ibid.*, No. 24.)

506.   Feb. 10, 5 Eliz. [1563–4]. Indenture[2] by which George Hall, merchant and Governor of the Fellowship and Mystery of Merchants and Mercers of the City of York, Christopher Harbart and John Hewson, merchants, Constables or Keepers of the same Fellowship, with the full assent of the Fellowship, demise and lease to Hugh Graves, merchant of York and brother (*broyer*) of the Fellowship and his assigns, all those lands and tenements with appurtenances in the parish of Peterlaynlytelle, namely, two tenements and a yard held by Dame (*uxor*) Sandwith, widow, a tenement held by Roger Shipton, a tenement and a stable by Robert Maskewe, a tenement by Jane Lokewood, a tenement by Thomas Nyccolson, a stable by Christopher Hewson, and a stable by Nicholas Haxope; to hold all the above to Hugh Graves, his executors and assigns, from Whitsuntide next following these presents for the term of 21 years and paying yearly to the Governor, Constables and Keepers of the Fellowship 28s. 4d. at Martinmas and Whitsuntide in equal portions; and Hugh shall repair and maintain the tenements with the stables, houses and buildings, and at the end of the term shall yield them up in satisfactory repair; but if the tenement and stables shall fall into ruin for lack of repair, and be so apparent after survey made by the Governor and Constables of the Fellowship, and if Hugh does not repair the same within the space of four months after warning by the surveyors, then this indenture to be null and void.[3]   (*Y.A.S.*, M^D 10, No. 14.)

---

[1] Seal: red wax, broken.   [2] In English.
[3] Seal: red wax, ₁⁵⁄₁₆ × ₁⁵⁄₁₀ in.; a figure rising from a rectangular box, and holding a tool, between the initials H G.

APPENDIX.

Original Text.   No. 446.

Frontispiece.

Eboracensi archiepiscopo totique capitulo sancti Petri et omnibus sancte ecclesie filiis . Gillebertus del Meinil de Turkillebi salutem. Sciatis me assensu et concessione Stephani primogeniti et heredis mei et Idonee sponse mee dedisse et hac presenti carta mea confirmasse Deo et sancte Marie Bellelande et monachis ibidem Deo seruientibus totam illam culturam terre mee quam predicti monachi sartauerunt in terrura de Turkillebi uersus Angotebi per easdem metas et diuisas quas Walterus del Meinil pater meus perambulauit. Concessi etiam eis et confirmaui sartare ad latitudinem predicte culture uersus orientem in longum . quantumcumque heredes mei uel ego ipse uel homines de Turkillebi terram nostram iuxta predictam culturam uersus orientem sartando prolongauerimus. Hanc autem donationem feci Deo et predictis monachis in puram et perpetuam elemosinam propriam . liberam . solutam et quietam ab omni terreno seruicio et exactione seculari in perpetuum pro salute anime mee et vxoris mee et patris et matris mee et omnium antecessorum et heredum meorum. Et ego et heredes mei hanc donationem manutenebimus et gvarantizabimus predictis monachis contra omnes homines in perpetuum. His testibus. Willelmo Darel. Philippo fratre vxoris mee. Stephano filio meo. Petro fratre meo. Waltero canonico cellarario de Nouoburg. Oliuero filio Vincentii de Tresc. Symone dispensatore meo. Roberto clerico filio Roberti de Busci.

SEAL: red wax, diam. 2 ins.; a mailed equestrian figure with sword uplifted; SIGILLVM GILEBRTI DE MAINIL DE TURKLEBI *Endorsed in a contemporary hand*: C. Gilb' de Meynil de quadam cultura terre sartata. Turkilbii B'l, iiii.

A pedigree of the Meinils of Thirkleby, a presumed younger branch of the Meinils of Whorlton, is given by Farrer in *Early Yorkshire Charters*, ii, 134. It is clear that Thirkleby is the place of that name in the North Riding, Osgoodby (*Angotebi*) lying in that parish.[1] The fact that the Meinils of Whorlton had a holding in Thirkleby (E.R.)[2] is merely a coincidence.

A gift by Walter de Meinil to Byland of common pasture in Thirkleby, made with the consent of Gilbert, his son and heir, was transcribed by Dodsworth from the original; the date assigned by Farrer is 1160–70.[3] This suggests that the date for the present charter is towards the end of the century.

---

[1] See *V.C.H., N.R.*, ii, 56.

[2] *Feudal Aids*, vi, 159; *E.Y.C.*, ii, 136.

[3] Farrer MS. for Stuteville-Mowbray fee, from MS. Dodsworth vii, f. 105d.

INDEX

For EU product safety concerns, contact us at Calle de José Abascal, 56–1°,
28003 Madrid, Spain or eugpsr@cambridge.org.

www.ingramcontent.com/pod-product-compliance
Ingram Content Group UK Ltd.
Pitfield, Milton Keynes, MK11 3LW, UK
UKHW010338140625
459647UK00010B/682